CW00550868

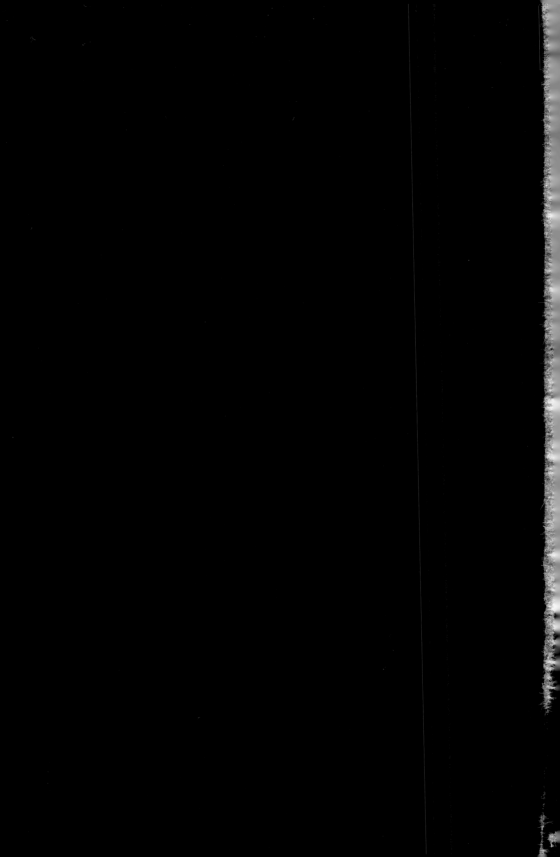

THE
PASSIONATE
IMPERIALISTS

The Passionate Imperialists

Published by The Conrad Press in the United Kingdom 2018

Tel: +44(0)1227 472 874
www.theconradpress.com
info@theconradpress.com

ISBN 978-1-911546-39-9

Typesetting and Cover Design by:
Charlotte Mouncey, www.bookstyle.co.uk

The Conrad Press logo was designed by Maria Priestley.

Printed and bound in Great Britain
by Clays Ltd, Elcograf S.p.A.

THE PASSIONATE IMPERIALISTS

the true story of SIR FREDERICK LUGARD,
anti-slaver, adventurer and founder of Nigeria
and DAME FLORA SHAW, renowned
journalist for *The Times*

RORY O'GRADY

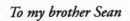

To my brother Sean

'And what,' said Gobind on Sunday evening, 'is your honoured craft, and by what means earn you your daily bread ?'

'I am,' said I, 'a kerani – one who writes pen upon paper, not in the service of the Government.'

'Then what do you write?' said Gobind...

'I write of all matters that lie within my understanding, and many that do not. But chiefly I write of Life and Death, and men and women, and Love and Fate according to the measure of my ability, telling the tale through one, two, or more people.'

Life's Handicap Rudyard Kipling 1891

By the Same Author

Stonecutters Bridge,
Gateway to Hong Kong's Port

(Bonham Media, Hong Kong, 2010)

Contents

LIST OF PLATES

1. Flora Shaw, the journalist 1890
2. Captain Frederick Lugard, the explorer
3. Vanity Fair Spy cartoon, 'Men of the Day No 639' Dec 19 1895 © The National Portrait Gallery, London
4. Travelling up the River Shire 1888, a sketch from *The Rise of Our East African Empire*. 1893 by Captain F. D. Lugard
5. Emin Pasha, a sketch by Nell Lugard from *The Rise of Our East African Empire* 1893 by Captain F. D. Lugard
6. The Rt. Hon. Joseph Chamberlain, Secretary of State for the Colonies 1895-1903, half-plate negative by Harold Palmer for Histed & Co. Rotary Photographic Co. Ltd. ©The National Portrait Gallery.
7. The Rt. Hon. Winston Churchill, Under Secretary of State for the Colonies 1906-1908
8. Colonel Willcocks and WAFF staff at Lokoja, Nigeria 1900
9. Battle of Tofrek, Sudan 1885, oil painting by Edwin Fripp © The Rifles Berkshire and Wiltshire Museum, Salisbury, England
10. Landing of the Belgian Refugees 1914, oil painting by Signor Frantoni © the Folkestone Museum, Kent, England
11. Lugard family photograph, England 1864
12. Sir Edward Lugard, uncle of FDL, photograph taken around 1890
13. Lugard aged around 16
14. Edward Lugard, brother and alter ego of FDL
15. 9th East Norfolk Regiment, 2nd Battalian, Afghanistan 1880
16. Captain Frederick Lugard 1893, after his return from Uganda
17. Sir John Kirk , leading anti-slaver in Africa and mentor to Lugard
18. Sir George Goldie 1899, founder of The Royal Niger Company, oil

painting by Sir Herbert Von Hekkomer © National Portrait Gallery, London

19. WAFF staff at Lokoja 1898. Courtesy of the Bodleian Library, Oxford

20. First British nurses in Northern Nigeria at Lokoja 1900. Courtesy of the Bodleian Library, Oxford

21. Nigeria Amalgamation Day procession 1 Jan 1914. Courtesy of the Bodleian Library, Oxford

22. Lugard, Governor of Hong Kong, receiving Viceroy of Canton 1908

23. Flora Lugard in Hong Kong 1912

24. Flora Lugard in England 1907, an oil painting by J. E. Blanche 1907, location unknown

25. Mr H.N. Mody, a Parsee businessman and major benefactor to the building of Hong Kong University

26. Hong Kong University shortly after opening in 1912

27. Architect's plan of the University 1907

28. Coat of Arms of the University 'Wisdom and Virtue'

29. Durbar at Kano, Northern Nigeria 1913. Courtesy of the Bodleian Library, Oxford

30. Nigeria Amalgamation Day, Lagos January 1 1914. Courtesy of the Bodleian Library, Oxford

31. Rudyard Kipling around 1895

32. Dame Flora Lugard, photo taken around 1916

33. The Rt. Hon. Baron Lugard 1929

34. Emirs' visit to Little Parkhurst 1931, Sultan of Sokoto, Emir of Kano, Emir of Gwando, Governor of Uganda, Governor of Nigeria

35. Lugard in his study at Little Parkhurst about 1930

36. Little Parkhurst 1940

All photos are from the Lugard family collection unless otherwise stated

MAPS

1. Route to Lake Nyasa, Nyasaland 1888
2. Route to Lake Victoria, Kenya 1890
3. Route to Lake Albert, Uganda 1891
4. West Africa 1891
5. Niger Basin - Route to Nikki 1894
6. Kalahari Trek 1896
7. Northern Nigeria Campaign 1903
8. Cameroon Campaign 1914

PREFACE

This book tells the true story of Sir Frederick John Dealtry Lugard and his remarkable wife Flora Shaw, who were at the centre of British colonial development at the end of the Victorian era. He was born in 1858, at the peak of the British Empire, at the very beginning of the 'Scramble for Africa'. He influenced and saw massive changes over his lifetime, and played a vital part in the development of East and West Africa in the early days, especially Nigeria. Flora was born in 1852, and had an outstanding career as a journalist, culminating in becoming the first colonial editor of *The Times*. She married Lugard in 1902, and the two became a formidable and famous couple in the early part of the twentieth century.

The British Empire presents something of a quandary to most British people today. The former empire is largely dismembered and disbanded, but is still a topic of fascination and fierce debate. Most people believe nowadays that nations should not have empires at all, and that those born in their country should have the right to govern their own nation, and make their own mistakes. The great Indian nationalist leader Mahatma Gandhi once said, '*Yes, we will have problems if we are granted independence, but they will be our own problems.*'

Yet it is too easy to be scathing about the British Empire and the people who administered it, especially in a Britain whose prosperity is still partly a legacy of colonial days. Yes, there were certainly colonials who enjoyed the rich trappings of a wealthy life gained at the expense of the subdued nations of imperial conquest, but there were also many who did not, and gave their all for the benefit of those nations.

Even those colonials who enjoyed a comparatively high standard of living found that their lives in hot, humid, foreign and indeed alien lands were often a poor compromise compared with the lives they could have enjoyed back home. And when they did finally retire to Britain, appeasing a yearning for their mother country which might have persisted for decades, they often found themselves suffering a new homesickness for the distant land they had left behind and which was now in many ways their real home.

What is certain is that these early colonials endured all manner of physical and mental hardships; stifling, uncomfortable climates, unfamiliar foods, deadly tropical diseases, and the constant threat of a sudden and violent death. Many travelled during the age of sail, became ill on board ship, died and were buried at sea and soon forgotten, while others suffered lonely deaths thousands of miles from their homes and families.

Lugard experienced all these hardships. He has fascinated me for over twenty years, ever since his name was first mentioned at a gathering of some of my Australian cousins in Brisbane in 1995.

Lugard's nephew, Charles Brayne, married my great-aunt Blodwyn Price and they retired to Brisbane after Lugard's death. On a later visit, I met their daughter Elizabeth Richmond, who was in her eighties at the time, and who had met Lugard when she was a girl growing up in Surrey, England. As she related the family legends, I found to my surprise that I had been inadvertently following in Lugard's footsteps for much of my life, having worked in both Nigeria and Hong Kong for some years, unaware of the great man.

Here I tell the story of Lugard's life as a soldier, adventurer, a builder of nations, a writer and a statesman. He was never looking for fame or capital gain in his life but was instead driven by enormous energy and passion. Like most people he acknowledged that the most powerful forces he experienced when he was younger were sexual ones, and he frankly confessed that he had great difficulty dealing with the feelings for the first woman he ever loved, feelings which lasted for some years, indeed for the rest of his life. It was only when he married Flora that he found true love and contentment. He had a vision, but it was Flora who inspired him and encouraged him to achieve many of his goals.

At the height of Lugard's fame in 1893, thousands came to hear this steely, quiet, and modest man, who was never comfortable with public speaking, enthral them with readings from his book, *The Rise of Our East African Empire* published in 1893, about his extraordinary adventures in East Africa. He was a prolific writer, finishing his two-volume 350,000-word best-seller in six months. The book was based on his meticulously-kept diaries. He described the land, animals and tribes encountered, interspersed with digressions on history and opinions on slavery and his recommendations for future administration - the first germination of ideas for Indirect Rule.

The last three chapters are directed at the British Government, pushing the case for making Uganda a Protectorate.

The number of copies sold is, as far as I'm aware, not known. The book got good reviews from newspapers and magazines, but as it consisted of two hefty volumes costing two guineas together, it was not a financial success for its publisher, William Blackwood.

Through the book, Lugard met writers such as Rider Haggard, who enjoyed enormous fame at the end of the nineteenth century with adventure novels such as *Allan Quatermain* (1887), and who incorporated Lugard into the heroes of his books. Lugard's fame as an adventurer was enhanced further when he ventured on an expedition to the Kalahari Desert in search of diamonds.

After further expeditions in Nigeria, Lugard was appointed the first High Commissioner of Northern Nigeria in 1900. He had already worked out a system of government which was a further development of his ideas of Indirect Rule. It allowed the existing rulers to remain but gave the British government a veto with the authority to remove the Emirs if necessary. Native institutions would be retained, with native courts and local laws and customs, but the death sentence could only be carried out with the agreement of the British Resident (the name for regional administrator adopted by Lugard). Slavery was abolished, liquor was prohibited, except in specific areas, and there was freedom of worship for all religions. This system had been used to a certain extent in India but was developed further by Lugard. Over the next thirty years it was adopted by many British colonies in Africa, until it was abused in east and south Africa with harsh restrictions and segregation which led to rebellions and eventually calls for independence. Enormous progress was made in infrastructure, education, public health and trade in Nigeria to 1906, but an exhausted Lugard was removed after a riot ended in a massacre in a small village near Sokoto.

In 1907, Lugard was offered the post of Governor of Hong Kong and with Flora by his side during turbulent times in China, he pushed through the construction of a railway to China, and the building of Hong Kong University which led to a lifetime passion for education. It was an enormous achievement.

He was recalled to London to prepare for the unification of Nigeria in 1912, and in 1914 raised the flag in Lagos, a city he disliked from the start. He immediately wanted to move the capital to Zungeru in the north. He tried to unify the two systems of the north and the south but was foiled by the sophisticated and wily Lagos chiefs. He had success with educational reforms, but struggled with judicial reforms and the introduction of taxes.

The outbreak of World War I caused further turmoil and after riots and many deaths in Abeokuta, further clashes with the Colonial Office were inevitable. He resigned in 1918 tired and frustrated.

Lugard retired to Abinger with Flora and put down his ideas for Indirect Rule in a book he wrote called *The Dual Mandate in British Tropical Africa*, which was published in 1922, and dedicated to Flora. The first part of the book covers a brief history of Africa and a survey of the peoples and the different governments. The second part sets out the special problems in Africa and his ideas for dealing with them. The book is the work of a practical administrator derived from his own experience. It is comprehensive and solid and above all showed that the Empire was not insensitively monolithic but had many layers of administration which could interact with the hundreds of tribes in Africa. Lugard firmly believed that Indirect Rule would soften the contact and give economic benefit to both sides. The book drew a mixed response, but influenced many colonial rulers right through to the start of the independence of the colonies.

The future always fascinated Lugard, much more than the past. Politicians found him difficult to deal with when he was younger, but his views on Africa were regularly sought once he became an elder statesman. During World War II, he came close to being blown to smithereens by a flying bomb that landed near his home. He was formulating ideas at the time about how Britain could work together with the old colonies as they became independent – the beginning of the Commonwealth of Nations. He was busy all his life; he wrote his last letter only a few days before he died, on April 11 1945, at the age of eighty-six.

Some of the problems Lugard faced during his long life are still with us. He worried about the tribal frictions in Kenya and Uganda that have held back those countries he traversed and explored in 1893. The descendants of the Mahdists he fought in Sudan are today uttering much the same violent religious rhetoric that he heard in 1886. Afghanistan is still the same political football he experienced in 1880, except with new protagonists, who are now using more sophisticated technology to kill each other.

Today, Nigeria is the richest and most populous country in Africa, as Lugard envisaged it would be in 1914 when he united the north and the south. It survived a horrific civil war from 1967 to 1970, and is slowly winning its battle against Moslem extremism in the north-east of the country. Despite the continuing political, economic, religious and tribal challenges that Nigeria faces today, it is still a united country and the optimism and pride that Lugard saw, and wanted to build on, is still there.

Europe itself needed two or three millennia to overcome tribal divisions and internal wars, so it is extraordinary what has already been achieved in Africa in about a hundred years, despite the inevitable setbacks. This progress will surely continue, and Africa will eventually become a thriving continent in the twenty-first century, as Lugard had hoped.

Lugard guided Hong Kong through five turbulent years and left a lasting legacy with the implementation and opening of a world class University.

The highly respected Oxford historian Dame Margery Perham wrote Lugard's biography in two voluminous tomes. They took her over twenty years to write and were crafted with great scholarship and detail. The first volume, *Lugard: The Years of Authority 1858-1898* was published in 1956, and the second volume, *Lugard: The Years of Authority 1898-1945* was published in 1960.

Margery Perham developed a close relationship with Lugard and I think came to really understand him. Lugard in turn held a high opinion of Margery as a historian, and came to look on her as a daughter, even successor. However, Margery Perham did not hold back on criticism of some of his decisions in Nigeria which, after long, painful discussions, Lugard also accepted.

This book takes another, even franker look at the extraordinary lives of Frederick Lugard and Flora Shaw, supplemented with new material from Nigeria, Hong Kong, and the Lugard family, that has come to light since 1960.

CHAPTER 1
Sanctuary

O n the third of August 1944, a few minutes before eight o'clock in the morning, Abinger Common, a quiet little village in southern England, experienced a violent reminder that World War II was, despite the successful Allied landings in France, far from over.

A deep hum came from the south, growing louder all the time. The hum turned to a harsh rattle. It was a V1 German pilotless flying-bomb, nicknamed by the British 'the doodlebug', powered by a simple jet engine, with a steel fuselage, stubby plywood wings and tailfins. It was travelling at about 400 miles per hour and carried a one-ton warhead containing an explosive mixture of TNT and ammonium nitrate, capable of enormous destruction.

After a few seconds the rattle stopped abruptly. There was silence. This was the moment everyone dreaded when they heard a flying-bomb, when the engine cut out. About twelve seconds later, the flying-bomb plunged in a steep arc towards earth. It plummeted down over the trees towards the village, only a mile away, and landed with a huge explosion and a plume of smoke.

Sir Frederick Lugard had dealt with danger all his life. Mementos could be seen around his mansion in Abinger, carefully placed to remind him of his own mortality and close brushes with death. There were the various spearheads on the wall, some barbed, but luckily not the one that a warrior plunged into his skull in Nigeria in 1894. The lion and leopard skins on the floor, overlooked by heads of the regal antelopes mounted on the walls, told of the many hunting expeditions in East Africa.

His large, heavy, monogrammed multi-bladed knife was in the drawer. He had always worn this on his belt when trekking. It had saved his life when a crocodile attacked him in Kenya. The knife also gained fame when highlighted by the famous Victorian cartoonist 'Spy' from the magazine *Vanity Fair* in December 1893. At the foot of the stairs was the large ominous Bugandan war drum, the membrane reputedly consisting of human skin, given to him for helping the King of Buganda in a civil war in Uganda many years earlier. Lugard still used it to summon guests for dinner.

A variety of African shields hung on the walls, a reminder of numerous skirmishes with warring tribes, and near to the front door, a large, beautifully-carved teak screen brought back from Kano. This had been presented to Lugard in Kano, Northern Nigeria, after this ancient city was besieged in 1902 and became part of the British Empire. One of his favourite mementos was a sword he kept in the study. It was given to him by his comrades after he led a fight against slavers on Lake Nyasa in 1889. Lugard had been severely wounded. He had stared death in the face that fateful day.

It is almost certain Lugard did not hear the doodlebug - he was now hard of hearing - but it is likely his loyal secretary, Violet Townshend, did. She had been working for Lugard for fifteen years, was a resident in the house, and took care to keep him informed of anything of importance happening in the village. He was used to the destruction of war, but he must have felt despair that it had followed him to his sanctuary in Abinger, Little Parkhurst. He was concerned for his family who lived in the village, especially his younger brother Ned, with whom he had a very close bond, and who had shared so much of his life.

At eighty-five years old, Frederick Lugard's gnarled, aching body still functioned well for its age, considering the punishment he had inflicted on it in his early years. He was five feet eight inches tall, and had a straight back and a taut frame, his posture still erect from military training. His hazel eyes had lost their youthful fire, and were now lighter, mellow and showed more compassion. The hair on top had long gone, leaving a bald island surrounded by neatly-groomed white locks. He needed a hat to keep his head warm. He preferred a simple, woolen peaked cap, buttoned on the top. He still wore his white, bushy Edwardian moustache. It was much shorter than the flamboyant style he sported as a young man, when the journalists pursued him for a good story, and he had been a favourite target for the cartoonists.

Abinger Common is a small, picturesque village only a few miles from the bustling town of Dorking, nestled under Leith Hill in the Surrey Hills. It is one of the oldest villages in England, with a prehistoric Mesolithic burial site nearby. The remains of a Romano-British villa lie hidden beneath the earth, and Abinger Common is recorded in the Domesday survey of 1086, valued at seven pounds. The village had seen much English history swarming through its streets.

Following the explosion, huddled groups gathered outside the village's only pub, the Abinger Hatch, a picturesque seventeenth century inn. They were mostly older people, with a few younger men in military uniform, talking animatedly and with concern as they looked across the green. The flying-bomb had exploded opposite the inn, blowing its windows out, damaging several other houses nearby, and had demolished most of the church. As if by divine providence, nobody was killed.

The church of St. James was built from attractive, yellow Leith stone and had stood there from at least the twelfth century, comforting the villagers, chronicling their rites of passage; details of baptisms, marriages and deaths had been recorded since 1559. The flying-bomb's blast had brought down the belfry with its three ancient bells cast in 1674, the roof of the nave, the Lady Chapel and parts of the walls. In the churchyard the World War I memorial, designed by Sir Edward Lutyens, had been blown completely off its pedestal and now lay in three pieces. The rector, the Reverend Lionel Meade, had been delayed that morning and had only just left the rectory to take Holy Communion.

Lugard's concerns were for his brother Ned, and sisters Agnes and Charlotte who lived in the village, and any possible damage to the family graves close to the walls of the church. The road from the church wound up through the trees towards Leith Hill, where Lugard had spent many happy days exploring the area with his beloved wife Flora, debating and planning his tasks in Africa and Hong Kong with her. The small track to Little Parkhurst was off this road, to the right, lined by trees and easily missed. The house was set back a few hundred metres from the junction, hidden by thickets, giving a delightful welcome on rounding the bend.

Little Parkhurst had originally been a two-storey cottage dating back to 1760. Flora had rented it in the 1880s, after she came upon it during a walk when she was single. After Lugard and Flora married in 1902, they built a large and impressive extension that in effect converted the cottage into a mansion. It was a fine example of the design of the time, with a grand Edwardian façade influenced by Lutyens. He had already designed Goddards in the village, which became the headquarters of the Lutyens Trust. There were now five apexed roofs, tall chimneys and well-balanced leaded windows in oak frames. Ten bedrooms, and seven bathrooms were added to cater for the many guests and the servants, with a large reception hall, drawing-room, sitting-room and a dining-room. The exterior was faced with local Leith Hill yellow stone, and red brick quoins framed the doors, windows and walls.

The house was now of a standard and quality to receive guests of Baron Lugard of Abinger, who had been the fourteenth Governor of Hong Kong and the first Governor-General of Nigeria.

An old man now, he tired more easily, but he still liked to keep to his routine. He tended to get up early, retire late, and exist on only a few hours' sleep, just as he had throughout his working life. He liked to start work in his study before eight o'clock, covered by a rug and wearing mittens if it was cold, to save electricity. His favoured time for tea was at five o'clock in the late afternoon, served in Chinese porcelain tea cups he'd brought back from Hong Kong.

Lugard's opinion and advice were still being sought on many topics in those tumultuous times. He was formulating his thoughts on the turbulent global changes that were going to occur after the war was over, with growing calls of independence from colonies around the world. Violet would have come in with the morning post, and picked up any typed letters he had left for her the previous night. She gave him any messages she had for him. He asked after her family, and gave any help where he could. It had been a long, fruitful and comfortable partnership that worked well for them both.

A large photo of Flora dominated Lugard's writing desk. This photo was his favourite. Flora was in her prime when it was taken, and she had retained her beauty. Quite tall at five foot eight inches, she was elegant, slim, with striking dark-blue eyes and thick auburn hair. It was sixteen years since Flora had passed away, but he still missed her deeply. He knew if she were here today, she would still be out there fighting some cause, helping the refugees, chasing politicians, urging him on, and keeping up his spirits.

CHAPTER 2
Flora's childhood

F lora Louise Shaw was born in Woolwich, in south-east London on
December 19 1852, the third of fourteen children. She inherited her
beauty from her Mauritius-born French mother, Josephine Adrienne Marie
Junot des Fontaines, descended from an aristocratic Catholic Parisian family
who had escaped from the French Revolution to Mauritius. Their family
saying was, *'Courage should be the distinguishing trait of nobility, and if
women could not fight they could at least die in their posts,'* and came from
Flora's spirited grandmother, Flore d'Epinay, who remained in Paris all
through the revolution.

Her father was Major-General George Shaw who came from an old
Anglo-Irish Protestant military family, whose influential father was Sir
Frederick Shaw. He had graduated from Trinity College, was a Member
of Parliament for Dublin from 1830 to 1848, and the leader of the Irish
Conservatives. A cousin was the famous writer George Bernard Shaw
(1856-1950), who used to visit the Shaw ancestral home at Bushey Park
in Dublin, until his alcoholic father was banned for overindulging.

Flora's parents met in Mauritius when her father was posted there
with the British Royal Artillery Regiment, and they were married in Port
Louis in 1846. In the early years of her childhood her father was away
frequently, first in Jamaica and then Crimea, where he fought and distinguished himself at Sebastopol in 1854 before returning to the Military
Academy in Woolwich.

It was an unusual and happy childhood. Every year from May to October
the family went back to the family home at Kimmage Manor, now a
built-up area in Dublin. They were magical days for Flora, and she used
those experiences when she wrote her first book, *Castle Blair*, in 1877, about
her childhood days in Dublin. The children had little formal education, but

they learnt French from their mother, and received lessons from a governess who taught Flora everything she thought young ladies should know.

Each winter the family returned to Woolwich, which was a busy, polluted industrial town at that time. The old shipyards were gone, but the famous Arsenal armaments factory was in full production. Flora would have watched ships coming up the turgid River Thames bringing their exotic cargos from all over the British Empire to be processed in the factories of England. She also saw the poverty of the working people in Woolwich, crammed into rows of terraced slums near the river and witnessed all the social and health problems.

When her father was made Commandant of the Military Academy in 1861 they moved into a larger house in Woolwich, and it allowed Flora to have access to the officers' library. She read enthusiastically and widely, encouraged by a sympathetic librarian who guided her through the labyrinth of books. As she grew older, she would occasionally creep into the back of the lecture rooms and listen to guest speakers who had come to lecture the young officers.

It was here she first heard John Ruskin speak when she was nineteen years old. She had met him briefly at a party two years earlier, and was entranced by one of the most brilliant social thinkers of the Victorian age. His views were to influence her for the rest of her life. He was not just the leading art critic of the day who was a keen supporter of the Pre-Raphaelite movement and J.M.W. Turner, but Ruskin also wrote extensively linking his observations of nature with art, architecture and society. He enjoyed the company of adolescents, which raised controversy, especially with his tragic obsession with Rose La Touche, but his greatest joy was teaching the innocent and opening their eyes to nature around them. This certainly is the impression given in surviving letters from Ruskin to Flora written around 1871.

Ruskin quickly saw that young Flora had an intelligent, enquiring mind, and was eager to learn, so he prepared a reading list for her. He monitored her progress and gradually introduced her to some of the most influential intellectuals of the age.

This included visiting Thomas Carlyle, philosopher and writer, and one of the most important social commentators of the day. Ruskin introduced Flora to him and said, '...*I have brought this little girl to see you and she will remember it all her life. I want you to say something nice.*' Carlyle replied in his Scottish brogue, '*Well, remember this little girl; I have seen and talked with Goethe. When you are old as I am, you can say you knew a man who knew Goethe.*' The memory of that visit remained with her into old age.

She started reading Carlyle's books and claimed that after she had read *The French Revolution* (1877) sitting up a tree, she climbed up a Royalist, and climbed down a Democrat. She also read his book *On Heroes, Hero-Worship, and the Heroic in History* (1841), which expounded the need for society to have heroes that were worthy of admiration.

She looked for this in men throughout her life, and was drawn to men of such qualities. Through Ruskin, Flora learned about art, philosophy, economics and ideas to help alleviate the poverty of the working class that she had observed in Woolwich. Ruskin was a proponent of emigration to the colonies to help to escape poverty in the cities, and instilled in her his belief in Positive Imperialism, an idea which she developed through the rest of her life.

She visited the Arsenal factory at Woolwich to see the conditions for herself. She asked the women what they ate and found they were being overcharged for their groceries. After discussing with Ruskin, she opened a co-operative store, buying the food in bulk and helped to cut the prices substantially

Ruskin helped Flora through the trauma of losing her mother when she was just eighteen, probably from exhaustion of delivering fourteen children. In 1870, Flora's closest sister Mimi married Charles Brackenbury, a lieutenant in the Gunners, so she found herself with the responsibility of looking after all the younger siblings. In 1872 her father remarried. His new wife was Ellen Little, a widow of a surgeon, and from the beginning it was clear she and Flora were not going to get on, so she took up the job of governess with Charles Brackenbury's cousin at Waltham Abbey, close to where her sister Mimi lived.

Flora enthusiastically pursued her writing, encouraged by her friend Ruskin. She started to produce articles for magazines, and in 1877 Ruskin helped to get *Castle Blair* published. The book was a great success. In return Flora helped Ruskin get over his doomed relationship with Rose, and later supported him through a mental breakdown in 1883. He gave her a little watch which she wore right to the end of her life.

CHAPTER 3
The early years

On Thursday March 5 1863, five-year-old Freddy Lugard embarked on his first epic voyage with his mother and four siblings. He never forgot it. Many years later he recounted details of this nightmare journey, recorded in his mother's letters to his father.

They left Madras (now Chennai), on an old wooden sailing ship called *The Trafalgar*, packed with troops returning from India, many of whom were ill even before they embarked. As the Suez Canal was still being built, the ship had to navigate round the horn of South Africa. *The Trafalgar's* crew were a motley lot, poorly paid, with drunkenness frequent and fights common. Cockroaches scuttled throughout the ship as if they owned it. Lugard's family of six, himself, his four sisters and his mother, had to share one cabin for the four month voyage.

The journey began with a series of abnormal calms. The intense tropical sun beat down on them for twelve hours a day. Two thirds of the water stored in casks below decks was found to be contaminated, forcing the ship to implement rationing. There was little left for washing. The children were continually thirsty, and babies cried constantly. To replenish the fetid water, the ship had to divert to Mauritius, where it ran straight into a severe tropical storm, the worst the captain had encountered in over twenty years at sea.

The howling wind tore into the sails, forcing the ship back forty-five miles. A tree was lashed to the mast to stop it breaking. Cries were coming from injured people who were being thrown around the cabins. The children were terrified, tossed about like puppets. Almost everyone suffered from sea-sickness. The wind was so strong it took five attempts to get past Cape Agulhas. Mary didn't panic, but called on her spiritual strength, reciting texts from The Bible to the children to keep them calm. Young Freddy took strength from his mother and didn't panic either. His mother wrote later, *'Freddy is quite well and hearty.'* He had taken on this hardship as a challenge.

Three months later the horrendous journey was still not over. By now infectious diseases were rampant on the ship, with some of the children contracting chickenpox and others whooping cough. The ship's doctor had only basic medicines, opiates and herbal remedies. Freddy had both diseases and was in severe danger for his life. The only medicine consisted of homeopathic pills and blackcurrant jelly. There were many burials at sea, mostly of young soldiers. There was overwhelming relief on the part of crew and passengers when the ship finally docked in London in early July.

The first British trading stations in India had been set up soon after 1600, when the East India Company was granted a monopoly of all English trade to Asia. The great Moghul Empire ruled India at that time, but went into rapid decline after 1739 when Nader Shah, the Shah of Persia, invaded India and soundly defeated the Moghul army at the Battle of Karnal, and took Delhi.

As the Moghul Empire disintegrated, the British started interfering in Indian politics, gaining influence to increase their trade in cotton, sugar and opium from the main settlements in Bombay, Madras and Calcutta. Huge local armies were set up by the East India Company, a total of 300,000 men, mostly sepoys - Indian soldiers usually of the middle to higher castes - and supplemented by British regular troops. The East India Company, ever hungry for growth and money, embarked on aggressive territorial expansion, playing off neighbouring states against each other. There was growing resentment over the Company's tactics and the haughty British attitude. It came to a head in the bloody revolts of 1857.

The first started on February 26, when sepoys of the 19th Bengal Infantry stationed at Berhampur refused to accept the issue of new cartridges, because the protective grease was a mixture of both beef fat and pork fat. The soldiers had to bite off the end of the cartridge, so the beef fat offended the Hindus, and the pork fat the Muslims. The revolts escalated rapidly, soon becoming a call for a religious war. Many were killed and terrible atrocities were committed on both sides, with the rebellions brutally crushed by the British. Some prisoners were tied to the end of cannons, which were then fired using powder only and no balls. This was an old Moghul punishment for mutiny. The explosion itself was enough; the bodies were torn apart.

The revolt shocked the British Government, who took swift action by nationalising the East India Company in 1858, and starting to rule its 'jewel in the crown' directly. The Company's Indian possessions and its armed forces were taken over. A new Indian Civil Service was created under the control of a Secretary of State, and the Army regiments were reorganised. The red and white striped flag of the Company was lowered and the Union Jack raised.

In the midst of this turmoil on January 22 1858, Frederick John Dealtry Lugard was born in Fort St. George, Madras.

Frederick was the son of the Reverend Frederick Grueber Lugard, a devout chaplain who had been working for the East India Company. One of seven children, the Reverend Frederick had attended St Paul's School and Trinity College, Cambridge, completing his BA in 1831 and was ordained the next year. A handsome man with a serious nature, he was physically strong with a liking for sport, and excelled in rowing and athletics. Once ordained, he held two brief curacies in England and then went to India as an Army chaplain in 1837.

Lugard's father stayed there for twenty-seven exhausting years. Conditions were harsh, with the heat, humidity and appalling hygiene conditions of Madras gradually wearing him down over the years. His close friend in Madras was Bishop Dealtry, who commissioned a bas relief in Madras Cathedral in recognition of the Reverend Lugard's work in the city, and from whom Freddy gained his middle name.

At the age of twenty-six, his father married an attractive young woman who worked at the mission, Grace Price Morgan, but after giving him three children in seven years she ran off with another man, and left the children with her husband. This was, not surprisingly, deeply humiliating for the Reverend Lugard. He became angry and bitter, and, unusually for that time, he divorced his wife in 1845. This caused him serious financial problems from which he never recovered.

Through his work with the Church Missionary Society he met and married again in 1849 to a missionary called Emma Cameron. They had two daughters, Lucy and Emma, but tragedy struck again when their mother contracted cholera and died in 1852, after only three years of marriage.

Aged forty-six, with five children to support and with continuous money problems, things looked bleak for Lugard's father, but he was affectionate and conscientious, and at the same mission in Madras he was lucky enough to meet his third wife, Mary Jane Howard, with whom he found enduring happiness. They married in 1855. Over the next five years they had five children, including one who died in infancy and another who was stillborn.

LUGARD FAMILY TREE

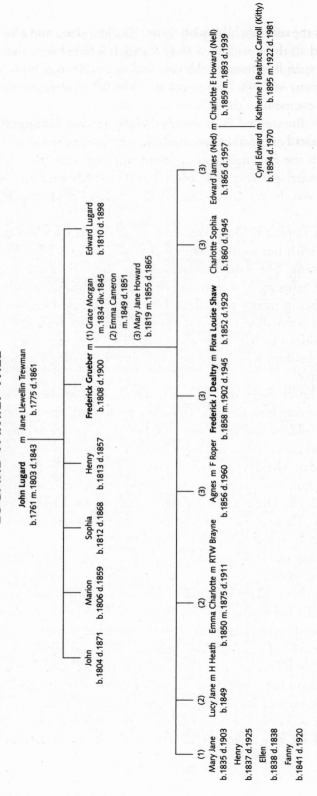

John Lugard m Jane Llewellin Trewman
b.1761 m.1803 d.1843   b.1775 d.1861

John
b.1804 d.1871

Marion
b.1806 d.1859

Sophia
b.1812 d.1868

Henry
b.1813 d.1857

Frederick Grueber m (1) Grace Morgan
b.1808 d.1900   m.1834 div.1845
                    (2) Emma Cameron
                        m.1849 d.1851
                    (3) Mary Jane Howard
                        b.1819 m.1855 d.1865

Edward Lugard
b.1810 d.1898

(1)
Mary Jane
b.1835 d.1903
Henry
b.1837 d.1925
Ellen
b.1838 d.1838
Fanny
b.1841 d.1920

(2)
Lucy Jane m H Heath
b.1849

(2)
Emma Charlotte m RTW Brayne
b.1850 m.1875 d.1911

(3)
Agnes m F Roper
b.1856 m.1960

(3)
Frederick J Dealtry m Flora Louise Shaw
b.1858 m.1902 d.1945   b.1852 d.1929

(3)
Charlotte Sophia
b.1860 d.1945

(3)
Edward James (Ned) m Charlotte E Howard (Nell)
b.1865 d.1957   b.1859 m.1893 d.1939

Cyril Edward m Katherine I Beatrice Carroll (Kitty)
b.1894 d.1970   b.1895 m.1922 d.1981

Frederick was the second child, with Agnes his elder sister and Charlotte his younger, and all three remained close for their whole lives. They were a happy family, spending most of the year at Fort St. George, built by the East India Company in 1644, living a colonial life. When it was particularly hot they would escape into the hills above Madras.

It was a hard climate and their mother Mary became exhausted with fevers that relentlessly sapped her strength. It was agreed she would return to England with the five youngest children to recuperate (the children from the first marriage were now adults) and that her husband would follow her. This was the traumatic journey that young Freddy experienced in March 1863.

On arrival in England, Mary Jane and the children travelled to York hoping to stay with her mother, who was now a widow. Mrs. Howard was not welcoming. She would allow only the three children from the marriage to stay, refusing to accommodate Lucy and Emma, the step-children. Despite being nearly penniless, Mary Jane refused her mother's hospitality, and immediately found another house in York for herself and her five children to live in. It was small but Mary organised it well, and had a tiny garden, which she divided into five little plots for each child to look after.

She wrote a letter every day to her husband, but refused to send a photograph, knowing how thin and frail she now looked. She made all the clothes for the children and somehow raised enough money to employ an eighteen-year-old governess to teach the children at home. A timetable was drawn up each day. The days started with prayers at seven in the morning, followed by five hours of schooling, dinner, walking, tea and reading, with bed at nine o'clock. The studies included Geography, English History, Ancient History, Themes, Parsing (analysing the structures of sentences), Arithmetic, French, and half an hour of Scripture.

Even on Sunday the children had to get up at seven, when there were more prayers and worship at church at ten-thirty, where they had a Lugard pew assigned to them. Mary Jane called this *my day of love and leisure.*

With the family belonging to the Missionary Society, they followed a puritan path, based on the Baptist doctrine, with much debate on religious matters and the evils of slavery. Their father would send regular letters to each of the children trying to guide their spiritual welfare. The routine was not overly repressive, but deep Victorian values were instilled in the children of duty, respect for others, order and love for the family.

Young Freddy was desperate to do things 'right' and took a great interest in The Bible to look for guidance. One time, at the age of six, he was found crying, because he had been dreaming that an angel was coming for him and was worried he had not yet confessed all his sins.

Early in 1864 his father returned from India. Mary Jane still loved her husband deeply and had longed for him to come home, but she was concerned about the consequences of the return. She was still physically weak and the thought of another pregnancy filled her with dread. After an idyllic holiday in the mountain meadows of Switzerland, she became aware another baby was on the way. She became weaker as she progressed through the confinement and went to Malvern for the birth, hoping the spa waters would help. On June 12 1865, she gave birth to her sixth child and second son, Edward.

Three months later tragedy struck once more. Mary died of exhaustion.

Young Freddy was seven years old, bewildered and traumatised. His father was grief-stricken, sobbed uncontrollably and found great difficulty in functioning. To lose three wives and have six children to look after was just too much for his mental state to bear. He withdrew into himself, aged prematurely and lost any affectionate interest in his children. Further financial problems arose, which brought more worries and uncertainty for the family.

Fred's older half-sister, Lucy took over the maternal role, but she was strict with the younger ones. Fred was closer to Agnes, and always felt a comfort with his elder sister. Agnes lived a long life and in later years, as an old lady, lived with Fred in Abinger until he died, spellbinding the younger generations with her tales. She was still driving at the age of ninety, and died at the grand old age of 103.

These difficult times prepared Fred for the challenges that lay ahead in his adult life. He was always frugal, and already appreciated how quickly misfortune can strike and change your life drastically.

His education continued in a haphazard fashion. He was first sent to a small school in Worcester, run by two elderly ladies. He stayed there for a year, then, at the age of ten, to a mercifully cheap preparatory school run by some Moravian brothers at Fairfield, near Manchester.

It was a deeply unhappy period for Freddy. A violent regime ruled, with a senile headmaster and brutal teachers from Germany; where thrashings were arbitrary and unjust and continuous boxing of his ears led to Freddy going partially deaf, giving him hearing problems for the rest of his life. The experience of this cruel institution gave him a sharp, personal understanding of injustice and tyranny.

In 1871 at the age of thirteen, he was sent to Rossall School, located on a bleak stretch of the Lancashire coast near Fleetwood. As it was a Church of England school and his father was a vicar, he benefited from a reduction in fees. They reduced further after a story circulated that an Irish boy had attempted to kill one of the masters.

Freddy's new headmaster turned out to be a kindly and humane man, a brilliant scholar both in Classics and Science, and who believed in teaching boys how to think. The bullying culture was still endemic though, and Freddy suffered further violence and degradation meted out to the new boys. He survived, but around this time he started to suffer from intermittent depression, when black clouds descended on his mind, and he would occasionally have panic attacks with which he would battle throughout his life.

He often wrote to his half-sister Emma during this time, now in her early twenties, who had taken over the maternal role of the family from Lucy. He revealed his feelings and started questioning his spiritual values. '... *when you feel the agony of bitterness,*' he asked, '*what would it be for a mortal if he had no spiritual comfort added to his lack of earthly comfort?*' He questioned, '... *what reason should you have for such a misery? ... but it shows how very little one mortal can read the heart of another.*'

He contemplated suicide, sadly a not unusual train of thought for adolescents throughout time. His school results were poor and he feared he was disappointing his father. Emma was his one consolation. She wrote to him, '...*and you will succeed Fred dear, I am persuaded, and all the better for your bitter experiences now. Work on with that highest motive (of pleasing God).*'

By the end of 1875, Fred's work had improved due to the influence of the new headmaster. He won prizes for Modern History and (to be expected), Divinity; also a prize for an essay, which the headmaster, who was leading his final prize-giving considered '...*a remarkable essay written by Lugard.*' His talent for writing was beginning to emerge.

In 1876, another headmaster arrived at Rossall, Dr. James, a distinguished Welshman, educated at Marlborough and Oxford. He was a striking man with a deep, resonant voice that was mesmerizing. He made a lasting impression on Lugard, who remembered Dr. James' first speech, and even sixty-nine years later could still recite it. Dr. James revolutionized the school that year by changing the staff, the syllabus, the house system, and cleared the school's debts. '... *I wish I had met him earlier,*' Lugard commented many years later.

At the age of seventeen, the continuous shortage of money and financial pressures on his father greatly concerned Frederick, and he contemplated his own future. To earn money to help the family, he first considered going to work for the husband of his eldest half-sister Mary as an assistant in a sugar factory. Had he gone down that route, the history of West Africa would have been considerably different.

This idea did not last long. Instead, he sat the Indian Civil Service examination the following year. His school had very little interest in the Civil Service, concentrating on getting boys into University, so Fred was given little advice and failed. However, this failure brought him into contact with an important member of the family.

That meeting changed his life.

CHAPTER 4
Learning the game

In the corner of Lugard's study at Little Parkhurst was a small, striking, white marble bust of his uncle, General the Rt. Hon. Sir Edward Lugard GCB, PC. He was always indebted to his uncle for the advice he gave to him as a young man, which led him to India.

Sir Edward was a legend in the family. He had joined the Army in 1824 and had taken part in some of the greatest military endeavours of the nineteenth century. He had served in the disastrous First Afghan War and the Battle of Kabul in 1842, campaigns in India in 1845 and 1846, and the relief of Lucknow in 1858. Despite being wounded in the Battle of Moodkee, he saw action again seven weeks later at Aliwal. He was described as a cool, intrepid and trustworthy soldier, and young Frederick was in awe of him.

His uncle was now sixty-seven years old, an eminent and famous man, and had retired as Permanent Under-Secretary of State for War at the War Office. He heard from his brother that Frederick had failed the Indian Civil Service exam, and invited him to his club in London for dinner. Frederick was extremely nervous, but was soon put at ease by his uncle in a large comfortable leather chair in the corner of the club. Sir Edward had little hair remaining on top, but boasted a large white moustache that looped round and joined up with the mutton-chop whiskers, the fashion popular with gentlemen of the early Victorian period. In addition he sported a neat white goatee beard that framed an interesting face, with thoughtful, experienced eyes. Dressed impeccably for dinner, Sir Edward cut a striking figure.

He asked Fred what he wanted to do with his life, and listened carefully to the options Fred said he was considering. Weighing up the young man's intellectual and physical abilities, he saw a similarity with himself. With Frederick's half-brother, Henry, a cousin already serving and doing well, and another uncle having reached the rank of Lt. Colonel, the Army was an obvious option.

Fred enjoyed the experience of dining at the club enormously, and even more so when his uncle announced he was taking him to the theatre afterwards. Fred had never been to the theatre before. It is not known what play he saw, but it was a truly memorable night and left a deep impression on the young man, and gave him a clear idea of the direction in which he wanted to head.

Fred travelled back to Rossall, excited at his prospects, and sat the Sandhurst exams at the end of 1877. The first part was straightforward, but the second was an extremely competitive test, where there was little time to prepare. Over one thousand candidates had entered. Fred was not confident he had passed, and told his father he thought he had failed. It wasn't until a friend congratulated him a few days after the results were announced, that he found, to his astonishment, he had come sixth.

Lugard entered Sandhurst in February 1878, determined to do well. He was just twenty years old, short in height and of average build, but physically strong. He had little knowledge of world affairs, which at this time were particularly complex.

The empires of Europe were competing for power around the world, especially Russia, who was marching armies into Turkey and looking for ways to gain advantage over the British in India and the Far East. Afghanistan became a centre of 'The Great Game.' The British wanted to boost the number of troops on the North-West Frontier, but with other military commitments, this resulted in a serious shortage of manpower. As a result, young Lugard had only eight weeks training at Sandhurst before hastily being given a commission and ordered to overseas postings. An American paper wrote at the time,

'England has let loose one hundred war pups from Sandhurst. Let Russia tremble!'

Lugard was given a commission in the 9th Regiment, the East Norfolk, and he joined the 1st Battalion at The Curragh. In September 1878 he set sail in the troopship *HMS Euphrates,* passing through the newly-opened Suez Canal, and arrived in India a few months later. A train took the battalion to the terminus at Jhelum. From there they marched the 150 miles to Peshawar, situated close to the eastern end of the Khyber Pass on the India (now Pakistan) Afghanistan border. Such long marches were usual at the time.

Peshawar was the gateway to the North-West Frontier, adjacent to the famous Khyber Pass, and located at the foot of the snow-covered Hindu Kush and Himalayas. It was an historic and well-established city, with acres of gardens planted with sweet-scented roses, jasmine, peach and plum trees, orange and pomegranate. This natural beauty contrasted with the local people suffering great poverty and disease. These were Lugard's first vivid impressions of India, and he never forgot them.

Lugard spent that first winter supplementing his meagre military training at Sandhurst with hours of hard drilling and understanding the basics of warfare. He studied the geography and history of the area. He came to understand its cultural and tribal life, and the caste system, which relegated millions to lifelong ignominy creating a complex social hierachy. He learnt about the dangers, symptoms and treatment of tropical diseases. Cholera and malaria were endemic and there were many different fevers of which there was still little knowledge.

Lugard was introduced to a vibrant new social life. Horses were an essential part of both work and recreation, so racing and polo were particularly popular. He acquired two of his own ponies, which he called Snowball and Stamp, despite a lack of funds, and quickly became an accomplished rider. He bought himself a small dog called Nettle who was, as he wrote to his sister Emma, *'my constant friend and companion,'* a luxury he had never been able to enjoy in childhood.

He observed the regiment's wives going about the daily dull routines of overseas rituals. With abundant servants, they had little to do themselves except issue orders and exact discipline, whilst preparing for endless rounds of coffee mornings, tea afternoons and dinner parties. This life was already well-documented in the sharp, acerbic stories written by Rudyard Kipling, whom the young subaltern was to meet, and be entertained by, years later.

In 1879 the political games of Russia in Afghanistan were escalating. The British Resident in Kabul was murdered and riots broke out across the country. Troops were sent to Kabul to quell the riots, including the 9th Regiment, but, much to Lugard's chagrin, shortly after leaving his barracks, he fell extremely ill. In a letter to his sister Emma he wrote, *'... a rattling headache, continuous vomiting, no appetite, could not eat for a fortnight ... could hardly stand.'*

Peshawar had its own special fever that sucked the strength from men in days. Carried by sandflies, it struck within hours, bringing acute pain to the joints and bones. The fever was intense, the head feeling it was going to explode with pain, red eyes staring out of a tortured skull. The local Punjabis had a strong immune system against the fever at a time when the immune system was still a mystery. New recruits arriving fresh from

England would all go through the painful delirium. If they did not quickly build up their own immune system they would continually suffer or die. Funerals were common. Disease was a far more serious deadly enemy to the British Army than the sharp sword of an enemy soldier.

Lugard was bitterly disappointed in his first experience of war, having to be carried back to the hospital in a litter. By the time he recovered, Kabul had been taken and the fighting was over. The regiment was quartered in the Amir's palace, and he spent the winter in Kabul rebuilding the city infrastructure. The nearest he got to action was shooting ducks on the frozen flood plains of the Kabul river.

There is a photograph taken at that time of Lugard and his fellow officers in Afghanistan in 1880. It is an informal shot, some men standing, some sitting, unsmiling, looking distant, thinking of home. They are wearing an assortment of quilted jackets and gloves to keep warm in the bitter weather, and hold a variety of swords and sticks. They look more like an impromptu group of militia volunteers than officers of the East Norfolk Regiment. Sporting a fashionable new moustache, Lugard stares intently into the camera with a challenging and determined air. It is the look seen in pretty much every fresh generation of soldiers wanting to test themselves and resolved to acquit themselves with honour.

This Second Afghan War, although short, was badly handled by the politicians in London with the cost overrunning to a full £6,000,000 (about £600,000,000 pounds today). It became a major issue in the British elections in 1880, when the government fell and William Gladstone swept into power. The troops were withdrawn, Kandahar was given up, and little of any benefit had been achieved; a result continuously repeated by future optimistic politicians thinking they had a solution for this feudal country. Lugard marched back out of Kabul with his regiment in August 1880 through the Jugdulluk Pass, where he could almost touch both sides of the narrow precipitous rocks, and found himself once more in Peshawar.

Lugard was sent to England for recuperative leave and returned to India in 1881 for an unusually peaceful three years, a time he would look back on later with great nostalgia. From his letters to Emma, we know that one of Lugard's favourite postings was to Umballa (now known as Ambala), situated in the foothills of the Punjab, on the railway line to Simla, nestling under the mighty peaks of the Himalayas, some over 8,000m high.

The British had a large base at Umballa with many facilities for both training and social events. Lugard needed to earn extra money, so he passed exams in Hindi and Urdu, and took a transport course to become a transport officer. He excelled in his understanding of complex logistics, which became invaluable during his future exploits.

He threw himself into social activities, with race meetings, polo matches, gymkhanas, bridge evenings and mess dinners. He bought a grey mare called Delusion, which he trained for racing and jumping, getting good results. Hunting was extremely popular at that time, with plenty of game around, especially boar. The pastime could be dangerous to both horse and rider. Lugard was drawn to the risk and skill required to succeed, to overcome the wiliness, aggressiveness, and sharp and filthy tusks of the boar, a deep injury from which could easily be fatal.

He was not interested in taking leave in fashionable Simla, and instead accepted an invitation from his half-brother Henry, from his father's first marriage, to go to Nagpur, much further south. It was their first meeting, and Henry had risen to Deputy-Commissioner in the Indian Civil Service. Henry took Lugard on his first tiger shoot, nurturing in him a passion for hunting. Hundreds of beaters accompanied the hunters on their elephants, slowly driving forward an abundance of wildlife. This behaviour seems reprehensible to us today, when so many animal species are in danger of extinction, but at that time few of the animals hunted were under serious threat. The British claimed, not without justification, that they were reducing the number of dangerous predators. It was true that a tiger which had enjoyed tender human flesh rarely went back to eating four-legged prey with rough skin or fur that needed to be bitten through.

Lugard observed the privileged lifestyle of the senior civil servants of the Raj, who would never have dreamed it would end within their lifetime.

For two more years Lugard continued his work as a transport officer, building up his expertise and experience, getting good reports and earning promotion to Lieutenant. On January 22 1885, his twenty-seventh birthday, he rejoined his regiment at Sitapur, near Lucknow.

Four days later he heard that General Charles Gordon had been murdered in Khartoum. Lugard was playing bridge when he was handed a telegram. It informed him he was to serve as a transport officer with the second Suakin Field Force, and to prepare to leave for Sudan immediately.

CHAPTER 5
The governess

By the time she was thirty, Flora was earning enough money to rent a small cottage of her own. One summer's day in 1882, she went to visit a friend in Abinger, and after climbing Leith Hill, came across a pair of semi-detached cottages surrounded by pines. She knew immediately this was where she wanted to make her home, and rented a large bed-sitting room in one called Parkhurst Cottage. This led to another close and important relationship.

George Meredith was fifty-five years old when he met Flora. He was by then a well-known English novelist and poet. He was a friend of Colonel Brackenbury and lived on Box Hill, within walking distance of Parkhurst Cottage. A lover of nature, he wrote many of his famous works in his cottage, including the poem *The Lark Ascending* in 1881, which inspired the music of Vaughan Williams. So a knock on the door of Parkhurst Cottage one Saturday afternoon by the tall poet with a greying beard and dressed in tweeds was an auspicious one.

Flora and Meredith spent hours on the hills of the South Downs discussing literature, philosophy, music and poetry. Meredith encouraged her to seek the truth and to train the mind to see it, for he considered that was the ultimate value. She wrote extensively in her diaries during this time, noting, *'As we walked along the summit of Box Hill, he seemed to raise our spirits to corresponding heights, rough, pure, and keen, where footing was not easy, but invigorating and every breath was sharp and good to draw.'*

In Meredith, Flora found another father figure and intellectual sparring partner that she needed. She discussed her experiences in the slums of London with him, and her ideas that, by encouraging emigration to the colonies, this would enable the poor to build new lives for themselves.

The colonies would be enriched. She argued that the purpose was not to subjugate people but to uplift them.

Meredith disagreed. He said the solution must come through the intellect and progress would be slow, possibly taking millennia. It was stimulating talk, and encouraged Flora to develop her ideas of Positive Imperialism further.

Flora was introduced to other well-known writers through Meredith, including Robert Louis Stevenson, the Scottish novelist, poet and essayist. He also knocked on the door of the cottage, and to Flora's surprise she found '...*a most weird looking little person, something of a cross between a Polish Jew and an Aztec, and quite fantastically dressed, with parted hair hanging in locks on his shoulders.*' They became good friends and Flora would visit Stevenson and his American wife, Fanny Osbourne at their house, which she described as unusual '...*with the décor being dire, the food inedible and the conversation brilliant.*' He had recently published *Treasure Island,* which was an instant success. One dinner party with Meredith and Stevenson she described as '...*the greatest dinner party in my life.*'

She met many Liberals, as their leader, Lord Farrar lived nearby. He introduced her to the famous Royal Navy Admiral, Frederick Augustus Manxe. He was also a political writer and wrote, '*Come and see Flora Shaw, to know whom is to look through an eyelet into the Promised Land. In matters of abstract thought as well as in warm feelings for the poor, muddy fry of this world, you will find her unmatched. She is Irish and French – that's why. Quite delightful to talk to as to look at.*' Flora spent the next few years learning much from her new friends, and honed her writing skills.

In 1886 she accepted an invitation to accompany old family friends, the Younghusbands, to winter in Gibraltar with their daughter, who was stationed there with her husband. She had never been to Gibraltar, and it was her first taste of life in a British colony. Through her contact with Meredith she had already met William Stead, editor of *The Pall Mall Gazette,* and he had agreed to consider any interesting stories she came across on her trip, to use as newspaper articles.

She researched the history, geography and economy of the Rock and spent weeks exploring the backstreets, seeing the prosperous garrison from every viewpoint. One day she scrambled up the eastern face of the rock and came across an isolated cottage guarded by men in Arab robes. It was the house of Zebehr Pasha, an important leader and slave-trader from Sudan. He had been suspected of being involved in the assassination of General Gordon in Khartoum in 1885, and had been brought to Gibraltar by the British and put under house arrest. Here was the story Flora was looking for.

Permission for an interview was granted, and she nervously returned to the cottage accompanied by an interpreter. Zebehr was sitting in a chair smoking hashish and suffering from toothache. He was tall, slight and dark, dressed in swirling Arab robes. The Pasha started telling her his life history in Arabic, and she was soon impressed by his sincerity, intelligence and original thought.

She asked him whether the death of General Gordon could have been avoided. The Pasha retorted with a furious response, blaming the British for being arrogant and ignorant. General Gordon had wanted him to come to Khartoum to take over as ruler and it was blocked by the anti-slavers in London. If he had been allowed to go to Khartoum, the massacre would never have happened. The English papers had branded the Pasha an evil, decadent, ruthless tyrant, surrounded by slaves, a harem and exotic pets. Here was a chance to tell the other side of the story.

Flora left the cottage exhilarated. She quickly transcribed her notes into an article for *The Pall Mall Gazette* to see if they were interested, and if she could follow it up. The paper had been critical of the Pasha, but William Stead replied swiftly with a positive response.

Over the next four months she visited the cottage once a week. She covered the Pasha's life story, his travels into unknown areas of Africa, and let him expound on his religious and political beliefs. Their last interview left an indelible impression on her when he said, '*What I like in the English is their justice. They are often ignorant, but when they know, they act faithfully. Therefore I should be greatly indebted if you could tell my side of the story.*'

Her first article was published in *The Pall Mall Gazette* in June 1887 under the title *A Lady's Interview with a Captive Chief* and it was well received. She wrote, '*There was a double positive result. Firstly Zebehr Pasha was released because of the effects of my articles on people in Government, and before my last article he was returned to Cairo. Secondly, I had discovered my vocation to which I have devoted my life ever since …I learned what it meant to be a journalist, and of his [Stead's] own brand of journalism which he calls investigative journalism.*'

Flora and Zebehr Pasha remained friends for the rest of his life. As a result of these articles, William Stead employed Flora as a full-time journalist. She learnt his disciplined methods of investigative journalism, research and analysis, which had not been employed before. He was a ground-breaking journalist, and ironically, he died on *Titanic* after carrying out an investigation on the shortage of lifeboats on cruise liners.

After her stay in Gibraltar, Flora visited Morocco, Tenerife and Cairo, where again she acted as a travelling companion to the Younghusbands whilst carrying out her research and writing articles for *The Pall Mall Gazette* and *The Manchester Guardian*. In Cairo, she also met Charles Moberly Bell, a correspondent of *The Times,* who had influence to open more doors for her, and his wife Ethel, who became one of her closest friends.

For the next three years Flora wrote extensively and widely on social, political and economic subjects. She could absorb information quickly and always hit her deadlines, often working late into the night. She started to get known, received invitations to social events and parties, which she enjoyed, and she was gaining respect as a journalist. By 1889 she was recognised as an authority on Mediterranean matters and was taking a deep interest in colonial developments, especially in 'the Scramble for Africa.'

In the summer of 1889 she met Cecil Rhodes, who was in London lobbying for his chartered company. Impressed with his vision for the imperial schemes that he wanted to implement, she met up with him several times. He held strong views on the slave trade, on the possible conflicts between Christian and Moslem and the harshness of the Dutch in South Africa.

In the autumn of 1889 Flora was asked to represent *The Manchester Guardian* at an international conference on anti-slavery in Brussels trying to agree a code of international laws. It was a unique occasion, and even more so for a female journalist speaking fluent French. She impressed many with her knowledge on the subject and was quickly accepted by the other journalists.

During this time Charles Moberly Bell returned from Cairo to take up his new post as the Assistant Manager of *The Times*. He wanted the paper to become a mouthpiece for colonial policy, and he wanted Flora to lead the imperial articles for the newspaper that was often known popularly as 'The Thunderer.'

CHAPTER 6
Tofrek

The murder of General Gordon at Khartoum in 1884 was a ghastly and bloody event which need not have happened.

In April 1880 the Liberals won a landslide victory at the General Election and Gladstone became Prime Minister for the second time. The Liberals had a large majority, but due to divisions within the party there was procrastination, and a reluctance to spend money on foreign expeditions.

The Mahdist uprising had started in Sudan in 1882 led by Muhammad Ahmad. He declared himself '*The Mahdi*', one of a continuing series of men, a prophesied redeemer of Islam, who would, as his followers believed, rid the world of evil.

By December 1883 the situation had become so serious that the British government ordered the evacuation of all personnel from the country. General Gordon was appointed in January 1884 to supervise the evacuation. He was at the end of his career, having gained fame in wars in Crimea and China, but there was a clamour from the public that he was the man who could save Sudan. He was unconventional, passionate and an intensely religious man whom Gladstone disliked, but Gordon was popular with the public, and with Queen Victoria.

He arrived in Khartoum, which is situated at the confluence of the Blue and White Nile and the capital of Sudan, in February. Over the next few months Gordon evacuated about 2,500 people from the city, and tried to negotiate with an influential local leader to take control, but with no backing from the British Government, he failed. The politicians refused to send troops to open the Suakin to Berber route, Gordon's only escape, and the garrison at Berber surrendered. The Mahdi army moved in, surrounded Khartoum and put it under siege for nine months.

Gordon had organised the defences of the city as best he could. There was still time to send troops to relieve him, but it was not until November that, after a public outcry, a relief force was eventually sent out under Field Marshall Garnet Wolseley. Gordon did not help the situation by sending his last message dated December 14, '*Khartoum all right, could hold on for years. C. G. Gordon.*'

By the time Wolseley arrived in Khartoum on January 28, it was two days too late.

Gordon, about ten thousand civilians and the entire garrison had been brutally slaughtered. A famous painting by George William Joy depicts Gordon making a last stand coming out of his house. After the scene in the painting, he was speared and beheaded, his head stuck on a tree, and his body hacked to pieces and never found. Wolseley's small relief force quickly surveyed the slaughter and was forced to retreat. Only then did Gladstone agree to send a much larger field force to Sudan to re-establish the route to Khartoum. Lugard was part of this force and in the following months, he sent detailed letters of his experiences to his brother Ned in England.

The Suakin field force comprised 13,000 men, consisting of a variety of British regiments, four Indian regiments and a contingent from Australia. They assembled at Suakin port on the Red Sea coast on March 12 1885 under the command of General Graham. Lugard heard the stories coming from Sudan as he travelled from India, and felt a mixture of anger and fear at what lay ahead. He read about Gordon, who was a devout Christian, and felt a certain religious zeal to defeat a force of evil. He was eager to fight, but had little knowledge of his enemy.

The Mahdists had mustered in their tens of thousands and were led by an experienced commander, Osman Digna, who was riding on a high from his recent successes against the British. His followers were completely obsessive about their cause and had no intention of giving up.

On arrival at Suakin, Lugard suffered an immediate setback. He received a message in his tent that General Graham had decided that, as a departmental officer, he was too valuable to lose in action. He was forbidden to join the impending attack on Hashim, some seven miles inland.

It was only a short battle, but it involved 8,500 men and 1,500 transport animals. They achieved their objective and only sustained a small number of casualties. Lugard wrote to Ned the next day, '*I went to bed feeling utterly down on my luck. They are apparently having a big fight and the action is so close... horse after horse coming riderless back to the camp, and here am I writing letters like a damned old woman ... You can tell Father that his precious boy is safe - as if he was attending Divine Service in Norton Church.*'

He met General Graham the next day and used all his persuasive powers to allow him to join in the next advance upon Tamai, only twelve miles south-west of Suakin, where 7,000 Mahdists were assembled. This attack required two supply bases to be established en route to support the main assault, the first to be near a small village called Tofrek. The General gave this task to Major General Sir John McNeill, a tough Scotsman who had won the Victoria Cross in the New Zealand Wars in 1864. He was Lugard's commanding officer, and the following days are well documented by a fellow soldier, William Galloway who wrote *The Battle of Tofrek: Fought Near Suakin March 22 1885* shortly after the battle.

McNeill left the safety of Suakin at dawn on March 22 with 3,000 men, heading towards Tofrek. His army was a combination of mounted infantry, lancers, Royal Engineers, a battalion from the Royal Berkshire Regiment, a battalion from the Royal Marine Light Infantry, four battalions of Indian Infantry, a company of Madras sappers and, most important, four naval Garner machine guns with their own naval crews. There was no artillery and no squadron of scouts.

Progress was slow along the hot, narrow, sandy track, with dense mimosa bushes, low-hanging branches and sharp thorns handicapping both troops and animals. After six miles they found an open area suitable for the first temporary stockade, known as a *zeriba*. The plan was to build a stockade about 200 metres square, with two redoubts at opposite corners to take the machine gun posts. The engineers organised the construction of the stockade from the mimosa trees, which were cut down and tied together to prevent them from being dragged away when attacked. A further cordon of sandbag parapets was then placed around the inside perimeter of the stockade.

Work was brisk and by two o'clock the north-east redoubt was complete, and work was concentrated on the south. Trees were still being cleared on the western side, while the south and east sides remained open. Lugard was organising the storage areas on the east side for the supplies, and the corralling of hundreds of camels and mules.

Forty-five minutes later scouts reported that the enemy was gathering on the south and east of the zeriba, and was advancing towards them. McNeill immediately ordered all personnel to return to the half-completed zeriba, and to take up positions. At the same time, the cavalry came galloping back into the camp from the south, with about 5,000 Mahdists hard on their heels. All hell let loose.

The Bengalese contingent on the south side retreated into the stockade, and the north, the west and the redoubts all held their ground as the attackers swung round to the east. The Mahdists stampeded the camels and mules into the stockade. An eyewitness recalled, '*Everything seemed to come at once; transport of all kinds, water carts, ammunition, mules, 17th Native Infantry, Madras sappers, sick-bearers, transport corps, cavalry and fighting arabs ...The dust raised by the crowd was so thick I couldn't see anything beyond the zeriba.*'

Lugard was right in the thick of the chaos, and now living the reality of war. The machine guns ripped into the Mahdists, who were screaming the jihadist mantras that had echoed down the ages. The Mahdists advanced so fast that within minutes hand to hand fighting took place all around. Lugard felt the fear and desperation of defending himself with a sword against someone intent on killing him, and the shock of receiving his first wound in battle.

He wrote to his brother the following day, '*Do not tell Father that I was in the fight on 22 March... They fight like demons. Even women (two or three were found among the dead yesterday)...worst of all is that my shoulder is so bad that I only feel half myself, and in a hand to hand encounter I could not slew [wield] my sword about. I felt much handicapped, but our fate lies with a higher power and so it must befall. It's real desperate work though. Don't let Father know; he is old and worries about things now.*'

The entire battle lasted no more than twenty-five minutes. The Mahdists suffered heavy casualties, estimated at over one thousand dead, due to the horrendous efficiency of the machine guns. Hundreds of dead camels and mules littered the blood-stained battleground.

The enemy threatened to launch another attack but after another hour withdrew, leaving their dead and wounded behind. On the British side there were seventy men killed, including four officers and thirty-four followers (non-combatants providing logistical support). A total of one hundred and thirty-three were injured, and eighteen followers and thirty-six men were missing.

Further isolated attacks were attempted by injured Mahdists and an officer was killed by one feigning death. Another eyewitness reported, '*... when our men sought to afford aid to some of the enemy who could not walk, the latter crawled towards them with spears between their teeth, striving even yet to slay a Kaffir (non-believer).*'

Lugard was taken back to Suakin, with a far better understanding of the realities of war, to have his wounds dressed. He sent another letter to Ned that day, describing the carnage. '*Today the usual convoy has gone to take water and stack provisions in the zeriba where we had the fight. Each time they have had some fighting, and today we can see that they are going at it hard. I confess I am hardly so keen as I was, after seeing all that I saw that day! But I do hope I get into the battle at Tamai… it is getting stinking hot here and the place is simply fetid with latrines, stale horse standings, and dead animals of all sorts… I believe that if they hang out at that zeriba, cholera will break out, for the stench when we left of hundreds of human corpses plus hundreds of camels and mules was suffocating … by gad I should like to see London again.'*

The Mahdi commander Osman Digna did not reach Tamai. He had suffered too many casualties and retreated, which allowed General Graham to take Tamai without resistance. Back in London, Gladstone realised that there were not enough resources to retake Sudan, while the Russians were again advancing in Afghanistan. The British troops were pulled back to Suakin, except for a small contingent left to guard the port. It was thirteen years before the British returned to exact bloody revenge on the Mahdi at the Battle of Omdurman in 1898, the consequences of which have never left us, and reverberate down into the twenty-first century.

Lugard quickly recovered from his wounds, and, as the searing heat of the Sudanese summer approached, he was allowed sixty days of much-needed leave back in England. On his return to Sudan, the Indian contingent was preparing to leave Suakin.

Lugard sailed back to India, a much wiser man.

CHAPTER 7
The summer of the siren

Lugard was subject to strong passions. Towards the end of his life, when he was eighty-two years old, he reflected on the traumatic year of 1886. As he wrote to his biographer Margery Perham, *'The real key to the story of life lies in the knowledge of the emotions and passions which have sometimes disfigured, sometimes built up character, and in every case, influenced the actions recorded. Of these the sexual instinct is recognized as the most potent, for good or ill, and it has certainly been so in my life.'* Lugard sublimated his sexual passions most of his life, pouring enormous energy into his other works, but when these passions were released they were life-changing.

On his return to India from Sudan in April 1885, Lugard was ordered back to his regiment, which had moved to Benares (now called Varanasi). It was a cold winter, and as it was quiet on the military front, he put in a proposal to his colonel to carry out a reconnaissance survey across the surrounding district of Azimghur. This was approved, and Lugard started a detailed and meticulous exercise, interviewing the local civil servants to understand how the various administration systems operated in India. He saw and noted the complexities and inefficiencies of the systems. This fostered his increasing interest in the administration of large provinces. He presented the report to his Commander-in-Chief, and it was well received.

Lugard was now an experienced transport manager, responsible for organising the scheduling and selection of all modes of transport to move personnel and equipment, before the time of trucks and computers. The following year, in March 1886, he was offered a post in Lucknow, the largest and capital city of Uttah Pradesh, in Northern India. He accepted readily.

The station in Lucknow was a much larger regional centre and Lugard was given authority to reorganise the whole transport system, which he did with enthusiasm. His responsibilities included the tricky logistical problems of how to manage sixty elephants, and find the optimum way to feed them. Solving this made future problems with motor transport seem easy. For Lugard this period was a relatively peaceful time, and he was able to turn his attentions to enjoying a more varied social life.

Since the 1857 rebellion, almost thirty years before, Lucknow had expanded into a large, well-established garrison. There was a thriving British community, with many more wives and families than Lugard had encountered on previous stations. The wives introduced more culture, with book and poetry readings, an amateur dramatic society and discussions on literature and philosophy by contemporary writers. Travelling companies such as those run by the London impresario Charles Du Val sometimes toured India from London, and if they were lucky, the Lucknow garrison was entertained by a Gilbert and Sullivan operetta or a Shakespeare play.

Lugard remained on the periphery of the Lucknow social scene, observing the courtship games between the men and women with curiosity, hiding his shyness and inexperience behind cynicism. He was still only twenty-eight, and while it is not possible to be certain that he had never made love to a woman, the evidence suggests that he hadn't. Margery Perham gives us a pen-portrait of Lugard at this crucial time of his adult life. We know that this portrait derives from conversations between Perham and Lugard himself and from letters he wrote which no longer survive. She describes Lugard as enjoying watching '... *the couples go by, to flirt in the dark plantations. The only joy he finds worth lyricising are his horse, his dog and his pipe... But his cynicism, as he watches the moves of the social game which he will not play, is reserved mostly for women, a subject to which he returns again and again.*'

Lugard also wrote poetry, in the time-honoured fashion of amorous but emotionally and sexually frustrated young men. Perham saw a few of the surviving verses and commented, '*In one production he writes at length, burlesquing the full, honeyed sentimentality of the eighties, rhapsodising about the love-light in the blue eyes of a woman in which a man sees his own image and reads of a love that will endure until death... then suddenly breaking off, and asserts that there is not much of that love to be seen... anywhere in this damned country where love is either of the promiscuous sort or to be bought for annas and pice.*[These were Indian currency, subdivisions of the rupee, one anna was one-sixteeth of a rupee.]'

The combination of respect and indeed awe Lugard had for women, combined with his (by modern standards) repressed middle-class religious upbringing, meant that it is highly unlikely he resorted to brothels. When he finally did fall in love with a woman, he quickly became infatuated.

The day indeed arrived when he was introduced to a woman who would change his life forever. Lugard deliberately obscured the name of the lady in question, possibly to protect her, but also under strong pressure from his brother, who detested her. He told Margery Perham the real name of the lady but insisted she collude with him in preserving her actual identity, so Perham refers to her as Celia. In fact her real name was Francis Catherine Gambier, and she signed her letters as simply C.

Catherine was only twenty-seven years old when she met Lugard. There is much in Catherine's life that is uncertain, but what is certain is that she was an incandescent influence on him.

He described her in a letter to his brother in 1938. '*There was in Lucknow in 1886 a lady who was greatly admired by all men. She was a divorcee and the wife of a Colonel there. She had an extraordinarily romantic life, had been painted as a noted beauty by one or more of the great English painters, had been ship-wrecked, been under fire in S. Africa, trained horses over exhibition jumps, drove a four-in-hand* [a four-horse carriage], *wrote for the press including poems of undeniable merit, and I don't know what else besides. She was always the centre of attraction at the evening gatherings in the Club grounds.*'

Catherine had been born in Seville in Spain. There are no details of her first marriage, but she married her second husband George Gambier, the previous year in 1885. He was a Colonel in the 1st Regiment of the Royal Horse Artillery ('The Chestnuts') and fifteen years older than her. Rudyard Kipling had probably heard of Catherine when he was a journalist on *The Civil and Military Gazette* in Simla, and wove her character into one of his many short stories.

In the same 1938 letter, Lugard, still obviously brooding on, and possibly obsessed by, events that happened a full fifty years earlier, wrote to his brother, '*I was not drawn to women's society, and I think she was piqued that I was one of the very few who had not sought an introduction. It is extremely difficult – indeed impossible - to say how it all came about – truthfully as I recollect it - without being guilty of the utter meanness of seeming to shield myself at a woman's expense. In the end we carried on a guilty liaison. She was at the time sexually attracted to me, and I by her, though I was not deeply "in love".*'

Margery Perham spoke more with him about the affair when she was writing his biography. She wrote, '*They rode together; they discussed all things under the sun; they read verse together and wrote it for and to each other; they watched the splendid settings of the tropical sun with an emotion that seemed to fuse their identities. Above all, his deeply affectionate and generous nature found at last an opportunity to give and this meant more to him than to accept.'*

If this, by Lugard's standards, was not being 'in love', one wonders what was.

Where did they meet for their romantic trysts? It is not known for certain, but the popular venue for an affair was, at that time and in that place, a discreetly-located bungalow. The traditional bungalows had large corrugated roofs spilling over a wide verandah, with bamboo chairs and tables placed outside. Inside, there would be a spacious living-room and a dining-room, with large airy bedrooms kept cool by the wooden fans operated by servants from the next room. The rooms smelt of sandalwood and the scent of jasmine wafted through the half-open windows. If you were in love, it was an agreeable place to be.

None of the love letters between Lugard and Catherine survive, having most likely ended up on the fire, and there is no doubt that Lugard's mind and body were on fire too. While we can only guess at the true nature of their physical relationship, we can readily imagine that twice-married and once-divorced Catherine was more skilled at love-making than Lugard was. It is likely she knew exactly what she wanted, and how to guide her new, passionate but inexperienced lover, both metaphorically and literally. We can imagine them lost in each other's ecstasy, with Lugard thrilled beyond excitement, as the wooden fan rotates slowly and hypnotically above them, doing little more than moving the warm tropical air from one part of the room to another.

Immersed in their mutual rapture, they would most likely have been unaware of the *punkawallah,* the servant operating a fan via a series of pulleys on the other side of the thin bedroom wall. It was the case that *punkawallahs* who were deaf were, for obvious reasons, regarded as especially prized. So perhaps the unknown and unnamed *punkawallah* heard little or nothing of what was going on through the wall that fateful day.

Or perhaps he was only pretending to be deaf? In any event, Lugard's life was changed forever.

He and Catherine met regularly over the next few months, with the passionate relationship continuing, and the poetry flowing from Lugard's pen. By all accounts Catherine went about her daily life as though everything was normal, which perhaps for her it was. For Lugard though, things were anything but, and never the same again.

The affair was soon noticed, but Lugard did not care, ignoring the pleas of his fellow officers to beware of a woman to whom they referred as 'a siren', whether out of jealousy or the time-honoured male hypocrisy of blaming a woman's atractiveness on her own sex appeal rather than on their own lustfulness.

As for Lugard, when he visited Catherine, he now left his size eight shoes outside her door for cleaning. It is not too hard to spot a man who has suddenly been smitten, who is distracted, wearing that distant look of being somewhere else, and taking risks he would never before have contemplated. By all accounts, Lugard fitted into all these categories.

The idyllic summer days in 1886 lasted less than six months. They came to an abrupt end in October, when Lugard received orders to travel with a field force to Upper Burma.

CHAPTER 8
Into the mists

In 1878 the King of Burma (now called Myanmar) died, leaving forty-eight sons. The following year his successor, Thibaw, went on an orgy of murder, killing eighty leading members of the family and some of his brother princes to secure his position. The British evacuated their Resident in 1885, and after Thibaw threatened fines on a major timber company, the Viceroy ordered a flotilla invasion up the Irrawaddy River. There was little resistance and the war was over in two weeks. Thibaw was deported and the country annexed on January 1 1886. As there was now no obvious successor, and the Burmese people showed little enthusiasm for the British, the situation remained tense, so further troops were dispatched to keep the fragile peace. This was the uneasy situation that Lugard found when he arrived in Rangoon (now called Yangon) in October 1886.

Placed in charge of two river paddle steamers full of men, equipment and animals, Lugard sailed up the Irrawaddy to the base at Kynetyat. During the voyage, cholera broke out and the doctor died. Water was rationed. The bodies of the dead were launched over the back of the steamers. Lugard felt he was reliving the childhood trip from India on *The Trafalgar*.

At Kynetyat, he organised the transport for a two-hundred mile march through almost impenetrable jungle. Watching for warlike local Shan tribesmen, they climbed about 1,000 metres up the mountains to Mogok, to reach the Ruby Mines district, to the east of Mandalay. His commanding officer, Colonel Cather, was frequently ill, along with many of the men, so Lugard took charge of the transport most of the time, working long hours in debilitating conditions for months on end. A telegram sent to his headquarters that year recorded his transport strength as: '*10 elephants, 697 mules, 149 ponies, 370 bullocks, 385 drivers, plus assorted local and transport staff.*'

Lugard also had to organise transport to the malaria-infested, jungle-covered mountains on the west side of Mandalay, which led to him suffering frequent fevers. The prescribed medicine was chlorodyne, an opiate which had many side-effects, including inducing hallucinations and depression. He corresponded with Catherine frequently, and in this fever-induced state, created in his mind a wildly distorted image of Catherine as his goddess whom he worshipped - his ideal woman. He recounted this in a statement to Ned in December 1938. '*We corresponded voluminously... I gradually grew to endow her with all the traits of perfect womanhood which my imagination created, and to fall really in love with my Ideal.*'

It was during this stressful time in July 1887 that Lugard received a letter from India. He continued in his statement to Ned in 1938, '*... I received a letter in which she* [Catherine] *described a terrible carriage accident which nearly severed one leg — due to recklessness of which I was the cause — I was thrown into a state of grief and anxiety which was more than I could bear. I absolutely worshipped the Ideal I had created.*'

He immediately applied for leave, which his commanding officer rejected due to his crucial role as transport manager. After threatening to resign, he appealed to General Lord Roberts, who sent orders for his relief with the reason: 'Urgent private affairs.' Burning with a raging fever, he set sail for India.

Landing in Calcutta, he went straight to Lucknow and found no trace of Catherine. She had sailed for England, presumably to have further treatment. He immediately booked a passage for London. He wrote, '*... the strain on the voyage broke me down altogether. I arrived* [at her address in London] *to find a somewhat cold reception* [from Catherine], *and a growing attachment to another man. Later* [this would have been 1889] *I found she was living with him and had a child by him.*'

There was no apology, no sign of contrition. Catherine had moved on from Lucknow, and was back in a hedonistic London set she knew well. It was a short meeting. Lugard had nothing to say, and left immediately. Catherine's expression gave nothing away, but underneath the mask she knew she had hurt him deeply, and there was regret.

Lugard wandered off, dazed, shocked and devastated. He could not believe that someone who had professed to love him with such heartfelt words could inflict such mental torment. He tried to reason with himself, but he was now incapable. He fell into a period of anger, not hatred, but intense self-criticism, sending him spiraling into a deep depression. For two months he did not go home, and cut himself off. He was still suffering from the effects of the Burmese fever and having to take chlorodyne, disturbing his mind further. He was losing touch with reality, and needed immense mental strength to avoid complete self-destruction.

His chosen solution was simple. He would find a distraction that would provide danger, be physically challenging and required no commitment. So he joined the London Fire Brigade as a part-time volunteer. He contacted the Superintendent of the fire brigade, Captain Eyre Massey Shaw, who had formed the brigade in 1865. A popular, gregarious Irishman, Shaw was well known on the socialite scene, had appeared in *Punch* magazine, and was even referred to in a song by the Fairy Queen in *Iolanthe* by Gilbert and Sullivan written in 1882:

> *Oh Captain Shaw!*
> *Type of true love kept under!*
> *Could thy Brigade*
> *With Cold Cascade*
> *Quench my great love, I wonder!*

By coincidence Captain Shaw was also a cousin of Flora Shaw.

Captain Shaw was hesitant to accept him initially, but changed his mind and eventually wrote, '*Your profession was an introduction in itself and your letter so frank and manly. I have no hesitation in promising to help you.*'

So, in that delicate state of mind, Lugard went out fighting fires in London, going out night after night, not caring of the dangers or consequences, taking each day at a time. That was until his uncle, Sir Edward, found out what he was doing. He invited him around to dinner a few months later, and was disturbed by the change.

He wrote to Lugard's brother Ned, who was stationed in India. '*Fred turned up last evening looking better than when he first came home but I thought rather wild ... I wanted him to stay and dine but he said he had an engagement and at last it came out that he had joined the Fire Brigade and went out every night (when they called him) to fires etc. - on the engine!! I was rather astonished and questioned him to his motive etc. He said it was for the excitement, and that he could not rest without excitement so he went to the Headquarters of the Brigade at Southwark every evening and remained all night, sleeping in his clothes ...In truth I am rather, indeed, very anxious about him and the risks he runs: he is out almost every night at great London fires and he is so fearless and daring I dread his coming to grief.*'

Sir Edward found out that Lugard had not resigned from the Army, but had only been allowed compassionate leave. After further discussions, Sir Edward persuaded him to report back to his regiment, which was about to set sail for Gibraltar. Lugard reluctantly reported to Aldershot, sailed for Gibraltar, and once there, found he had been awarded the D.S.O. for his achievements in Burma. But nothing could bring him out of the dark depression into which he had sunk. His benevolent Colonel could see he was in no fit mental state to handle his job, and recommended him for sick leave.

Lugard knew that his obsession with Catherine was not over. She was there deep in his soul, and he needed to get away from England, from India, to avoid any place that she may visit, for him to have any chance of recovery. Africa had always been an attraction to adventurers, with plenty of danger, excitement and challenges. This is where he decided to go.

Lugard had read about Sir John Kirk, the Consul in Zanzibar who had known the famous Scottish explorer David Livingstone, and was continuing his work in Africa battling to end the Arab slave trade. This appealed to Lugard on many fronts, so he wrote a letter to Sir John to ask him if he could get involved, to help him end this evil practice in Africa. He added he would be willing to do so at any cost. His anguish would then not be in vain.

Sir Edward was none too impressed by his nephew's '*wild projects.*' He considered that he was throwing his career away, which had such good prospects, and bringing grief to his family. There was a last plea to him in a letter in January 1888 '... *to throw off that morbid affliction.*' It was to no avail. Lugard had made up his mind.

Whilst waiting for a reply from Zanzibar, Lugard read that the Italian Army was about to invade Ethiopia, a major base for the slave trade. He had another impetuous idea, not thought through, but he didn't care. He would join up. It would bring the excitement he was craving.

He packed a small suitcase, gathered together his entire savings of forty-eight sovereigns, his medals from Afghanistan, Sudan and Burma, and boarded the first ship from Gibraltar bound for Italy. He disembarked at Naples and went to the British Embassy in Rome. The officials there curtly informed him that his idea to join the Italians was futile, for if he got to the front line, he would be treated as a spy and shot. So he returned to Naples and travelled on to Suez, still not entirely convinced. He was back in Africa, and on his way to Zanzibar.

CHAPTER 9
Battling the slavers

By the time Lugard reached Suez, he was already low on funds, and about to experience life as a deck passenger. Whilst waiting for a ship he looked for cheap lodgings and was grateful for the kindness of strangers; first a Greek restaurant owner who offered him a room for free, and then a German family. They invited him to eat and pray with them, and asked if he would travel with their son under the German East Colonisation Scheme. He agreed and together they caught an old Italian tramp steamer called *The Pandora* going to Zanzibar.

It was a miserable journey, sharing a searing hot, open deck with Arab coolies, Italian labourers, cockroaches and fleas. The steamer passed through the Red Sea into the Indian Ocean, hugged the East African coast, and a week later arrived at Massawa in the Italian zone of Ethiopia. Lugard was desperate to get off the boat. He cleaned himself up, and, despite the advice of the consul in Rome, decided to make his way to the Italian front line. He caught a train, and by sheer bluff, and the aid of a Somali guide who spoke Hindustani, he got through to the front line, where he dined with *The Times* correspondent and an Italian General. He found no fighting, no job available, and a peace mission about to start; but the General gave him the best meal he'd eaten for months before returning to the coast.

The next stop was Aden, where he found his half-pay had been granted. He had just enough money to get to Zanzibar, by second class, a big improvement from the fetid deck of the steamer. He was becoming more focused, read further on the history of the slave trade and started to understand the consequences in East Africa. He researched which companies were working on the east coast, and by luck found that the Zanzibar Consul, Colonel Charles Euan-Smith was on board. Despite Lugard being a rather disheveled second-class passenger, Euan-Smith met him, and was impressed enough to put his name forward to The African Lakes Company based in Mozambique, working on Lake Nyasa in an area controlled by the Portuguese. (In 1907 this became the British Protectorate of Nyasaland, and gained independence as Malawi in 1964.)

On arrival at Zanzibar, the Consul gave him a letter of introduction to the Consul in Mozambique, Henry O'Neill. A quiet and studious man, O'Neill impressed Lugard. He was an ex-naval officer who had served in anti-slavery patrols, an experienced geographer and explorer, and had known both explorers Livingstone and Stanley. O'Neill had only recently returned from the north end of Lake Nyasa where he had led a group of Europeans and local allies against Arab slave-traders, so was an ideal person from whom to learn the history and problems in the area. The slave-traders had hundreds of well-armed men who had recently attacked the post of The African Lakes Company. They were beaten off but further attacks were imminent.

O'Neill detected the intelligence, courage, and training of an experienced military man. When Lugard asked O'Neill if he could be of any service to the Company, his immediate reply was, *'You would be a God-send to them!'*

Lugard was delighted. The challenges ahead contained all the elements he craved. He probed further to ensure that the Company had the legitimate right and authority to attack. O'Neill gave him full assurances. Lugard wrote to Ned '… *that for the first time since my return from India, I am as comfortable and as happy as my state of mind would permit.'*

O'Neill made one request of Lugard - to write about the country and his experiences as he travelled. He would forward Lugard's dispatches to the British press to show the public the sort of problems they faced in East Africa. Lugard agreed enthusiastically, and those dispatches were later included in '*The Rise of Our East African Empire',* the book he published in 1893.

He left the port on March 31 1888, and headed south along the Mozambique coast in the British India ship *Dunkeld,* arriving at Quilimane six days later. This small Portuguese port lay on the Kwakwa river, a tributary of the Zambezi, too shallow for steamers but navigable by canoe. Lugard was short of money, but persuaded the local agent to pay for transport and provisions to his next stop, Blantyre, the headquarters of the Company.

Lugard set off from Quilimane in a long, wooden dug-out canoe. He sat at the back under a small awning that gave him meagre shelter from the scorching tropical sun, lit up one of his thin acrid Indian cigars and observed the crew.

The coxswain sat in front of him on a box, steering, urging on six oarsmen from the local Tonga tribe. They sat three each side in the middle of the boat, stripped to the waist, one man guiding with a punt pole on the bow of the canoe. Every so often the coxswain would sing in a deep, melodious voice, the crew joining in harmony as they ploughed up the river, the sun beating down relentlessly, sweat pouring down their backs. This Africa was completely new to him, and he felt an affinity with it. *'Great limbed acacias festooned with giant creepers. River and forest were alive with butterflies and birds - kingfishers, highly-coloured reed sparrows, bitterns, storks, cormorants all watched over by the magnificent white-headed fish eagle, with its haunting cry.'*

Nature balanced this with vicious hippo-flies whose bite could draw blood, the ever-present threat of crocodiles, dangerous groups of wallowing hippos and incessant clouds of stinging mosquitoes that descended every evening.

They joined the wide, majestic Zambezi River for a short length, paddling furiously against the rapid current to reach another large tributary, the Shire River. It took six weeks to paddle to Blantyre.

Lugard talked to traders en route, learnt more about slavery, saw the evidence of its existence from passing boats, and found that Europeans were still involved. It was known that the Arab/Swahili traders were using some of the stronger tribes to attack and capture or kill the weaker ones, but from talking to the settlers along the river he realised Portuguese traders and soldiers were also actively involved in transporting the slaves to the coast.

Even worse, some British ships were transporting untied slaves when British men-of-war were in the vicinity, confident that even if they were seen, they would not be stopped. Lugard wrote, *'Thus our British ships actually become the medium of carrying slaves for the Portuguese… It was no use trying to free slaves at the ports or at sea… we must go to the root of the evil and crush the traders.'* He continued, *'Our horror-stricken outcries in Europe against the unspeakable atrocities of the Arab slave-raider ill become us when we look back at the history of the past, and recall the fact that for two and a half centuries we ourselves stained our hands with this traffic, and pocketed the gold which was the price of human blood. We thus have a duty of expiation to perform towards the African.'*

During the journey, he heard much criticism of the African Lakes Company and its owners, the Moir brothers; that they were mean and corrupt. Lugard decided to keep his distance. He refused to travel on their steamer to Blantyre, and went by canoe instead with two excitable Polish exiles he had met on the journey up.

The Shire River meandered through marshland, with large swathes of matted grass floating past carrying birds and small animals hitching a ride. One day he ventured into the tall elephant grass to look for an antelope to shoot, and was told there were four lions nearby eating a kill. He inexplicably went looking for them, pushing himself into the face of immense danger.

He was watched closely by the Tonga men who thought he was either crazy or extremely brave and protected by a spirit. He met men from the Maklolo tribe who had come up from the south with Livingstone thirty years earlier, and who talked of the famous man with great affection. He experienced the hypnosis of African drumming, dancing, and singing and started to learn about the tribes and cultures of the region. He was trying to understand the power of animism, and what issues were important to the African.

The marshy area was a breeding ground for fever, and Lugard inevitably went down with another bout of malaria. At thirty years old, he was now an old hand at dealing with the various fevers he contracted and had devised his own treatments; always keep out of the sun when resting, protect the stomach, liver and spleen against chills, and continually smoke the cheroots! Lugard noted in his diary: *When the fever comes, take five grains of quinine and pile on blankets to sweat it out.*

The geography gradually changed as he travelled north, the marshlands giving way to wooded areas, culminating in the Shire hills, with mountains in the background. He was mesmerized by the magnificent sunrises and sunsets, but it brought back the vivid memories and trauma of Lucknow.

They arrived at Katunga in May and Lugard climbed up the steep track to Blantyre joined by two other Europeans, Alfred Sharpe, (later to become Governor of Nyasaland) and a friend called Burton. They were greeted by the unexpected sight of a small mission built by the Rev. David Scott of the Church of Scotland, constructed in traditional Scottish style. It comprised a rectangle of houses built of local red brick for the minister and families, with a space left on one side for a church that was to be completed seven years later in 1895, to become the pride of Blantyre, named after the small town in South Lanarkshire where Livingstone was born.

At the offices of The African Lakes Company they were met by John Moir. His brother Fred had been badly wounded in a recent attack and had returned to Scotland. John was delighted to see Lugard, and asked him to lead the next expedition. After hearing more details, Lugard realised the mission was far more complex than he had first assumed.

Around Lake Nyasa lived a number of peaceful tribes including the Tonga, Nkonde and Bemba, and two aggressive tribes, the Ngoni and Yao, of Zulu origin who had moved into the area from the south. Arab and

Swahili slave-traders had arrived from the north thirty years earlier, and based themselves at the northern part of the lake. They used the Ngoni and Yao to attack the other tribes and capture slaves for them, paying them with guns and goods. The village raids would be carried out at dawn, the older men killed, and the women, young men and boys captured to sell.

The slaves were taken both north and south, and to new routes which were opening up the west to Lake Tanganyika. One Swahili slave trader, Mlozi, controlled a well-defended stronghold fourteen miles west of Karonga. It was his aim to eliminate the African Lakes Company from his area.

Lugard was asked to lead the attack on Mlozi's stronghold. He was happy in principle, as he had the support of the Rev. Scott, but the Acting-Consul, John Buchanan was not willing to give his approval. An appropriate British solution was found. A dinner was held at Blantyre, and Buchanan was invited. He was happy that Lugard was leading the expedition, but the Foreign Office was nervous about the fragile political situation. It did not want to set off a mini-war between European powers, especially Germany and Portugal, so could not officially approve it.

Lugard made a heartfelt plea. *'The African Lakes Company are nothing to me. My grounds for going are because I think the cause so great and a good one. But see the risk you make me incur if you compel me to go without your authorization.'*

Buchanan was persuaded, and would agree if they could demonstrate the whole of the community was behind the decision. The Company and the Scottish missions voted and all agreed with the expedition as long as Lugard was leader. A letter was sent to Buchanan. He approved the plan, but nonetheless began his reply, *'That Her Majesty's Government will not be held responsible for the expedition but...'* Lugard wrote in his diary, *'I was most proud of thus having succeeded in uniting all parties, and lifting the expedition from an enterprise by a trading company into a crusade in which both the political and religious sections equally approved and supported, and which had the earnest wishes for success from the one, and the prayers of the other.'*

In reality Lugard had little authority, and would have been entirely blamed by the Foreign Office if it were to go wrong. This was confirmed by a letter he received from his cousin, Colonel Henry Lugard, six months later, which showed he had been using his cousin as a mole to get the unofficial view from the mandarins. *'The Foreign Office learnt from the Consuls near you that you were knocking about in East Africa and they wrote to the War Office asking who were you and what were you doing? The War Office replied that you were on half-pay on recommendations of the Medical Board and suffering from debility and great mental depression. F.O. then wrote asking if some communication relative to your state of health should not be made to the African Lakes Company... It is a case in which the Government are evidently not able to do or say anything which might in any way fix responsibility for what is being done on them - but nevertheless I gather they would not be displeased (quite the contrary) if your efforts to oust the slave traders prove successful.'*

He was beginning to understand the duplicity of Her Majesty's Government.

Lugard left Blantyre on May 18 1888 with John Moir and Dr. Cross, the mission doctor, on the steamer, *Ilala*. There were fifteen members in his task force, a mixed bag of men, a marked contrast to his comrades in the Norfolk Regiment. Seven were tough mercenaries of various nationalities recruited in Natal who had cut their teeth in the South African goldfields and fought in local wars. Seven were experienced Scottish company men, who spanned the religious spectrum, knew the local problems, and could speak the native language. The last man was Alfred Sharpe, who Lugard had already met. He was a crack shot, highly reliable, and considered a good man to have at your side.

The majority of the men were all new to him. From his diaries, we know he studied and got to know their strengths and weaknesses quickly, and worked out who to put together. His life may well have to depend on it.

They boarded the already-overloaded steamer, which was belching smoke and sparks and could be seen for miles. The steamer headed for Mlozi's stronghold at Karonga. They stopped at a Free Church mission at Bandawe and met another dedicated Scotsman, Dr. Laws, who ran a church, hospital with training facilities, and a school for a thousand pupils with his wife and a few supporters. They were surrounded by hostile tribes and slavers, were seven weeks from the coast but determined to overcome adversities with quiet resolution. Many such missioneries never saw Scotland again.

The Karonga stockade had six employees led by a fierce, stocky, bearded, bull of a man called Monteith-Fotheringham. Few would have guessed he had come from England as a missionary to this desolate and dangerous outpost. Lugard soon found he was an enormous asset, totally reliable, having great courage and tenacity, but, as discovered later, had a fierce temper.

The stockade was chaotic, with housing, stores, ammunition and medical facilities built ad-hoc. It was vulnerable to attack, inefficient, and the lack of hygiene a potential health hazard. Lugard had the stockade and walls rebuilt, the compound areas redesigned, a fireproof magazine built, and separate medical and surgery facilities constructed. All this completed within a week.

He wanted to unite this wild bunch. One night he donned his medals, assembled the group together and made a small speech to explain his priorities. His first was the suppression of the slave-trade; his second, to save the local tribe, the Nkonde, from further persecution. Third was to save the lives of the missionaries and his final priority was to uphold British honour. He demanded total loyalty from the men, and to give the local community their full support. He received an unequivocal response, and prepared for the attack.

The next evening he set off with a scouting party of Fotheringham and five Tonga to recce Mlozi's position - in his tennis shoes. At the stronghold he took note of all the defensive ditches and watchtowers. As they moved away they were spotted, and an alarm was raised. A large number of attackers poured out of the stronghold, firing at them. Lugard's men hastily retreated, bullets skimming over the top of their heads. He fired a shot back into the melée of slavers, and they scattered, allowing the scouting party to return to the camp safely.

The following day was Sunday. Bizarrely, the Scottish half had a complete day of rest, whilst the remainder were repelling a party of Arab slavers' scouts (who had completed their Moslem day of rest.) Lugard checked the ammunition, and manufactured grenades from food tins rammed with mud and assorted steel parts. Alfred Sharpe had been sent out to recruit from the local Tonga tribe and he returned that day with 190 men.

Sharpe had attacked a slaver caravan train and freed three women, a boy who had been in a gori-stick manacle clamped around his neck, and had taken an Arab prisoner. The Tonga wanted to execute the prisoner, but Lugard stopped them and kept him in chains to use as a guide. The women looked extremely frightened, as they had heard rumours that all white men were cannibals. Lugard quickly made the decision to reunite them to their tribe, before any harm befell them.

One of the Natal men died of fever so it became essential to launch the attack before any further losses. Lugard assembled the local tribesmen, and with the aid of an interpreter, told them they would be paid, but there was to be no looting. Any loot taken afterwards would be equally divided by the Company agents. He stressed the need for discipline and insisted they obey the orders of the white men, otherwise there would be chaos. Finally there would be no stealing of women; this was not the white man's custom.

Lugard recorded, '*With such arguments we carried the day and, finding out their war cry, I said when I shouted, they must charge side by side with*

Fig 1. Flora Shaw,
the journalist c. 1890

Fig 2. Captain Frederick Lugard,
the explorer

Fig 3. Man of the Day No 639, Dec 1895, Vanity Fair Spy Cartoon
© The National Gallery

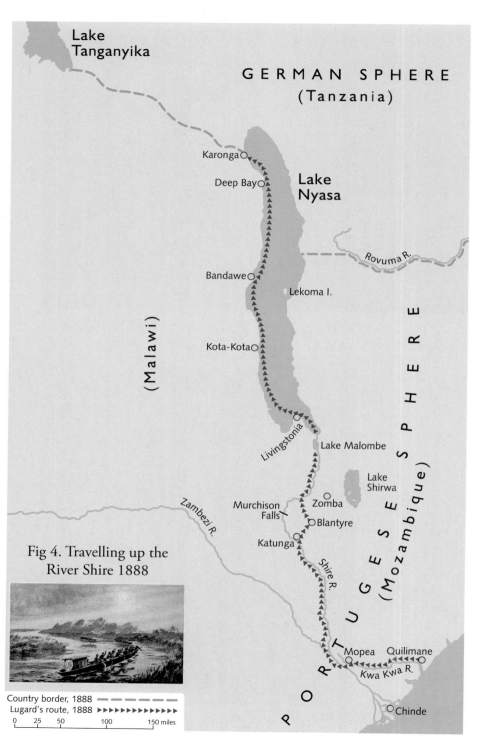

Lake
Tanganyika

GERMAN SPHERE
(Tanzania)

Karonga○

Deep Bay○

Lake
Nyasa

Rovuma R.

Bandawe○

Lekoma I.

(Malawi)

Kota-Kota○

Livingstonia○

Lake Malombe

Lake
Shirwa

Zambezi R.

Murchison
Falls

Zomba○

○Blantyre

Fig 4. Travelling up the
River Shire 1888

Katunga○

Shire R.

P O R T U G E S E   S P H E R E

(Mozambique)

Mopea○   Quilimane○

Kwa Kwa R.

Country border, 1888 ▬ ▬ ▬
Lugard's route, 1888 ▶▶▶▶▶▶▶▶▶▶▶▶

0   25   50   100   150 miles

○Chinde

Map 1. Route to Nyasa, Nyasaland 1888

Map 2. Route to Lake Victoria, Kenya 1890

Fig 5. Emin Pasha, leader of the 'lost army'

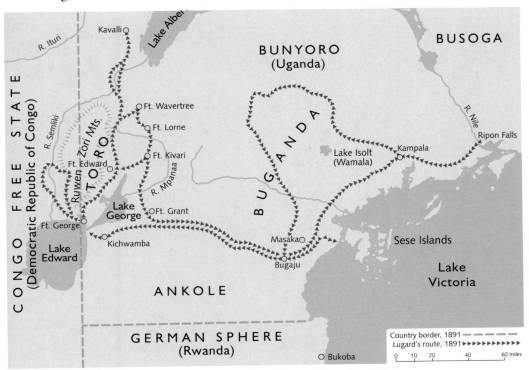

Map 3. Route to Lake Albert, Uganda 1891

Fig 6. The Rt. Hon. Joseph
Chamberlain, Sec. of State for
the Colonies 1895-1903.
*'When he screwed in his eyeglass
you felt as you were going to
be sifted to the marrow'*

Fig 7. The Rt. Hon. Winston
Churchill, Under Sec. of State
for the Colonies 1906-08.
*'It seems ridiculous that a boy of
his age should have the power
that he has'*

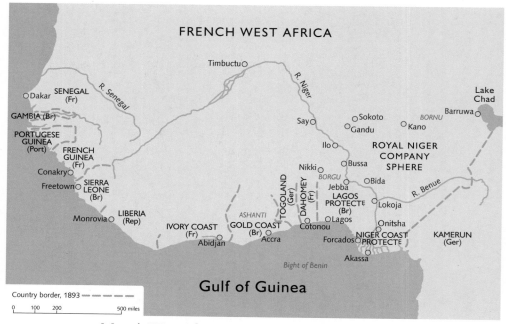

Map 4. West Africa 1893, 'The Scramble for Africa'

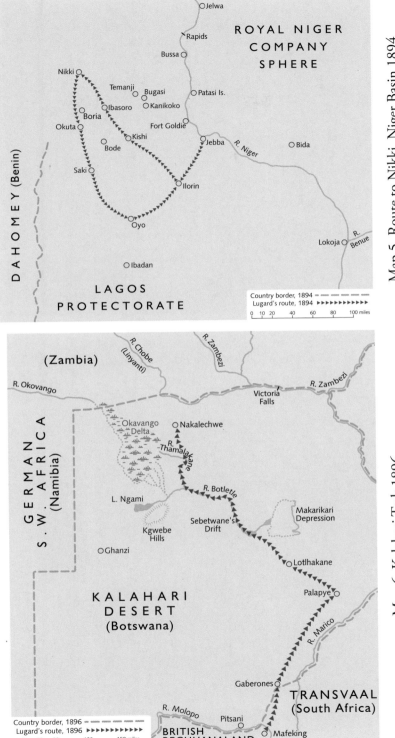

Map 5. Route to Nikki, Niger Basin 1894

ROYAL NIGER
COMPANY
SPHERE

○ Jelwa

Rapids

Bussa ○

Nikki ○
Temanji ○   ○ Bugasi
                        ○ Patasi Is.
○ Ibasoro   ○ Kanikoko
Boria ○
Okuta ○   Fort Goldie ○
            Kishi ○   ○ Bida
Bode ○   Jebba ○   R. Niger
Saki ○
            Ilorin ○

DAHOMEY (Benin)

○ Oyo

Lokoja ○   R. Benue

○ Ibadan

LAGOS
PROTECTORATE

Country border, 1894 ▬ ▬ ▬
Lugard's route, 1894 ▶▶▶▶▶▶▶▶▶▶
0 10 20   40   60   80   100 miles

Map 6. Kalahari Trek 1896

(Zambia)

R. Chobe
(Linyanti)

R. Zambezi

R. Okovango

R. Zambezi

Victoria
Falls

GERMAN
S. W. AFRICA
(Namibia)

Okavango
Delta
R. Thamalakane

○ Nakalechwe

L. Ngami

R. Botletle

Kgwebe
Hills

Sebetwane's
Drift

Makarikari
Depression

○ Ghanzi

KALAHARI
DESERT
(Botswana)

▼ Lotlhakane

Palapye ○

R. Marico

Gaberones ○

TRANSVAAL
(South Africa)

R. Molopo   Pitsani
                        ○

BRITISH
BECHUANALAND

○ Mafeking

Country border, 1896 ▬ ▬ ▬
Lugard's route, 1896 ▶▶▶▶▶▶▶▶▶▶
0   25   50   100   150 miles

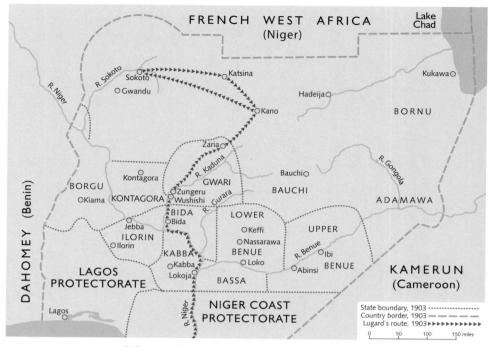

Map 7. North Nigeria campaign 1903

Fig 8. Colonel Willcocks and WAFF staff, Lokoja 1900

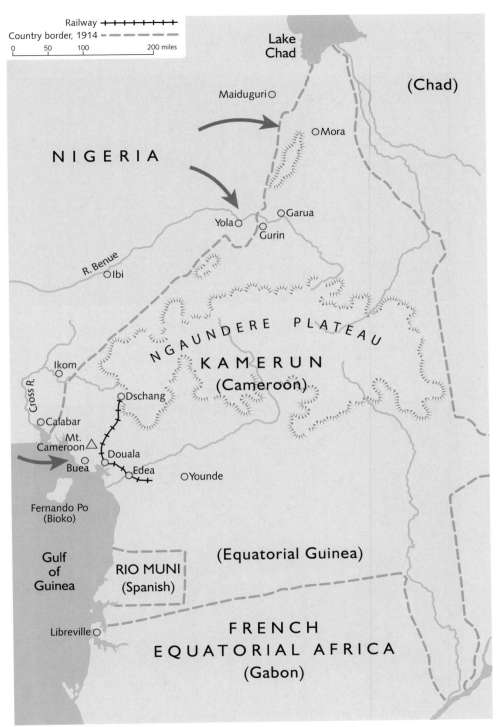

Lake
Chad

(Chad)

Maiduguri ○

○ Mora

NIGERIA

Yola ○   ○ Garua
        Gurin ○

R. Benue
    ○ Ibi

N G A U N D E R E   P L A T E A U

KAMERUN
(Cameroon)

Ikom ○

Cross R.

○ Dschang

○ Calabar

Mt.
Cameroon △

        ○ Douala
Buea ○   ○ Edea
                        ○ Younde

Fernando Po
(Bioko)

Gulf
of
Guinea

RIO MUNI
(Spanish)

(Equatorial Guinea)

FRENCH

Libreville ○

EQUATORIAL AFRICA
(Gabon)

Map 8. Cameroon campaign 1914

Fig 9. The Battle of Tofrek 22 March 1885 by Edwin Fripp
©The Rifles, Berkshire and Wiltshire Museum, Salisbury

Fig 10. Landing of the Belgian Refugees at Folkestone 1914
by Fredo Frantani ©The Folkestone Museum

the white men. They went half mad with excitement… Yet I think there was something fine in the sight of the Englishman standing up for the right of superiority, the rooted custom of centuries, saying that they would have no carrying off of slaves and women and urging the wild passion of these savages to seek a nobler channel.'

The Tonga men were divided into companies, each under a Tonga chief and a white man who knew the language. On June 15, in the late evening, they set off towards the stronghold led by the captured prisoner. They reached the stronghold at one o'clock, set up a medical post, and took up positions to attack. Lugard shouted a loud rallying cry and the charge began.

It did not go according to plan. They reached the wall of the stronghold, but the Arabs reacted quickly and let out a volley of shots from the slit holes in the walls. Grenades were to be thrown in, but the men with the explosives had fallen too far behind. A quick decision had to be made. Heart pounding, Lugard grabbed hold of a branch and started scaling the wall.

He heard a deafening shot, and instantly felt a violent, burning sensation in his chest. He crashed down into a sitting position. His arms went limp. He was bleeding profusely, and he was convinced he was mortally wounded. He called to Sharpe *'I have got it… I am no more use here… I am off to the rear to the doctor … You take command.'* He begged Sharpe to see the attack through and not give in.

He staggered into the darkness, the razor-sharp spear grass slashing his face, but he could walk. His loyal servant Mahea eventually found him and helped him to limp away, his useless arms dangling at his side like a rag doll. Unable to find the medical post they made their way slowly along the track back to Karonga. As the sun rose, a raging thirst set in, and with no hat he began to hallucinate. A friendly local tribesman saw the state he was in, and offered him his red tam o'shanter hat to keep off the sun. It was in this desperate condition that the doctor found him on the track, almost unconscious from loss of blood. He was stretchered back to the camp, arriving at three o'clock, fourteen hours after he had been wounded.

Meanwhile, Sharpe had been unable to take the stronghold and made an orderly withdrawal with minimum casualties. A Natal man was shot through the head, and another wounded. Five of the Tonga were killed and nine badly wounded; lucky, considering the fierce resistance.

The next morning the extent of Lugard's extraordinary injuries became apparent. The bullet had gone through his elbow joint, but not fractured it, into his chest, then, deflected by a rib, missed his heart and a major artery, and emerged above his breast pocket, causing a tearing wound. Finally, it hit his left wrist, smashing the bone, cutting a minor artery and leaving pieces of a letter from his breast pocket embedded in his wrist. The discharge must have only been a few inches away, for his right arm was also blackened with gunpowder and two pieces of wadding were found forced into the flesh of his arm.

To say he had a lucky escape is an understatement. The bullet had only to be a few millimetres from its trajectory and it would have hit a main artery, paralysed an arm, or killed him outright. Dr. Cross had a difficult decision to make. With only basic medical facilities and supplies in the stockade, even if he carried out an amputation, Lugard would probably die from post-operation problems. He therefore carried out a series of delicate operations. To Lugard's astonishment, when he came round from the chloroform, he found he still had all his limbs intact. He was to carry the pain in his left arm for the rest of his life, a reminder of that day.

The following day Lugard summoned his men, to rally them, and to congratulate them on their courage. He ordered the stockade to be strengthened in case of a counter attack, and considered what guerilla tactics could be used against the slavers. Privately he knew there was little effective action they could take until they had a cannon to breach the slavers' stronghold. Moir was going to South Africa to purchase one but it would be months before he returned. In addition fever was running through the camp and many of the men were suffering, including the good doctor, who became severely ill. His assistant, a novice to first aid, had to take over dressing Lugard's wounds.

When the *Ilala* returned to Karonga on July 1, the Natal men left. Lugard should also have gone, but his mind was in turmoil that the whole venture could implode if he left, and that the fighting would all have been in vain. He decided to stay on.

During the next month arguments broke out between the remaining men leading to an attempted dual, broken up by Fotheringham. The stockade was overrun by a plague of rats, followed by snakes, and more fever broke out, not an easy situation for a healthy man to control, never mind someone with both his arms in splints and who could not even scratch his nose. He reorganised his Tonga men into three new companies and sent them on marauding parties, to boost morale.

The steamer returned on August 5, and as his wounds had still not healed, Lugard was reluctantly taken to the boat. Even this was not without incident, when a squall blew up as the transfer dingy took him across to the ship. Had it not been for the skill of the helmsman to beach the craft he would have been drowned.

He spent three weeks in Bandawe having his wounds dressed daily by

Dr. Laws, who was impressed by the courage and character of this strange soldier. Lugard had suffered a great deal without a murmur, and appeared to only have the good of his country at heart. He was transferred to Blantyre for further recuperation. The company doctor, Dr. Bowie removed the splint on his arm, which was now rigid, and massaged it back to life. He was helped by Mr. Scott and his wife who wrote to his sister Emma in October 1888, '*He is such a fine, straightforward disinterested man, and has really done good work at the north end against the Arabs; work willingly undertaken because it seemed to need his presence and help.*'

Lugard wrote in his diary how deeply affected he was by the kindness and generous hospitality of those that tended him, and that this period of convalescence was the most peaceful and pleasant he had known since he left Burma. Having come so close to death, Lugard started to value life once more.

Having recovered, he returned to Karonga and went shooting game at the northern tip of Lake Nyasa, which was not affected by the slavers. There he visited the Nkonde villages and saw how life had been before the attacks; the neatly laid out, well-constructed houses, villagers tending the herds of cattle, goats and fowl, growing crops; friendly people leading simple, rewarding lives. He felt only he and a handful of white men were between them and potential misery, and felt a heavy responsibility, and helplessness with so few resources.

Using the Consul's envoy in Zanzibar, Lugard attempted negotiations with Mlozi, but the slave-trader just used the time to stock up with more ammunition and supplies. Eventually in January, the gun arrived from South Africa, a seven-pounder breach-loading screw-gun, a mainstay artillery piece of the British Army. They were down to six Natal men, with some sick, including Fotheringham, but voted narrowly to go ahead with the attack.

The gun was hauled seven miles to a hill overlooking the stronghold and his three companies of Tonga took up positions in the long grass. They started firing early in the morning, penetrating the stronghold but caused little damage inside. It kept the Arabs pinned down, but little else. They found a lot of ammunition was found to be faulty, so firing was frustratingly erratic. After three hours they withdrew and returned to Karonga with little achieved.

External events had moved fast whilst Lugard was waging war in Karonga. The Germans tried to impose a coastal blockade on Arab traders after an Arab revolt, and wanted the British to join them. Meanwhile, the Portuguese were trying to extend their influence into Nyasa from Mozambique. In addition a new figure had appeared on the African stage, the controversial, ambitious businessman Cecil Rhodes, who was taking a keen interest in Nyasa. The British Government wanted the 'North End War' brought to a close as soon as possible to avoid antagonizing friendly Arab factions. As Henry O'Neill wrote to Lugard in November, *'Our quarrel is with Mlozi and his fellow robbers and slave-hunters ...not with Arabs in general or with Islam.'*

Lugard could see the direction in which events were tending, and after a meeting in Karonga he decided to leave. He felt certain his time would be better spent in England lobbying for support. His little band of brothers threw a party for him before he left on March 13 1889, with Dr. Cross making a warm and complimentary speech on behalf of the Company, saying he had gained respect from both white men and African alike. Fotheringham, who had served him so well, also spoke and presented Lugard with a sword and a pair of binoculars.

The sword was inscribed:

From the members of the Karonga Expedition to Captain F.D. Lugard D.S.O. Norfolk Regt. Commanding the Expedition as a token of their esteem. Karonga, Lake Nyasa, Central Africa, March 13th, 1889

A party started and they sang well into the night, of home, wives, foreign ports, lovers and all those they missed. The following day Lugard wrote in his diary, *'All were poor men - they were facing constant fever and exposing their lives for a miserable pittance; yet every one of them gave a large subscription.'*

The two gifts remained among the most treasured items of his life, with the sword later proudly displayed on a wall of his study in Little Parkhurst.

CHAPTER 10
The pearl of Africa

When he arrived in Zanzibar on June 5, Lugard read that Prime Minister, Lord Salisbury, was leading debates on anti-slavery, but Salisbury made no promise of military support or proposal to take over Nyasa. The directors of the African Lakes Company wrote to Lugard to say they could not raise enough money for another expedition, and gave him just one hundred pounds, which didn't even cover his boat fare. He was out of a job, and in need of an income.

Lugard started to write articles, and made presentations to the Royal Geographical Society, the British Association and various missionary societies, especially in Scotland. He lobbied politicians, met up with his old friend Henry O'Neill and stayed with Sir John Kirk, who had been in Zanzibar for twenty years. Sir John was a renowned botanist and doctor, and had been chief-assistant to Livingstone on major expeditions. He was considered the authority on slavery. He and Lugard developed a lifelong friendship, and in him, Lugard found his mentor.

Cecil Rhodes arrived in London in March, and began lobbying for a Royal Charter for his new company. He was not well known at that time, and the politicians were wary of his methods and motives. A pivotal figure linked with Rhodes was the colourful Harry Hamilton Johnston.

Johnston was the same age as Lugard, but a completely different character. He could speak a dozen languages, was a gifted artist, botanist, naturalist, and wit, and had explored East Africa with Henry Morton Stanley. He was also extremely ambitious. He had entered the colonial service in 1886 when he was appointed Vice Consul of the Cameroons and Niger Delta, and was well thought of by Lord Salisbury, who had sent him to Lisbon that year to negotiate with the Portuguese over their expansionist plans in East Africa. In his memoirs, Johnston recalled meeting Rhodes at a dinner party, and spent all night debating the policy in Africa. In the morning, he came away with a cheque for £2,000 to secure Nyasaland, and a guarantee from Rhodes to put in a further £10,000 a year. Rhodes wanted to form a new company with The African Lakes Company and immediately set up a meeting with Fred Moir on July 2.

Lugard read about this meeting in the newspaper two days later, and was elated - to start with. He met Rhodes, and put forward his estimates for a permanent station in Nyasa. Rhodes was impressed and, in his usual way, asked if he could put forward a plan without The African Lakes Company. This never came to anything, for shortly afterwards Lugard was informed by the War Office that he would not be granted leave to undertake a further expedition. Moreover, Harry Johnston had been appointed Consul in Mozambique to undertake a mission to Nyasa.

Harry Johnston travelled to Mombasa in July 1889, taking his new deputy, Alfred Sharpe, and found a new route up the Zambezi which could take a gunboat. On arrival, he found a large Portuguese force preparing to occupy the highlands. This forced Lord Salisbury's hand to declare the highlands a British Protectorate, which nearly led to a state of war. In 1890 a convention was drawn up, and in 1891 the Portuguese saw most of their inland empire taken from them. The slave-trading and murders continued unabated at Lake Nyasa. Johnston tried to negotiate with Mlozi, but the situation merely worsened.

It took seven years and the use of British Army officers, Sikh soldiers from India, trained African soldiers, artillery and two gunboats (as Lugard had predicted), to overcome the strongholds and defeat Mlozi. After a decisive battle, Mlozi was found hiding in an underground cell after he had murdered forty-five African hostages. He was by now an old man with a long white beard and was dragged in front of a military court. He had murdered and killed thousands of Africans, and many others of different nationalities. He refused to present any defence for his crimes. He showed no remorse or fear as he was sentenced to hang on the spot in 1895.

Lugard failed to complete his mission in Nyasaland, but set his sights on Uganda with the support of Sir John Kirk. He was on the board of the Imperial British East Africa Company set up by William MacKinnon, another devout philanthropic Scotsman who had founded the British India Steam Navigation Company. Kirk convinced MacKinnon the Company required a strong character and introduced Lugard to George Mackenzie, another director who was about to go to the Mombasa office as Administrator. They agreed to take Lugard to Mombasa for a few months on a flexible basis to use up the rest of his Army leave.

This suited Lugard, as he now had no desire to go back to humdrum military life in a British barracks. He did though get a warning from the War Office. He was '*not to overstay his leave, not to engage in any military employment and not to serve with any foreign troops* (underlined twice!).' That amused Lugard, who wrote to his brother, '*This child is going to do just as he pleases and the War Office be damned!*'

Lugard set sail again on November 5 1889 with George Mackenzie and Colonel Euan-Smith, the Zanzibar Consul-General he met on his first trip less than two years before. This was a totally different voyage, with long discussions on the best way forward for the Company, and proposals for an expedition into Uganda. By the time the ship reached Mombasa on December 6, Lugard had decided he was not going to return to the Army.

Mombasa was the main portal to the interior of Africa. It was only six years before Lugard arrived that the Royal Geographical Society had first commissioned to find a practical route from the coast to Lake Victoria. It was this route that the Company was interested in, for if they got to the Lake, it led to Uganda, which Stanley had labelled '*The Pearl of Africa*'.

Information about Uganda was sparse and confusing, even the name. The province being explored at that time was Buganda, a large area on the west shores of Lake Victoria - Uganda is the expanded area both sides of Buganda which eventually became the Protectorate. It had a large, civilized population, with a monarchy going back hundreds of years, possibly thousands, a thriving culture, rich soils and vast herds of elephants. Germany was also interested in gaining control there, and investing money into the area. They had recently installed a new German Commissioner called Hermann Wissmann, who wanted to mount an expedition to find a quicker route to Lake Victoria.

Stanley was also in Mombasa. Lugard had serious misgivings about him. Stanley had led a disastrous expedition in East Africa to find Emin Pasha, a Governor of an Egyptian province that had been cut off after the Mahdi uprising. Stanley did find him, but many lives were lost in the process, and Emin Pasha's troops under the command of Selim Bey were left lost in the interior.

Lugard was concerned that MacKinnon was about to ask Stanley to lead his expedition into Uganda. MacKenzie also wanted Lugard to meet Stanley. Lugard wrote to his sister Emma with his misgivings, '...*between ourselves I do not care greatly about meeting Stanley. Letters of his that I have seen (not published) had made me disinclined to fall down and worship him, so I went up country again... and did not wait for him.*'

Stanley turned down the offer and went to Egypt to write his bestselling novel *In Darkest Africa* (1890). Lugard's concerns about him appeared justified when a few years later accusations surfaced of cruelty and the killing of numbers of tribesmen during his expeditions.

Negotiations were concluded with Mackenzie, during which Lugard had to reluctantly agree to a secrecy clause, which made him an emissary of the Imperial British East Africa Company. He set off from Mombasa on December 20 1889.

He decided on a preliminary trek, before mounting the full expedition. This took five months, striking north-west from Mombasa up to Sabaki via two slave centres - Fuladayo and Makongeni. Lugard hired 120 Swahili porters and used a mixture of mules, camels and donkeys to find which combination worked best in the difficult terrain.

To survive they needed to shoot game as they advanced; the local tribes were not always willing to sell their crops. He noted the wide range of wild life and fauna in his diary and he collected samples as he went. They encountered lions, aggressive buffalo, rhinos, venomous snakes and poisonous insects, and had to be constantly on the alert.

Lugard liked to bathe regularly in the rivers, and in one incident a crocodile attacked him and tore his hand. He would walk up to twenty miles a day and in the evenings would sit in the tent writing his meticulous notes, with plenty of cigars to hand. En route he constructed a variety of stockades, similar to those in Nyasa, and entered into an agreement with a chief of the Kamba tribe for protection and trade.

On his return he received news from Mackenzie regarding Buganda. The Kings of Buganda had been Moslem until the arrival of the Christians in 1875. Protestant missionaries had arrived first from Britain, followed closely by Catholics from France. The Christian religion was received with sympathetic interest by King Mtesa who ruled at the time, but he was confused about the denominational differences. The King welcomed them both, but the chiefs were divided as to which to follow. To differentiate them they were called 'Wa-Ingleza' and 'Wa-Franca'.

In 1884 Mtesa died and his eighteen-year-old son, Mwanga succeeded him. He took a completely different stance. He started to play off the Moslems against the Christians, which led to a bloody massacre of the Christians. Mwanga was overthrown and his brother, backed by a Moslem faction took the throne.

Lugard's news was that after another recent battle, Mwanga had overthrown his brother and the Christian faction ruled again. It was backed by a clandestine British trader/missionary, Charles Stokes, who promised them arms. However, the French priests resented the British missionaries, and favoured a German protectorate.

Lugard needed to get to Buganda and make an agreement with Mwanga. He received a letter from Mackenzie on March 12 1889 saying, '*The Uganda caravan is placed under your control... I have telegraphed London informing them that I believe you to be the right man to undertake such work, and if given a free hand, that I had no doubt that you could do it in a shorter time than probably anyone else that could be sent there...*' Ten days later he followed this up with a second letter. '*If you succeed you will, as a work of lasting and practical good, put Stanley's late work quite in the shade. It is a glorious opportunity of establishing your name and adding to your fame...*'

Lugard was still over a week's trek away and the going was slow. After crossing the Tsavo, famous for its lions, he headed south and saw huge troops of baboons before they hit dense jungle. There was heavy drizzle and the paths were obliterated and they kept losing their way. Lugard's boots were falling apart giving him bad blisters. Thorns stabbed at his feet. His wounded left arm continued to give him pain, yielding splinters of broken bone, and needed a sling. On April 30 his feet were so painful he had to give up walking and was carried by his porters in a blanket slung on a pole, '*... Not an easy conveyance unless you know how to dodge it, legs hanging out on one side and head on the other is the only way, for you must wear a big hat in this fierce sun, and the hat won't go under the pole, or accommodate itself to the shape of the blanket!*'

Lugard was extremley relieved to reach Mombasa on May 11. Struggling into the town with his motley crew, he looked extremely disheveled, with torn clothes and a large hole cut out of his battered boots to relieve the painful blisters. He was looking forward to a hot bath and catching up with his mail.

The next few months were spent writing his expedition report, completing maps, and clarifying his status. A new, experienced administrator, Sir Francis de Winton (Crimea War, Governor-General of Canada, and Administrator of Congo Free State) arrived, and the two men immediately disagreed on the organisation of the next expedition. Lugard felt so strongly about this that he handed in his resignation.

De Winter was taken aback and sent a conciliatory letter that allowed Lugard to retract his resignation and add '*... It is due to the events of the last four years. These positions of constant responsibility, with men older than myself serving beneath me - together with a heavy private trouble which sent me adrift,... and made me reckless of my Army career and of wither money or* *ambition, fostered in that spirit of independence, which I know will not be in the advancement of my interests.'*

De Winton replied that he did not think that Lugard would have cause to regret his decision. Privately, he still had his concerns, but the Company did not. On receiving Lugard's report, they overruled De Winton and appointed Lugard in charge of the upcoming expedition.

Lugard expressed his satisfaction in a letter to his sister Emma. *'All is settled now, and as usual I have got my own way, entirely like an obstinate and self-willed man as I fear I am...'* He continued that he had sympathy for De Winton, who had been put in a difficult position.

Lugard won the day against a much more senior figure for something he felt was right. His confidence was high, his body was healing and he was ready for the next major expedition into the African interior.

CHAPTER 11
The court of Buganda

Lugard had no idea when he set off from Mombasa on August 6 1890 that it would be nearly two years before he would see the Indian Ocean again. His expedition reached places hitherto unseen by Europeans, he was involved in a bitter civil war, and brought back thousands of refugees from a lost army. Lugard wrote a detailed account in his book *The Rise of Our East African Empire*. Here is an abridged version of that extraordinary expedition.

Lugard's new team consisted of George Wilson, an Australian from his first expedition who had been in Africa about a year and whom he greatly liked and trusted, Fenwick De Winton, the younger brother of Sir Francis, who wanted practical experience (Fenwick was also suspected of being there as a spy), and two new employees, William Grant and Archibald Brown. He hired a tall Somali man, Dualla Indris in Mombasa, as an interpreter and assistant. A tough, shrewd and honest fellow, he spoke English, Swahili and Arabic, and had a working knowledge of some of the local languages. He had worked for Stanley in the Congo, and an eccentric Hungarian, Count Teleki on remote Lake Rudolph (now in Kenya).

He found a Sudanese officer, Shukri Aga, to look after the Sudanese soldiers, who knew Emin Pasha and his commander Selim Bey, who had been left somewhere in the north of Uganda by Stanley. Both these men were to play crucial roles in the months ahead.

It was estimated that the expedition would take one year. Lugard asked for 200 porters initially. Eventually only 140 were available and he intended to recruit more as they headed inland. In addition, he took seventy Sudanese soldiers and six Somali guards. He knew there would be desertions (usually early on when thieves had the best choice of goods) and estimated only thirty per cent would be fit and reliable. These were mainly the Swahilis from Zanzibar; the best could carry seventy pounds on their heads and walk twenty miles a day on difficult, rough paths. His friend Mackenzie observed with concern that '*no caravan has ever left the coast so ill-equipped in every way.*'

This long caravan retraced the route Lugard had returned on a few months earlier. He was happy to be back on the road, leading from the front, relying on his own decisions. He recorded a typical day in his diary in detailed prose. '*Daybreak brings a stir among the sleeping forms... You tumble out of your last unfinished dream and your camp-cot, and substitute the realities of a heavy pair of boots, leggings, knee breeches and khaki jacket with a pith helmet... You buckle around you the belt which contains your hunting knife and rounds of Winchester ammunition; you fill your haversack with the paraphernalia which only long experience has taught you to select... The dawn has hardly broken when we emerge from our tents to give the order to the caravan headman to take up loads... At the word there is a rush from all parts of the camp; every porter seizes his own load, laid out in long rows, and he seems to have a dread that it will be seized by another, however heavy and unwieldy it be... Just as the sun appears above the horizon I lead the way followed by the askari [the caravan.] The Wanyamwezi [tribe] strike up their strange but musical chant and in two minutes the camp, by now a scene of animated life, is deserted, the smoldering fires die out with the rising sun... giant beetles come from every quarter to roll up into balls and to carry away the bits of offal of the camp and the hyenas and the vultures come in to scavenge... Meanwhile we are on the march, following a narrow path, and pushing our way through bushes and thorns... Before the sun is well up we are wet up to the waist... If the caravan is proceeding along game tracks I select a bear(ing) in the direction I wish to go by my pocket compass. Each path that branches away is 'closed' with twigs of grass by the men who follow me. After some two hours there is a halt. By this time the caravan has opened out, the sick or lazy have lagged behind, and the halt gives them a chance to close up... At the end of the day the site of the camp is chosen by me with small flags. In half an hour the tents are pitched, the stockade of branches is in place, the inevitable cup of tea is made. Each little coterie of men select the small site for their bivouac; one goes off to collect material to build the huts, another to draw water, another for firewood and stones on which to place the cook-pot. The men, tired as they are, would then go off long distances fishing or trapping small game... Sharp at six, the sun sets, the headman blows his whistle to ask if all are present, and gets a lusty chorus of replies for every little fraternity of messmates. They would then lie down in the open, or if it was raining, under little shelters of branches of squares of cotton cloth and go to sleep.*'

Every night Lugard went hunting for meat, adjudicate over disputes or offences, or write up his notes, maps and diary. This routine gave some comfort to the porters to help tackle the many physical dangers and pain that had to be dealt with every day. Discipline was hard but Lugard tried to be fair. There was no police station, no court, so he was judge and jury. If anyone was caught stealing either their supplies or from the local tribes they were flogged. Lugard disliked the brutality of the punishment, making him feel physically sick when he saw it meted out. Occasionally he would carry it out himself, to show the local chiefs he was policing his men, and that he intended no harm to them. Gaining the trust of these chiefs was essential; he needed to make treaties with the tribes as he went along.

Near Sabaki he came across a caravan of slaves. He was reminded of his original intention of coming to Africa, and confronted the traders. The slavers scattered when they saw him, but he caught several and sent them to Mombasa for trial. He released three emaciated children, fed and clothed them, and they joined the caravan on a donkey.

At Sabaki, he turned north-west, followed the river, and skirted the sacred snow-covered Mount Kilimanjaro rising majestically in the distance. After only a few weeks, forty of the porters had deserted and many were struggling to keep up with the pace.

George Wilson's health had deteriorated. On September 12, when Lugard was out shooting, he received an urgent message to return to the camp. Wilson was unconscious on the ground, hardly a pulse, barely alive. He was carried back to Lugard's tent, his shoes and socks were removed and his feet rubbed with whisky, and a generous amount poured down his throat. They made a strong solution of carbolic oil and rubbed his torso and legs violently which jump-started his heart, sending him into a spasm. He shivered and suddenly '*revived like a dead man.*' Every few minutes he was given a brandy and after he had drunk nearly half a bottle, he opened his eyes, grasped Lugard's hand and uttered, completely inebriated, '*By George, I'm glad you came. I was determined not to go until you came, and when I saw you I knew it was all right!*' Wilson had further similar attacks that evening, and Lugard stayed up nursing him all night, almost certainly saving his life.

Eight days later Lugard arrived at Machakos. He picked up more supplies and stopped to give everybody a well-deserved rest. He completed a stockade and a shelter for Wilson, who needed further convalescence. Of the five hundred loads he started out with, only eighty arrived, and he realised there was organised pilfering on a massive scale.

Gaining the trust of the local chiefs was essential. Lugard found the local Kamba tribe friendly (as were the majority of tribes he met on his journey), and to complete the negotiations for a treaty he carried out a blood-brotherhood ceremony. Lugard described the event in his diary. '*A goat was killed and its liver roasted on the fire embers. The chief sat on a mat and I sat opposite him, our legs crossed over each other and face to face, close. His weapons - sword, bow and arrows etc. – and mine (a rifle) were held horizontally over our heads. The interpreter then, taking a knife, made a long speech, continually tapping the weapons with the knife as he spoke, and emphasising his words with the clink of steel. He said how we would always be friends, and help each other in trouble, how in Mkamba land I should never want for food, nor he in my country, and we would fight against the common foe etc. At each sentence the assembled chiefs and headman gave a chorus of assent, and my party joining in. This completed, my arm is cut, and his chest. A piece of the liver is rubbed in my blood and he eats it. I eat a piece rubbed in his blood. Then taking each other's hands we help each other to rise, and the ceremony is over.*' Lugard also gave the chief a flag as an emblem of friendship. This ceremony was repeated with several tribes as he moved north-west across modern-day Kenya.

He had been told that the Kikuyu tribe had a reputation for being hostile and tricky. Lugard lived among them for a month and in his opinion '… *I had no hesitation in trusting myself alone among them, even at considerable distances from the camp… I found them honest and straightforward.*' They helped him select a site to build a stockade which he called Dagoretti.

Lugard surveyed the area, predicting '*In the far future that it might prove suitable for white civilization.*' Little did he realise how quickly things would change. Once the railway was constructed, a town called Nairobi was established in 1907, and has grown to a city of over three million people. That year a settler brought a seedling tea plant from India. This was the start of Kenya and Uganda becoming major tea producers of the world.

He did not sign a treaty with the Kikuyu as he felt the wording of the official treaty was inappropriate. Instead he entered into a blood-brotherhood with some of the chiefs who he considered, '*extremely intelligent, good mannered and most friendly.*' Goats and presents were exchanged and another flag handed over.

The Kikuyu later turned against the British in a revolt against colonial rule during the bloody Mau Mau uprising from 1952 to 1960, and proved to be one of the most politically astute and important groups in Kenya. They produced the first president, Jomo Kenyatta, who led Kenya into independence in 1963.

One evening, as Lugard was writing letters to England, a tropical thunderstorm passed over, the rain beating down so heavily on his tent it gave him a bad headache. The hypnotic rhythm of the rain brought back memories of verses that Catherine had sent him, which had enchanted him so much. He had found them in England on his last leave from Nyasa, had cut them out and put them in his breast pocket. It was this shirt he was wearing when he was shot; the bullet had passed through the verses, covering them with blood and carried the paper into his left arm, causing constant pain.

With this poignant thought he wrote another verse in his tent, but left it unfinished. He noted afterwards, *'These are the lines that I jotted down in my field book, and it does one good to recall the thought, that it lies with ourselves who have to do 'the strong and steadfast duty', and leave it in higher hands to judge of the right and the wrong of the past.'* Even in a dark corner of the African interior, the voice of Catherine still haunted him.

At Dagoretti, Lugard received a letter from De Winter urging him to continue swiftly into Uganda, to go to Mengo, the palace of King Mwanga. On November 1 his caravan entered hostile Masai country with three Europeans, sixty-six Sudanese and Somalis, 285 porters, and a battered but workable Maxim gun with only a small amount of ammunition. He bade a reluctant goodbye to Wilson, as he missed his company, leaving him to complete the stockade with a small garrison. He was not confident that the Company would send provisions ahead. *'... I do not expect for one moment that things will follow me as arranged on paper - so far even the very mails have failed to reach though we were so long delayed at Sabaki...'* He itemised all the provisions he was short of, even boots and clothing.

After a few days' march they encountered the first party of Masai warriors. *'The Masai have most intelligent faces, and many of them clean cut features with sharp noses and high foreheads. They came out in war dress with huge-bladed spears and gaily painted five-foot shields... This fighting tribe, so striking in their attitude of proud self-containment, were strangely tolerant of peaceful European intrusion into the wide lands under their mastery.'*

Lugard refused to pay them *hongo* (Swahili for bribe), and after a brief discussion they simply let him pass. The caravan skirted Lake Elementia and the beautiful Lake Nakuru, animated by a mass of pink flamingos. A long, exhausting climb brought them up to the Nandi plateau on the edge of the Kavironda plain, perched 2,200 metres on the north end of Lake Victoria, where they woke up to cold mornings and clinging mists. They saw no sign of human life until they dropped down the steep escarpment to the great plain curving around Lake Victoria, and came to the village of Wakoli, close to the border of Buganda.

They halted there for two days to get further provisions, sent a request to King Mwanga at his palace at Mengo to assist with supplies and canoes, then pushed on to the Ripon Falls, the start of the almost 2,500-mile journey to the Mediterranean of the great River Nile. Such was Lugard's concern to get to the Buganda capital, he paid scant attention to this now famous tourist spot, noting briefly, *'It was a charming spot, with very beautiful scenery.'*

Having found most of the boats had been removed, his biggest concern was how to cross the Nile before the King delayed them further. Dualla, the Somali interpreter, found a small canoe hidden in the reeds, and paddled furiously against a strong current to get a few loads across to the other side. Larger canoes were sent by the local Sultan and the remaining loads were landed by sunset - except for two cows. It was only six weeks since they had left Dagoretti.

As Lugard entered Buganda and marched west around the north of Lake Victoria, he caught his first glimpses of the legendary 'Pearl of Africa'. *'The ground was very undulating mostly of marl and gravel, but the dips have very rich black soil. The valleys are spread out below with endless banana groves and villages... Bananas and sweet potatoes seem to be all that is grown together with tobacco. I saw the castor oil plant once more, which is wild on the Nile.'*

He descended into the forested lowlands and the swamps of black mud matted with beautiful plumed papyrus and water lilies.

Village life here showed a degree of civilization in marked contrast to the primitive life he had seen on the way. Roads were marked with tall fences, and around each hut was a neat banana grove which supplied food for that family. The people wore long garments of russet bark-cloth or imported cotton and had a dignified air, with fine manners.

As Lugard approached the palace at Mengo he surveyed the scene - a series of small hills ahead with the palace located on the highest. The Protestant and Catholic missions were about half a mile away on two smaller hills. His three hundred strong caravan was met by an envoy from the King accompanied by the royal band of flutes, drums and many kinds of gaily-decorated stringed instruments. Halting every so often, the musicians would transform themselves into dancers.

The King invited Lugard to camp in *'a wet and dirty hollow'* which he quickly declined and moved to a *'low gravelly knoll of untenanted ground just over a mile from the King's palace.'* It was called Kampala, eventually to become the thriving capital of Uganda, with nearly two million inhabitants. The site of this camp is still marked in the old Kampala district.

Lugard had been contemplating this important meeting with King Mwanga. Buganda was still very unstable. It had just experienced six years of bloody civil war between the Christian and Moslem factions. There

80

had been changes of kingship, and the King was playing the two factions off against each other. There was still friction between the two Christian factions, Wa-Inglesa (Anglican Protestant) and Wa-Franca (Catholic). Arms were being brought by Charles Stokes for the Christians, and political changes were afoot with the Anglo-German treaty just signed. With all these considerations in mind, Lugard arranged a meeting with the King the next day.

Lugard was concerned about what he would wear for the ceremonial meeting with King of Buganda. His clothes had been torn to pieces during the trek, and the only remaining respectable pair of trousers was a pair of Melton cords. The only other item that vaguely matched was a pyjama top, which he fitted with brass buttons to complete a rather eccentric air of authority! To make some form of dignified entrance, he assembled an escort with rifles, and a dozen Sudanese with bugles to accompany him, to try and match the drums and instruments of the royal court. With his interpreter Dualla, he entered the large Durbar hut and approached the King, surrounded by his Buganda chiefs (mostly Catholic supporters), in their white robes, who looked on curiously, and made sure he did not tread on the royal carpet.

He shook hands with Mwanga and to avoid any protocol problems with seating, he brought his own chair, sitting to the right of him. He studied the face of the King intently. This man was going to be of immense importance to him; he held the balance of power. Still a young man in his twenties, Mwanga already had a cruel, ruthless reputation. He had murdered many, was a heavy smoker of *bhang* (cannabis), and known to be addicted to sodomy, murdering some of his courtiers if they did not participate. Lugard was troubled by his off-putting habit of giggling and caressing his courtiers. This was not going to be an easy negotiation.

Lugard made a short speech saying he had come to bring peace and had the power to make treaties and to settle disputes. He read out three letters in English from the Imperial British East Africa Company, translated into Swahili and the local dialect by Dualla. No mention was made of flags, which he knew to be a sensitive issue, being interpreted as a sign of taking over the country. He concluded that this was merely a preliminary meeting and left with a polite farewell. He returned to his tent set up on Kampala, and spent most of the night writing two long letters to the two Christian missions detailing his proposals.

First, that the supply of arms was to be strictly controlled, that they were to be registered with only soldiers and used only by registered holders. Second, a British Resident would be set up at the King's court, who would have control over all white men. Third, a control board of principal state officials would be set up to collect revenues, with the Resident as chairman. Part of this revenue would be used to pay for the costs of occupation. Finally, there would be absolute freedom of religion, with all disputes settled by the Resident.

The next day he called on each of the missionary chiefs to explain in Swahili the proposed treaty in more detail, and to ask for their total support to bring stability, peace and prosperity to the country.

On December 24, he went back to the King's palace with De Winton and presented the treaty to the court. Many questions were asked, primarily on the control of arms and the mechanism for the collection of taxes. At the end of this lengthy session, Lugard asked Mwanga if he was ready to sign. He delayed, and an unsettling feeling ran through the crowd. Lugard tried to persuade Mwanga to sign by saying that if he would not agree, he would have to start talks with his enemy, Kabarega. The King became very agitated at this thinly-veiled threat, and it set off a commotion in the crowd, with cries that the country was being sold out. Ammunition was loaded and weapons were cocked. A gun was aimed at Lugard. At his diplomatic best, Lugard defused the situation by announcing he would come for an answer in two days. He then made a dignified, if not hasty exit.

On Christmas Day, the British held a party at their camp and invited various priests, missionaries and a German, Dr. Stuhlmann, who had been an assistant of Emin Pasha. The next day, there was a delegation from the Protestant chiefs who said they would sign the treaty, but wanted confirmation from the consulate on the coast on the British position in Uganda. They warned that the delays by Mwanga were due to Catholic influence.

Lugard was desperate to find a solution, so he returned to the palace with De Winton to get the King's signature. After further delays (including the King demanding presents which Lugard had promised were on their way!) he reluctantly agreed and signed. This treaty had little authority and was later superseded by another, but it was the first step that enabled the Company to offer protection, control arms and ensure freedom of religion. Lugard had hoped it would stabilise the country, but as he quickly found out, things were far from stable.

Over the following days there were a series of false alarms that an attack on Lugard's stockade was imminent. Lugard continued his shuttle diplomacy between the parties, concentrating especially on the Catholics, whilst completing the fortifications and training of his soldiers.

On January 31, Captain Williams and Dr. MacPherson arrived with reinforcements from Mombasa consisting of seventy-five Sudanese soldiers and another one hundred porters. On February 19 the two factions fell out again, and hundreds of men massed on the hills opposite each other.

Lugard contacted the Wa-Franca chiefs and demanded in the strongest terms that they disperse their men. He set up the Maxim gun and a line of his soldiers, which diffused the situation, and they dispersed. He noted, '... *Then I went to the King, and told him things were quiet and people were dispersing. He was very grateful for this and sent a messenger later to thank me. We returned to camp and breakfast.*'

Further disputes arose about the distribution of land between the parties, and Lugard could foresee endless arguments. By March he considered a possible expedition that could unite all parties. When reports started coming in of women being taken by Moslem raiding parties in the north, and confirmation that the European powers had placed Uganda in the British sphere, this was enough for Lugard to put his plan into action.

Despite doubts about Mwanga's loyalty, Lugard presented to him a large number of presents that had been brought from Mombasa, which included shotguns, and luxury cloth. In addition he read a letter from the Sultan of Zanzibar telling Mwanga to treat the British well as '*they are our very best friends, and we all have confidence in them...*'

On April 1, the sacred Wango war drums echoed outside the palace. An advance imperial guard assembled before the King, waved their weapons and shouted their loyalty, ready to go to battle.

One week later, in heavy rain, Lugard marched north to confront the Moslem raiding parties with Captain Williams, William Grant, Dr. Macpherson, 300 soldiers, 300 porters, and the rather unreliable Maxim gun.

CHAPTER 12
The Mountains of the Moon

As they headed north, thousands more warriors joined from the villages, until the army had swelled to over 25,000 men.

They passed through burnt-out villages and abandoned land, scarred from years of civil war, gleaning little food on the way. It rained every day, never giving them a chance to dry out. The heavy, black, glutinous mud sucked the energy from their tired legs. The Europeans became sick with chest infections, developing rasping coughs that left them gasping for air.

The gloomy weather played with Lugard's mind as he tried to keep warm sitting by the smoky fire, writing page after page in his diary in the damp night. He started to doubt his own virtues. Captain Williams was his second-in-command, slightly older and an experienced professional soldier who had established a good rapport with the Sudanese troops. Was Williams a better soldier, a better communicator? It was unjustified and illogical, but he continued to criticise himself in his diary. *'I thought that the bitter lesson of my life had taken away most of that contrariness, self-conceit, jealousy and opinionatedness, which I well know to be intolerable in a travelling companion and which I well know is one of my miserable characteristics. As he (Williams) says I am a very difficult man to serve with. He struck true and I had nothing to say, except that I had tried hard to study his feelings, and since we should probably fight together presently, we must try and make the most of each other.'*

Lugard was a harsh self-critic, but Williams clearly respected him and had written in a letter *'Lugard is a good man and we are more like brothers than first and second, so that the omelette won't be spoilt by the frying pan slipping.'*

In the quiet hours Lugard's mind wandered back to the days and nights in Lucknow, to the nightmare scene at the London house, to Catherine. Until that point, he had still expected some contact, but not now. *'Was it not those who feel such injuries most deeply,'* he asked himself, *'who view with dismay in the course of the years that the wound is healing and only a scar remains?'*

He reflected, with astonishment, on his state of mind three years earlier, *'... leaving for Aden for Africa, maddened with grief, reckless, almost insane, with a broken career behind me...an adventurer - possibly to find only navvies work with a bare subsistence...I was then a different man entirely...only five years between that old life and* this!*...Am I once more beginning to see with healthy eyes?'* He was healing slowly, but could not forget.

A few days later, when he was on a path that no European had trodden before, he came across a beautiful freshwater lake with little islands nestled inside it. It was a very peaceful place which the Baganda people called Wamala. He sat beside it and, inspired by Wagner's opera *Tristan and Isolde*, he renamed it Lake Isoldt. It showed on his maps as Isolt. We don't know why he misspelt it, but today the lake remains Wamala and only exists as Isolt on Lugard's map.

Tristan and Isolde had its first performance in 1865. It was considered scandalous at the time and did not have its next production until 1875. An opera of doomed love, it is a celebration of sexual pleasure between two lovers that leads to death and suicide. Tristan, the chivalrous and flawed knight, and Isolde, the princess betrothed to a King she does not love. Lugard saw himself as a tragic, flawed figure, and was drawn to this opera, appealing to his dark side. Catherine introduced it to him, and would have led him through the music, immersing herself in the tragic heroine role.

The time for retrospection swiftly came to an end when news came that the Muslim leader, Kabarega wanted to negotiate, and had sent a captured woman with a message to make contact. Lugard sent Dualla, who was a devout Moslem, to meet Kabarega and offered terms - to hand over their leader and surrender their arms in return for honourable treatment and offers of land. This was rejected by Kabarega. Lugard knew a battle was inevitable. That day came on May 5 1891.

Lugard and his well-armed troops were based on one side of a river, and the enemy overlooked them from the hills on the other side. It would have been suicide to attack directly across the swampy river, so Lugard found another ford downstream and created a diversion, whilst the others crossed under the cover of night. Safely over, the Buganda troops made a surprise attack, rushing the hill early in the morning and overwhelmed the enemy defences. Lugard meanwhile kept in the rear doing very little but harass the retreating force with rifle fire. It was a decisive victory, losing only thirty men and inflicting losses of over three hundred.

Lugard wanted to march straight on to Kabarega's capital, but was informed there were impassable swamps and rivers ahead and little food to feed the hungry army. The Buganda warriors were happy with their victory and eager to return home. Within a few days, the majority had drifted back to their villages.

Lugard was not to be deterred. He decided on a much longer route, going south into Ankole to friendly Christian chiefs to pick up more supplies and then headed north-west towards Lake Edward. This was unexplored country, but he imagined new trade routes opening up. Large salt deposits were reported to be in that area. It could also stop the arms trade into Buganda. Maybe he could find Selim Bey's lost Sudanese army in the north.

He took most of the men from Kampala, totaling 150 soldiers and 185 porters, and sent back Williams with a handful of men to reinforce Kampala, which was only defended with 220 mediocre men. He was to receive a lot of criticism for that decision.

On turning south, he returned to the green hills and plains of Buganda, where game was more plentiful to feed his 400 strong caravan, despite an epidemic of rinderpest which had caused famine in some areas. They needed seven or eight antelope a day to feed the men. The Protestant Wa-Inglesa villages gave him a warm welcome and food assistance, but the Catholic Wa-Franca villages contributed nothing, and hid any canoes he needed to cross rivers.

It was still a divided country, but filled with such potential. He noted as he travelled, 'With an era of peace and vaccination, the two destructive agents, war and smallpox will disappear, and as the people increase, there is no reason why they should not produce large quantities of grain, cotton etc. for export...' He did not believe in the distribution of cheap goods such as beads and looking glasses among the African people, but wanted '... to replace this by sound good cloth at a fair price, household utensils, coinage and writing paper (which was already in demand), which was a fair aim for commerce.'

It took two months' hard trekking westwards before they reached Lake Edward. It had only been discovered by Stanley two years previously - and they did not have the benefit of his map. All this is recorded on 265 pages of close-written foolscap in his neat, meticulous hand.

Arriving at Kichawamba Ridge, Lugard approached one of the most stunning areas of Africa, the ridge overlooking the edge of the Great Rift Valley. The plains and marshes were teeming with wildlife, crowded with herds of elephant and buffalo. In the valley below, two shimmering lakes were linked by the narrow Kazinga channel, where the waters rush powerfully through. Gazing through the mists across the southern lake, he could gradually make out the Ruwenzori Mountains - the legendary Mountains of the Moon, which had so mesmerized Speke and Stanley. The permanently snow-capped mountains rise to over 5,000 metres, retaining their mystery in the clouds until the right wind blows away the mists, and reveals them to the favoured traveller in all their glory.

Lugard descended the escarpment through a dense forest of trees smothered in tropical flowers. He came to the Kazinga channel, where the Banyaro people lived, hunting hippos and trading in salt. A few local warriors made hostile gestures but retreated after a warning shot. Lugard found some large canoes made from thin planks sewn together and caulked with grass, surprisingly watertight and strong, to get to the salt lakes at Katwe. He was fascinated by the deep claret colour of the water, caused by the various salts it contained, and the way the dried salt fringing the lake made it look like an iced cake. This contrasted with the adjacent, larger Lake Edward, with its clear blue water, surrounded by reeds, dotted with green islands.

The high lakes were located in a good strategically defensive position, and an ideal location for a stockade. He built it from timber gathered from a wide area, and named it Fort George, after his companion George Wilson.

Lugard continued his detailed surveys of the area and sent out messengers to try and contact the leader of the lost soldiers, Selim Bey, thought to be somewhere to the north. He received confirmation of this from three Swahili runners, who showed him mail they were carrying to Selim Bey. Further confirmation came from a group of slave-traders passing through to the Congo Free State. On August 7 he left the stockade under the charge of Dr. Grant and one hundred men, and marched into an area that no white man, even Stanley, had ventured. Heading for Toro, east of Ruwenzori and west of Lake George, he found himself in hostile country ruled by Kabarega. The tracks were rough, the loads were heavy, it was oppressively hot, and soon the caravan was spread out over several miles.

Lugard was near the front of the column surveying this new land, when he heard cries from the scouts shouting that an enemy army was approaching. He looked through his binoculars and could see the hills ahead swarming with natives running from the foothills of the Ruwenzori towards them, many armed with guns. He wrote, *'My heart misgave me that we had tried too big a game. It seemed impossible that we could beat these hordes with 450 men and there was no retreat anywhere. Defeat means annihilation.'*

He urgently ordered his men to bring the Maxim gun. He lined up one hundred troops and slowly advanced towards the attackers, holding fire. Some of the enemy started to outflank him along the hills to the left, so he drew up the Maxim gun and aimed into the group about 800 metres away.

To his relief and amazement the old gun burst into life, sending the red hot bullets into the centre of the attack with deadly accuracy. The effect of the deafening noise and the casualties was immediate, with the main mass of the enemy scattering in panic. A party of Sudanese and Buganda soldiers were sent to complete the rout. Not one man was lost, and they captured the enemy's abandoned camp with all its stores.

That evening they found a good location to camp between the hills and a deep river gulley, looking back down to the salt lakes and Fort George. The next day Lugard built another stockade at this strategic position and called it Fort Edward, after his uncle. Over the next few weeks he invited the local villagers to talks and to assure them that he wanted to bring a new era of peace and prosperity to the country, and that The Imperial East Africa Company would give them protection. Slave-trading would be banned, guns registered and a new legitimate king, Kasagama, would be placed on the throne to herald this new era.

In return, the Company would have rights to all the ivory. The tribes accepted this proposal, and brought gifts to the new King, who came to rule an enlarged and peaceful kingdom called Toro for thirty-seven years. Kasagama was later awarded an honour by the British Government.

Whilst building Fort Edward, Lugard set up his portable desk and sent to Kampala maps and reports, official letters, and personal letters to his family. He set out proposals of how to run the forts in the area and detailed figures on how many men would be required and an estimate of supplies needed to sustain them. He estimated it would require twelve Europeans and five hundred trained soldiers. This was not well-received by the office in Mombasa, struggling with the mounting costs of the expedition.

On August 26, he left Fort Edward under the control of a Sudanese sergeant with a small but well-armed garrison of three hundred men and headed north in search of Selim Bey. Two days later, he encountered a large number of Banyoro warriors, the main core of Kabarega's army. Heavily outnumbered, Lugard again lined up 150 men in a straight line and advanced upon them, keeping the Maxim gun in range. The Banyoro fired heavy, inaccurate volleys to no effect. Lugard kept advancing. This panicked the Banyoro, and again they fled in disarray without a single shot being fired. Lugard was proud of the valour and discipline his troops showed that day, considering only half were trained soldiers.

He saw this as a good opportunity to show captured prisoners how justice would be administered by the Imperial British East Africa Company. He gave stern lectures on the benefits of the new regime, then released them. At the same time he forbad the burning of villages or the looting of stock. This was especially difficult for the Baganda who believed, as did many others, in profiting from the spoils of war. They continued trekking north into difficult terrain. When they came to the Semliki River, over one hundred metres wide, they could find no canoes on the bank. They could see some on the other side of the river. They drove off the guards and two brave Somalis swam across the river battling with strong currents and menacing crocodiles, and retrieved them. With three canoes they somehow got all their supplies across the river, including a cow, much to the amazement of the enemy, who continued firing shots across the river to jeers from Lugard's soldiers.

This intrepid band battled dense swamp, sinking up to their waists in mud, lacerated by spear-grass and dodging swamp-wasps' nests, marched across undulating plains with the threat of attack by wild animals, hacked through thick forests, and clambered up sheer granite faces. Progress was just a few miles a day. Lugard marvelled at the endurance of the porters carrying such heavy loads, often in marshy ground, marching until sundown and yet still singing. They would shout in the mornings 'Mwaka, Mwaka' meaning 'years' – they were willing to follow him for years, showing incredible loyalty to a stranger from an unknown land, building an extraordinary bond of trust between two vastly different cultures.

They crossed the Ruwenzori and dropped into the Semliki valley to 600 metres, the lowest level since Mombasa, and came to the vast blue waters of Lake Albert. Here they were given a friendly welcome by an aborigine tribe who were unclothed, leading a simple life. They begged Lugard to build a fort to keep out the Banyoro who had recently attacked them. Lugard declined but did hire some guides from them for the last part of the journey north. They climbed out of the Semliki valley and on September 6 1891, at an altitude of 1500 metres, camped at a village on a lush, green plateau.

That morning they heard a shot, and out of the heat haze came a group of soldiers moving slowly towards them. Lugard came out of his tent and recognized the uniforms as Sudanese officers and men. They were part of 'the missing army' that Lugard had been searching for. He had found them. There followed exultant scenes with shouting, hugging, kissing, and as he noted in his diary, 'Everyone temporarily became a fool, and jabbered as is right and proper on such an occasion.'

A goat was slaughtered to celebrate and the story was recounted by the three officers of how Stanley and Emin Pasha had met on the shore of Lake Albert, and what had happened to Selim Bey and his army. Stanley had sent Selim north to evacuate the isolated equatorial garrisons from the attacking Mahdi forces coming up the Nile. The country was in turmoil, and the garrisons were so far apart it took much longer than anticipated. Stanley could not wait and went back to the coast, and Selim Bey, after great difficulty, led his troops down to Kavalli, where they had been living ever since.

The next day, Lugard climbed the 600 metre escarpment to Kavalli and found the large, mature encampment that had been there some years. He asked to see Selim, but was denied, with Selim demanding to see Shukri Aga first. Lugard refused and as there was no reply, he set up his camp with a Durbar hut, officers' and men's quarters, latrines, arms, provisions stores, and a flagstaff with a home-made Union Jack. Selim watched, and three days later sent a message to Lugard offering a meeting. Lugard agreed, but in his own hut.

Selim Bey was a jet-black Sudanese, around fifty-years old, six feet tall, with a large imposing girth. He had been employed by the Khedive of Egypt but had lost contact with Egypt since the Mahdi took Khartoum in 1885. For nearly ten years his army had not been paid but continued fighting the Mahdi under the Khedive flag. Stanley's description of him in his book was most derogatory. '...*a weak and distrustful character who had been disloyal.*' Lugard's assessment was entirely different, summing him up as '... *a Sudanese with no other blood. He is no fool, however, and I saw that in the first five minutes, and that I had met a man who was shrewd and suspicious and strong-willed.*'

Selim explained that since 1883 they had been cut off by the Mahdists in Khartoum and driven south. They had suffered a mutiny, been attacked by hostile tribes, endured starvation, and a breakdown in discipline had led to attacks on villages to survive. Originally there were three thousand men, now reduced to six hundred.

Selim was extremely proud of them, and insisted on a march-past for Lugard. He lined them up in two companies, with the remnants of a band beating drums and playing bugles. The troops were in a sorry state, most without uniforms, some dressed in just bark-cloth, many suffering from old battle wounds, and all had prematurely aged. Lugard was taken aback by their condition and noted, *'It was a sight to touch a man's heart to see this noble remnant who were fanatical in their loyalty to their flag and their Khedive.'*

Lugard was exhausted and suffering from a fever that did not even respond to his special dose of quinine. He spent days negotiating with Selim, telling him that the Khedive and Britain were now working together and that he could now serve under the British flag. Selim wanted a letter from the Khedive giving him authorization to do so, which would have taken a year to come. In the end he agreed to work with Lugard temporarily. Whilst awaiting the Khedive's answer, Lugard drew up a treaty. At the parade of Selim's troops he told them *'they would find the British kind and considerate masters but hard upon disobedience.'* In his notes he added, *'I do thank God that it has fallen to my lot to come to their relief and that I have been able to secure so fine a body of men for the Company service.'*

Selim dismantled his camp and prepared for the long journey to the coast. Lugard shot some elephants for meat for the journey, and collected tusks to trade for the Company funds. Fever still troubled him, and for the first time he felt terror whilst he was hunting. *'I fairly funked it. The strain is so great that I am trembling from head to foot and even my knees were knocking together.'*

The realisation of what he had taken on shocked him. Each of the soldiers had an entourage of wives, children, slaves and porters numbering from fifty to one hundred people, nearly 9,000 people plus livestock to take over rivers, hills, forests and swamps. Many of the women were emaciated and sick, naked, except for a few bunches of leaves strategically placed, and carrying babies, food and cooking implements. It seemed a biblical task as he watched the long line of humanity snake out of the camp heading south-west. The weary soldiers led the way, waving tattered flags of previous battles that had been fought against the Mahdi, and praised God that deliverance had come at last.

Lugard sent an advance party of 250 to the Semliki River to secure canoes for the crossing. He split the caravan into three groups, each one a day apart to make it more manageable; a single caravan would have been over seven miles long. With the help of the local tribe, they all crossed the river without incident. As he headed slowly south, Lugard found some of the desperate mothers were abandoning their babies. Every night he retraced the track they had taken, gathered up the helpless infants and put them in a crèche. Thieving continued to be a problem, especially from villages they passed through, and he dealt with the perpetrators severely, making sure the floggings were seen by the villagers.

He continued making treaties with the village chiefs and produced his detailed maps at four miles to the inch with only a watch and a prismatic compass. He established three more substantial forts, the first he called Waverley after Sir John Kirk's home, the second Fort Lorne, and the third, which was across the Mpanga River, he called Kivari. He left two thousand Sudanese soldiers and their dependents, and a good supply of provisions at each garrison.

Crossing the Mpanga River was a major challenge. *'… here the river flowed in a rocky gorge, some 700 or 800 ft deep, whose precipitous banks were clothed with the densest forest. Here the mists and vapours hung, and the trees dripped with continual moisture. Every class of fern-from the tree ferns to the moss ferns were to be found beneath the moisture laden trees, whose limbs were clothed with them, and with mosses and log bearded lichens and orchids. The flowers, familiar in our hot-houses, grew in these perpetual shades and gorgeous butterflies glanced like meteors through the forest twilight. Below foamed and eddied a seething torrent of water between its rocky walls. No trees grew on its banks which could reach more than a quarter a way across. I sat down on a rock to think the matter out.... Behind me were a mass of over 3,000 souls in a foodless country.'*

A simple solution was engineered. Midstream there was a projecting rock. Two fifteen-metre long palm trees were manoeuvered from the bank and wedged to the rock. Strong swimmers were sent across the torrent to the other side and the same method was carried out from the other bank. The palm trees were lashed together and transverse bars were fixed with creepers and packed together with rough grass. Long creepers were then fed across to form a stout handrail to complete the primitive, but workable bridge. The long line of men, women, children, goats and chickens were all led slowly down the steep gradient of the bridge to midstream and helped up the other side. It was remarkable feat of improvised engineering.

Whilst Fort Kivari was being completed, Lugard left Dr. Macpherson in charge with Grant, who was seriously ill with fever, and travelled to Fort George, a two day journey. There he met De Winton, who had come from Kampala with supplies of cloth and food, and quinine, desperately required for Grant. He also received mail from Williams describing the latest situation in Kampala. There had been various incidents between the Wa-Franca and the Wa-Inglesa but none too serious. Lugard felt reassured that Williams was keeping things under control there. However, one of the letters convinced him he had to return quickly.

The caravan pushed on east, with a more manageable 1,200 people. They were all desperately tired, covering just twelve miles a day. Lugard's boots were almost worn through. Thorns pierced his feet and his clothes were once again in tatters. On December 14 1891, he crossed into Buganda having travelled over 732 miles in six months.

He had brought all the country west of Buganda, and the salt lake, under the control of the Imperial British East Africa Company, gained the good-will of the people and made multiple treaties. He drastically cut the arms trade, and reduced the slave trade. He had built seven forts, established a route to Lake Albert and brought to safety the lost army of Emin Pasha. The cost to the Company had been nothing. The expedition paid its way with ivory and salt. He had hardly fired any ammunition in anger and to his great satisfaction, he had incurred only a minimum number of casualties. For him it was one of the high points of his life.

Lugard felt proud of what he had achieved, but as he approached Kampala on Christmas Day, there was great apprehension. The letter he had received from Williams was from the Imperial British East Africa Company in London.

It instructed him to evacuate immediately and return to the coast.

CHAPTER 13
War and peace

The letter Lugard received from Kampala confirmed that the Imperial British East Africa Company had fallen into serious financial difficulty. The Salisbury Government had reversed its decision to build a railway from Mombasa, the situation in Kampala was rapidly deteriorating and the country was heading for civil war.

The long, bedraggled procession limped into Kampala on New Year's Eve, exhausted from their trek. The men's clothes were in rags, boots were broken, and, to the disapproval of the Baganda, many of the Sudanese women were naked apart from a few discreet leaves. They had traded their only possessions, their clothes, for chickens.

Lugard was again escorted to the palace by musicians and dancers, singing and playing on their local instruments, but this time it was only the Wa-Ingleza who were celebrating.

Captain Williams greeted him warmly and they sat down to discuss the drastic decision by the Company. Lugard was angry that all his efforts had apparently been in vain, and greatly concerned that a withdrawal could result in a nightmare scenario of a civil war and a humanitarian disaster.

He wrote, *'This was a thunderbolt indeed. It is the second time now that a long spell of <u>very</u> hard work in Africa has been ended in reverse so complete that all my toil has seemed to be merely waste – and worse. <u>This</u> collapse will be <u>terrible</u> in its results …Does it lie with me in such a terrible pass to abandon everything connected with myself, and give my life to save these people ? This is the question I ask myself and I dare hardly reply to it …Am I to plunge into war again when my whole soul yearns for peace and quiet? Am I to more than risk my commission? It is a terrible sacrifice, God help me to choose alright!'*

Williams too was shocked at the Company's decision. *'I would be ashamed to hold my head up in any society of gentlemen if I were involved in any such breach of faith.'* He even offered to put in his life savings of 4,000 pounds, to which Lugard noted '*...and this is the kind of man which my colleague Captain Williams R.A, was!'*

Williams confirmed that religious tension was building again between the Christian parties. Since Lugard had left, the Wa-Franca Catholics tried aggressively to convert the Wa-Ingleza Protestants, considering them heretics. Further shipments of arms had arrived, which led to more violence. There was also a Pagan group known as Futabagi who were bhang smokers, had the King's ear, and were campaigning to get rid of both parties. Their involvement created yet more tension.

Mwanga meanwhile was vacillating between the various groups, causing further confusion. When a Wa-Ingleza chief was murdered, the perpetrator was tried and acquitted by Mwanga. Lugard reluctantly issued arms to the Wa-Ingleza for their protection. He continued to mediate between the parties, but it appeared the Wa-Franca were determined to fight. He could hear the war-drums beating.

On January 24, large groups of Wa-Franca gathered on Mengo Hill, which incited the Wa-Ingleza to set fire to Rubago. Williams set up the Maxim gun and as the Wa-Franca rushed the fort, Lugard ordered a short burst of fire; only a few were wounded but it was enough to scatter them. Williams moved forward with his Sudanese soldiers in time to prevent the King's palace being burnt down, and drove the Wa-Franca back down the hill.

Lugard could see the resident Bishop and eleven priests were in danger, trapped in Rubago, so he jumped on a horse, rode to them and led them back to sanctuary of the fort. He saw it as essential that both parties' leaders should survive for there to be any chance of peace in the future.

Mwanga meanwhile had escaped to his usual hideout on an island about six miles away. The priests insisted on joining him, leaving the next day under heavy fire. Lugard again sent Williams down with the Maxim gun to save them from massacre. There were more casualties this time, as it was a confused situation by the lake in thick reeds. Williams estimated up to a hundred were killed by gunfire and more drowned in the reeds, but the priests were saved and brought back to the safety of the fort. In the confusion Mwanga and the bishop escaped in a canoe, and made their way to Budda and into German territory to take refuge.

This skirmish was later described by the French as a massacre, with Lugard being blamed for the loss of life. The story reached London the following year, but he felt totally justified in using the Maxim gun; it had enabled negotiations to start with relatively few casualties suffered. The alternative would have been a bloodbath and chaos.

The situation stabilized in the capital, but all around the country the two Christian factions were on the move. The Moslems were watching the division between the Christian parties very closely, and started to mass in the north-west of the country. Lugard saw King Mwanga as the key to negotiating a settlement and sent streams of messages to him in exile, which met with very little response. With a stroke of inspiration he sent four of his wives as messengers with reports of their good treatment. This worked, and after sending ahead two senior chiefs, the King arrived nervously on March 30.

Lugard noted, '...*Presently a huge vast crowd in the wildest excitement appeared on King's Hill and surged down into the valley towards Kampala. I rode out to meet the King and found him being carried on a man's shoulders... from the main road up the Kampala gate I stationed all available askaris, mostly Somalis and Sudanese who were drawn up on each side of the road and presented arms, while my drummers and buglers executed a prolonged flourish...Mwanga in his dirty clothes, like a common peasant, travel-stained, unshaved, disheveled, and looked utterly played out, was a shadow of his former, sleek self. Dismounting, I led him to the house by the hand, for the poor devil was by this time almost in a state of collapse what between fear, excitement, anxiety and fatigue.*'

Lugard presented some small gifts to him, as this was the custom, which delighted the grateful King. The head of the Catholics embraced the Protestants and a scene of joy broke out. '*I told Mwanga that I wanted him to come to my place first because I wanted all of Uganda to see at once that we have come to an understanding and were friends...Outside were the French priests and several of the English missionaries who all shook hands with the King.*'

Mwanga expressed his full confidence in the future, and prolonged discussions started on how to achieve long-term peace. This involved partitioning the country between the rival factions. Lugard was impressed by Mwanga's shrewdness and knowledge in negotiating the new peace treaty which was signed on April 11 1892. For now, trust had been established by Lugard, with both sides expressing their faith in him.

The Moslems, who numbered as many as the combined Christian factions, also had to be brought into the agreement, and a meeting was set with the Moslem leader, Mbogo, on May 13 outside Kampala.

Despite suffering from toothache and neuralgia, and the other Europeans being sick or absent, Lugard rode out with 100 guards, 350 Baganda warriors and his two trusty envoys Dualla and Selim Bey. He found 10,000 Moslems waiting for him. Lugard and Mbogo finally met under a little shelter supported by poles on May 22. Mbogo appeared resplendent in his gold-embroidered robes.

Lugard tried to make the atmosphere as relaxed as possible. He offered the Moslems the north province of Singo which they already dominated, plus three smaller provinces within easy reach of Kampala. In return Mbogo (who was Mwanga's uncle) was asked to renounce the throne and to come to live in Kampala. The talks lasted for two days and eventually, much to Lugard's relief, an agreement was reached.

Mbogo and a large retinue marched with Lugard through suspicious and hostile crowds to the King's palace in Mengo. '... *The meeting was a curious spectacle. They held each other's hands and gave vent to a long drawn 'Oh! Oh!' in a guttural, then 'Ah! Ah!' in a higher note, then low whistles as they gazed into each other's faces. This went on for a long time ...then they fell on each other's necks and embraced and then again...meanwhile the same performances were going on between the chief and chieflets and common people on every side ...'*

The meeting was a success, and Mbogo added his signature to the treaty. They formally agreed to the prohibition of the slave trade and promised freedom of religion. Mwanga made an impressive conciliatory speech in which he said he was now impartial in matters of religion, and that the Moslems would be treated with justice.

Lugard had succeeded, knowing that The Imperial British East Africa Company had a deadline to pull out of the country by the end of 1892. He needed to get back to England as soon as possible to lobby the government either for further support for the Company, or to take over Uganda as a Protectorate. He also needed to contest any accusations he knew were coming from the French missionaries.

During these negotiations, he heard the sad news that Fenwick De Winton had died in the north province of Toro. This greatly upset him. *'Poor boy, it is very sad that he should die alone out there in the Mahommedan camp with no friend near to hear his last wishes. Four men left the coast with me last August year. Of these De Winton and Brown are dead. Wilson was as good as dead ...Grant has been so ill twice that we have feared for his life. Such is Africa!'*

At a farewell dinner, Lugard gave unstinted praise to his successor Captain Williams. In return, Lugard was given heartfelt thanks from all the different factions, which greatly moved him. Selim Bey and Dualla thanked him warmly and refused to stay in Kampala without him. Lugard was presented with an impressive royal war drum by Mbogo. King Mwanga sent a letter to Queen Victoria thanking her for sending Captain Lugard and bringing peace to his country, and requested he be sent back soon to finish his job.

Lugard never did return to Uganda. Eventually the British Government set up the country as a Protectorate, ushering in a time of prosperity, which was continued by Mwanga's son and grandson well into the twentieth century.

The royal war drum, with its decoration of tassels of hair and bells and its deep and ominous tone, was placed in the reception hall of Little Parkhurst, and beaten to summon guests to dinner.

CHAPTER 14
Trials and triumphs

In May 1892, Lugard set off on the trek to the coast in great despondency, missing the comrades with whom he had shared so much. He took with him Dualla, forty Somalis with their women and children, and some Swahilis; nearly two hundred people in all. He had to travel to Kikuyu with a caravan under the command of Captain J R L MacDonald (later Major General Sir), who had recently carried out a railway survey from Mombasa.

The two men did not get on from the beginning. MacDonald refused to take any advice from Lugard, despite never having been to Africa before, and over the next two months seriously endangered the caravan several times. It led to some heated exchanges. Perhaps foreseeing trouble ahead, Lugard recorded these events in his diary in detail. He could not have known that MacDonald would be asked to produce a report on the Uganda situation for London, which would have major repercussions for him over the following two years.

In Mombasa, Lugard met Sir Gerald Portal, the young Consul-General for British East Africa visiting from Zanzibar. Lugard expressed his grave concerns about the consequences of evacuating from Uganda. Portal listened intently, and sent a message to the Earl of Rosebery, the Secretary of State for Foreign Affairs, urging a meeting with Lugard as soon as he returned to London. Lugard set sail for England on September 14 1892, anticipating difficult times ahead.

Whilst travelling, the repercussions of the events in Kampala were being felt in London. The French priests had submitted a report to the French government implying that Lugard had carried out a massacre at Kampala. An official complaint was lodged with the British Government with demands for an inquiry. Rosebery duly ordered a report, and the task fell to the unfortunate Captain MacDonald. He was sent back to Kampala to gather the facts and submit his findings.

There was also a curious request from the French – that a psychological analysis of Lugard's mind be conducted. The Chargé d'affaires Baron D'Estournelles, who had an interest in the new science of psychology, had decided that Lugard had suffered an extraordinary mental reaction to the evacuation. The baron also stated that England was more concerned about the evacuation than the so-called massacre, which he insisted was France's greatest concern. He concluded that when Lugard returned, he did not react as he should, that he was far too calm, and they interpreted this as indifference. Lord Rosebery listened attentively to the report, and dismissed it.

Lugard learned of the main accusations in Mombasa and used the time on the boat home to prepare his defence. He was accused of deliberately provoking war, committing or allowing atrocities of all kinds in the course of the fighting, neglecting to protect the fathers and then ill-treating and imprisoning them, and cheating and oppressing the Catholics in the final settlement.

Other accusations were inaccurate, wild and vague; that he brought 800 soldiers to Kampala (in fact there were one hundred); that he sent troops to hunt the priests to death (no priests were harmed), and that he mowed down women and children with the Maxim gun firing wildly and continually for half an hour, which was not even technically possible.

Lugard was presented as a man of no pity and principles. He described this as '*Such contemptible trash, obviously a mere sensational lie, and not worth replying to …the fathers have painted me as a rancorous and fanatical Protestant though they well know the picture is untrue …to me Catholic, Protestant and Mahommedan have each of them much that is good, and I deplore and detest the narrowness of view which prevents the full appreciation of this good.*'

Using his meticulously detailed diaries, he was able to answer and dismiss each accusation. He did not appear to be distressed by the accusers; he knew he was in the right. The experiences he had endured during the last two years had hardened him, mentally and physically.

By the time he arrived in London he had prepared his defence. In a vigorous period of writing articles, presentations and letters, he hit back at his accusers. In an article for *The Fortnightly Review* in November 1892 he wrote, '*… after reading page after page of invective, I can truthfully say that the feeling uppermost in my mind at the conclusion, was one of pity and sorrow for men whose very bitterness of language proves the intensity of the interest they had in their work…*'

The report was read by the Cabinet with the Prime Minister, William Gladstone, commenting, *'Lugard seems to make a case against the R.C.'s. I hope he has right on his side.'*

The Catholic leader of the aristocracy, the Duke of Norfolk, tried to take up the matter with the Imperial East Africa Company, but it refused to supply him with information. The Duke asked unsuccessfully for a debate in the House of Lords. Lugard offered him a meeting but was swiftly rebuffed.

Lugard continued to lobby in the corridors of power in London, raising interest wherever he went. At the same time he started work on his book. His first speech was on November 3 at the Royal Geographical Society, and proved very successful.

His brother Ned, back from India, attended and wrote to his fiancée Nell, *'Last night's show was a huge compliment to Fred. Lords and Dukes and all sorts of swells were turned away at the door for want of standing room!'*

The Prince of Wales sent a letter of regret that he was unable to attend. The Archbishop of Canterbury and Henry Stanley did the same. His speech was so popular that he was asked to read it again at a special meeting of the Society later in November for those that missed it the first time.

Throughout November and December, Lugard toured the country lecturing at Manchester, Edinburgh, Glasgow, Aberdeen, Dundee, Newcastle, Cambridge, Liverpool, Birmingham and Norwich, being greeted by mayors, aldermen, bishops and peers. He received substantial and mostly favourable press coverage, and was invited to many dinners. His speeches concentrated on the geographical and commercial aspects of East Africa, avoiding political argument or jingoism, and always mentioned the good works of the missionaries, especially to the enthusiastic Scots.

The publicity generated loud public feedback, which reverberated through Parliament. Rosebery was forced to act. On December 1 he appointed Lord Portal as a special Commissioner to go to Uganda and produce a report. This was exactly what Lugard wanted. He could now finish his book, and present an even clearer view of <u>his</u> ideas for imperial rule in Africa.

Firing off long letters to *The Times,* Lugard confronted his critics. One of these was Henry Labouchère, a rich, colourful, English, Liberal politician, writer, publisher and theatre owner, who had been strongly critical and mocking of him. After reading a particularly libelous article, Lugard was so incensed he went to his house. The servant recognised him, tried to block his entrance, but Lugard was too quick. He burst through the front door, into the living room, and found Labouchère in a sheer panic, hiding behind a writing table. He was no adventurer and had certainly never faced wild lions on the plains of Africa. He looked into Lugard's eyes feeling distinctly unsafe. Lugard thundered, '*Mr Labouchère, you have called me a liar and a murderer. You well know that this is untrue and that I am neither.*'

'*Oh yes, yes,*' Labouchère replied, grateful that physical violence was not going to occur, '*but it makes good copy. It brings you before the public - you can always deny it!*'

Lugard was speechless, never having been the victim of such brazen cynicism, but it cleared the air and they continued with a civil discussion. Labouchère later became a useful establishment contact.

On March 20 1893 there was a debate in the Commons on the estimated cost of annexing Uganda. It broadened into the whole question of the benefits of imperial policy, with strong views being expressed on both sides. A new voice came out in favour, and gave a strong speech in praise of Lugard. It came from Joseph Chamberlain, an influential back bencher, who would go on to become Colonial Secretary in 1895.

Lugard finished the two volumes of his book in June 1893, calling it provocatively '*The Rise of Our East African Empire*', and dedicated it to his uncle Edward. It was over 350,000 words long and contained large numbers of illustrations and maps completed with the help of the well-known cartographer E. G. Ravenstein. It was a comprehensive analysis of the state of East Africa, and how it could be administered in the future at every level. There was a discussion on slavery, the pros and cons of chartered companies, the importance of a new railway, and the case for a new capital in Kenya, Nairobi. In Lugard's view, '*... the object to be aimed at in the administration of this country, is to rule through its own executive government. The people are singularly intelligent, and have a wonderful appreciation of justice and of legal procedure and our aim should be to educate and develop this sense of justice...*'

The book was reviewed by a wide range of newspapers, magazines and periodicals and generally favourably received. Lugard decided to visit *The Times* newspaper himself in London, as it was the leading daily paper, and he needed to ensure they understood his cause clearly. On November 22 1893, he met the editor Charles Moberly Bell, who took him to the office of the reviewer. To his pleasant surprise he was introduced to an elegant, striking woman dressed in black. Her name was Flora Shaw.

He was immediately impressed with her depth of knowledge on Empire issues, and how well-travelled she was. Flora had given the book a good review, and considered it '*...the most important contribution that has yet been made to the history of East Africa.*' She continued, '*The imagination will be dull to which the conflict of hostile barbarism and civilization fail to present* *itself with something of the grandeur of a modern epic.'* He thanked her for her generous review, and they met at regular intervals to discuss African affairs.

The publication of the book launched Lugard on a social whirlwind, fêted by the political hostesses of the day, and invited to dine with the high and mighty. He moved in circles he would never have dreamed of joining just a few years earlier. He came into contact with the world of art and literature, making some unexpected acquaintances. He was invited to join the Anglo-African Writers Club by Rider Haggard, which met monthly at the Grand Hotel in London. There he was introduced to other famous writers of Africa. He met John Buchan, became friends with James Barrie, (before *Peter Pan* was written), Charles Brookfield, a well-known author and playwright of the day, and with Frank Dicksee, a painter who was later knighted and gave him a copy of one of his famous paintings *The Viking Funeral*. Lugard wrote whimsically at the time, *'I wonder what these people think when they read of the deck passage and my gratitude to my pal the boatswain! I suppose they say he's a complete adventurer, started with fifty sovereigns as a decker out of some slum.'*

Lugard met other Africa experts including John Kirk, staying with him several times at his house in Kent, Horace Waller, another close associate of Livingstone, and Frederick Selous, a famous explorer and hunter in South Africa. He was reunited with his protégé from Kampala, Captain Williams, to make a joint presentation at the Royal Colonial Institute. He found these experiences in London enjoyable but he never lost sight of his objectives, of supporting Uganda and his desire to expand his knowledge of Africa.

Whilst waiting for the Portal Report, Lugard was approached by Sir Percy Anderson from the Foreign Office to undertake a short, delicate mission to France. The French were pursuing their own imperial ambitions in Africa. They dreamed of linking their West Africa colonies east to Somaliland. A famous French explorer Major Monteil (the nearest the French had to a Lugard), was trying to mount an expedition to the Upper Nile. He had mentioned to Poultney Bigalow, an American journalist he knew, that he was an admirer of Lugard. The Foreign Office felt Lugard was right man to find out more information about French intentions in West Africa. He was flattered. Cancelling his engagements, including one with the Duke of York, and despite speaking little French, he set off on his first diplomatic mission.

Lugard and Monteil met in Paris, and struck up an immediate rapport. On the first evening he was taken to Montmartre to experience the delights of the Moulin Rouge which had only been open for five years. The iconic red windmill drew him inside the club to watch the famous can-can cabaret. In a smoky corner he saw the unmistakable monocled and hunched figure of Toulouse Lautrec sketching the girls. He was appalled at the cost, but wrote '...*we really had some fun. I felt for a moment as if I had rolled off sixteen hard years and was the boy I was when I first came to London Town - but not quite! But I think it did me good. These ladies of Paris take life so* very *lightly. They are so happy and bright!*'

The two travellers parried each other's questions for two days. They exchanged a minimum of information, but it was enough to confirm the fears of the Foreign Office. Lugard submitted a memorandum to Sir Percy Anderson, who was delighted with the results and said he had handled the situation admirably. Lugard remarked to Ned '...*I was really quite proud, for it was my first diplomatic mission.*'

In December Lord Portal returned from his visit to Uganda and completed his report. He submitted it to Rosebery, who was loathe to release it. The report was critical of Lugard and he was not happy with the conclusions. Portal then became critically ill from typhoid contracted in Uganda, and died in January aged just thirty-five.

Gladstone was coming to the end of his long and distinguished career. The Grand Old Man retired in February, and Rosebery took over as Prime Minister in March 1894. Portal's report was eventually presented to Parliament on April 10, and came down in favour of the retention of Uganda. Two days later there was an official announcement that Uganda was to become a British Protectorate.

The debate in the House of Commons was set for June 1894. Lugard continued lobbying key people, especially Joseph Chamberlain and Claude Lowther, to ensure that they would not use Zanzibar as a base from which to rule, and that the legal status of slavery was abolished. There were long debates, and to Lugard's delight it was Chamberlain's eloquent, hard-hitting speech which swayed the crowded house. After ten long hours the Government won with a majority. Lugard wrote to his brother the next day, '... *I believe that my ceaseless efforts there and in England have produced a wonderful result... so many speakers (and many more crowded out for lack of opportunity to speak) so well informed on any possession of British Empire as there were about this little country in the centre of Africa... You'll be delighted Ned, I know, for you know how hard I've worked and, my boy, this debate to my mind is the greatest triumph I've ever scored.*'

His brother wrote later, '*This was undoubtedly Fred's finest hour.*'

The next day Chamberlain held a dinner party to which Lugard was invited. After dinner, Chamberlain took Lugard aside. He told him that all the knowledge for his speech in the House the previous day was solely derived from Lugard's book and from conversations with him. Lugard was honoured and felt immense satisfaction.

Now he needed new employment.

CHAPTER 15
The journalist

Flora had been grateful to William Stead at *The Pall Mall Gazette*, but by 1892 incompatibility of views on colonial issues between the newspapers became apparent and she decided to work for *The Times*. After a meeting with the editor George Buckle, he agreed to expand her scope, and she started producing a regular fortnightly article for *The Times* under the name of F. Shaw because of prejudice against female writers at that time. Her first articles were well received.

Flora began a long and fruitful period writing for *The Times*, undertaking three major trips to South Africa, Australia and Canada between 1892 and 1898. She was fully supported by Charles Moberly Bell, whose confidence in her consolidated her position as one of the leading foreign correspondents of the day. She researched her topics extensively and astonished those she visited with her intricate knowledge of the subject and her comprehensive analysis of the situations.

Moberly Bell sent Flora to report on the situation in South Africa. She met Cecil Rhodes again and was further impressed by his leadership and vision. She saw his willingness to work with the Dutch, defending them on occasions, and witnessed the intransigence of President Paul Kruger, a man who could barely write, was convinced the earth was flat and had no desire for change.

Flora travelled throughout South Africa talking to the various parties and sending back reports on the political, economic, social and labour problems she found. This included visiting a diamond mine at Kimberley to see the conditions the men were forced to work in.

She insisted on meeting a number of the Zulu chiefs in Durban, who still vividly remembered their great victory at Isandlwana over the British, and the Battle of Rorke's Drift, when eleven Victoria Crosses were won, thirteen years earlier. Flora heard and wrote about the broken treaties with local Xhosa tribal chiefs, the abuse of labour in the mines and the disputes over land.

She saw that major clashes were going to be unavoidable in the future. Her view of Cecil Rhodes was that he was a man of vision who could lead the country forward, and Rhodes saw Flora as a very useful ally in London.

On her return to London, she was congratulated by George Buckle for her dispatches. Some commentators thought they were so good that they must have been written by a man.

After the success of South Africa, Flora sailed for Tasmania in September 1892 for a tour of Australia. She started with the fruit orchards of Hobart, then visited the wineries of Melbourne and Adelaide, made a brief stop at Sydney and continued to Queensland. There she met the Prime Minister. She also toured the sugar cane plantations, and various sheep stations, interviewing the sheep shearers and union officials. On one train journey she interviewed an eccentric multi-millionaire called John Tyson, who was so enamoured by her that he proposed marriage at the end of the interview. She gently declined.

In Brisbane, Flora received a letter from her sister Lulu informing her that her father had died the month before after a long illness. She took a break for two weeks and went to the Blue Mountains outside Sydney to work on her notes and contemplate her next move. She decided not to cut her tour short.

Whilst in Sydney, Moberly Bell asked her to return to England via Canada. She first paid a short twelve-day visit to New Zealand, then caught a boat to Samoa. Also on board was her old friend Robert Louis Stevenson, travelling with his wife Fanny back to their new home in Samoa. He was very ill, and a shell of the man she remembered. He died within the year.

In San Francisco, she stayed in the most beautiful hotel she had ever experienced, later destroyed in the 1907 earthquake. On the train to Vancouver she was entranced by the spectacular coastal scenery, especially at Puget Sound, which, many years later, she was able to show to Lugard on their way to Hong Kong.

In Canada she found there was further support for the secession from Britain, a movement also growing in Australia, and she deliberately slanted her articles showing the advantages of remaining part of the British Empire than allying with America.

Flora saw Canada as a vast, underpopulated land with enormous reserves and tremendous potential for emigration. This was her last stop, and after nearly a year away, she returned to London to more enthusiastic reviews.

George Buckle was again delighted, and as soon as she returned, she was promoted to Colonial Editor of *The Times*.

Flora met Lugard for the first time on November 22 1893 when he came to her office to thank her for the favourable review of his book. She impressed him with her breadth of knowledge on colonial matters, and there was an immediate attraction and rapport between the two imperialists, with their shared passion for Africa. During her research Perham found a note from Flora written shortly after the meeting saying '... *we must meet again, I am nearly always at home late in the afternoon.*' Further meetings and exchanges of letters followed as they sought each other's opinion on Africa, but romance was not to blossom for another nine years.

In 1893, at the age of forty-one, Flora Shaw became the first woman to hold a major editorial position on any prominent newspaper worldwide. She found a house in Cambridge Street, Warwick Square, near her offices at Printing House Square, and invited her three sisters Lulu, Marie and Allie to share. This lasted for eight happy years.

Later in 1894, she nervously presented a paper on her findings in Australia to the Royal Colonial Institute. It was a full house, drawn to see one of the few women to make a presentation. Within a few minutes her nerves had settled, and her voice rang out clearly with confidence for nearly an hour. It was a resounding success and letters of congratulation came flooding in. These included one from her lover George Goldie, and another from her admirer, Captain Frederick Lugard. The following week she appeared the subject of a cartoon in *Punch*. She had arrived.

Cecil Rhodes and Dr. Jameson came to London in 1894 for further negotiations with the Government over his company, and Flora met them often. She continued to support Rhodes, and tried to win over those that did not trust him, including Lugard. Another was Joseph Chamberlain, who became Colonial Secretary in June 1895, but he assured her, '*I will work with the strong man if it is at all possible.*'

Throughout 1895, Flora continued working at her hectic pace, and was in charge of various correspondents reporting to her from all over the world. The Scramble for Africa was continuing apace, and the political crisis in South Africa was coming to a head. Flora was aware of the preparations that were ongoing but had not anticipated Dr. Jameson's ill-judged decision to attack early.

On December 30 1895, Leander Starr Jameson led two columns of armed, part-time soldiers across the border from a small town called Pitsani heading towards Johannesburg on a bungled raid that aimed to encourage an insurrection against the Transvaal government, then led by Paul Kruger.

It was a disaster from the start. A breakdown of communications and a failure of the raiders to cut one of the telegraph lines with Pretoria allowed the Boers advanced notice to prepare an ambush. Jameson was outnumbered six to one. After a brief fight during which he lost seventeen dead, fifty-five wounded and thirty-five missing, he surrendered on January 2 to the Boer commander, Piet Cronje. He was handed over to the British and sent back to England for trial.

There was a damaging political backlash. The plot was quickly traced back to Rhodes, with various documents and telegrams incriminating British Government officials. Flora had been in communication with Rhodes by secret code and had known the raid was imminent. The day after the raid she published in *The Times* the manifesto that would have been issued if the uprising had been successful. Chamberlain condemned the raid, despite having knowledge of it.

The Jameson Raid led to the first professional crisis in her life, implicating *The Times,* and questioning her relationship with the Government. Flora was to be called as a key witness in the House of Commons Select Committee Inquiry. She followed the trial of Jameson and his officers in July 1896 closely, and prepared for the Inquiry thoroughly. It commenced in January 1897. The main accusation against her was that she had passed secret cables between Rhodes and Chamberlain.

Flora received strong support from Moberly Bell and George Goldie, but her editor George Buckle sent her a letter on May 24 warning her not to say anything to damage the reputation of *The Times.* His lack of confidence in her shocked and disgusted her, but she did not show it.

On May 25 1897 Flora was called to give evidence. The Committee room at Westminster Hall was full and included the Prince of Wales and his retinue. Flora's performance before the fifteen-man committee was outstanding. She kept calm and collected under immense pressure for three days, answering questions clearly but deftly, deflecting the awkward ones. There was a crowd outside who cheered as she drove away. The press had a field day. When the report came out, she was exonerated. So was *The Times* and Joseph Chamberlain. Rhodes was severely censured and forced to resign as chairman of the BSAC, and had to stand down as Cape Prime Minister. It was an impressive performance, making her a cause célèbre, and was reported in papers around the world.

A direct result of the raid was the Second Matabele War in 1896 when hundreds of Europeans and Africans were killed, and the start of the Boer War in 1899.

Just before Flora left for South Africa in 1893, she had met George

Goldie for the first time when she interviewed him for an article on the Niger Basin. She was again drawn to a strong, magnetic character with similar imperialist views and a clear vision of what he wanted to achieve. He was out to seduce her. They quickly became lovers and it was the beginning of an eight year intermittent affair that both excited and drained her. Goldie had taken over the role of her advisor and mentor from Charles Brackenbury, and it was through Goldie she heard more of the exploits of a certain Captain Lugard.

In late 1897, George Goldie's wife, Mathilda suddenly died at the age of fifty-one. Goldie was distraught and locked himself away, refusing to see any friends. Despite his philandering, this complex man never lost the love for his wife, and he was wracked with guilt. Flora offered her support and kept her distance for a while, but she was convinced he would now want to marry her. When she eventually raised the subject of marriage with him, she was abruptly and callously refused. Flora was devastated. The strain of events of the previous year, combined with this rejection, caused her to have a mental breakdown. She could not eat or breathe properly, developed a fever and was in bed for weeks, nursed by her sisters. They were confounded how such a strong-willed woman, that had travelled the length and breadth of Australia and South Africa on her own, could succumb so quickly to her mental torment.

There was concern at *The Times* too, and it was Charles Moberly Bell who helped pull her through. He went to her house and found her sitting in a chair looking pale and thin. His view was there was only one way to get her back on her feet. Producing a bunch of flowers, he announced that *The Times* had an important assignment for her. She was to go to Yukon for five months and report on the Klondike Gold Rush, and its effects on Canada. Her eyes lit up and she agreed straight away.

This was the most physically arduous trip she would undertake, and while regaining her strength she wrote various articles. These included one on the urgent questions arising in West Africa which were being debated by Lugard and Chamberlain. Flora's backing helped secure Lugard his new post as leader of the West Africa Frontier Force, and he came round to her house to thank her before he left for Nigeria in March 1898. Flora was pleased to see him again, and after a fond embrace, Lugard left promising to write to her every week, which he duly did.

The Klondike lived up to its reputation of being hard, wild and challenging. Lulu was especially concerned for her safety, but Flora reassured her sister, writing, '*I want you to fully realise that I shall take every necessary precaution ...If I were to allow myself to come to grief either through exposure* or violence they would get no letters ... *They have not gone to the expense of my journey for the purpose of leaving my bones in Canada.*' On the voyage out she met '*an expert Klondiker of disreputable appearance but I believe honest habits and great experience. For the last twenty years he has been in and out of the Klondike region and knows every way to Dawson City.*' He recounted tales of large, fierce mosquitoes, gunslingers, seas of mud, falling rocks and raging rivers, and advised her to carry a gun. She considered him '*rather pessimistic,*' but she did add to her luggage a beekeeper's hat, canvas leggings and stouter walking boots. Her planning was meticulous, checking all the different modes of transport, informing government officials, the Hudson Bay Company and even the Mounted Police.

Flora sailed to New York and took the train to Montreal, which connected to British Columbia. From there, she headed west across Canada by train to Victoria, calling at Winnipeg to get a toothache sorted out. There followed a nine-hundred mile journey by steamer to Skagway in Alaska, where she watched whales, puffins and sea eagles, and caught her first glimpse of the aurora borealis. At Skagway, she arrived just after a shoot-out with 'Soapy Smith' and his boys, and observed the marauding gang being escorted onto her boat. Ahead of her lay the six-hundred mile journey across the glacial mountains to wild Dawson City - by horse.

Flora joined a long caravan of fortune hunters and suppliers. They immediately had to climb the precipitous White Pass, '*...scrambling along granite ledges with mountain torrents thundering in our ears, before winding into the stillness of a pure forest...*' At night she declined the bunkhouse and slept under the stars wrapped in a blanket and '*slept like a log on a pile of chips ...and the sound of the waterfall was delicious...*' They continued climbing the next day, walking along narrow ledges, sometimes crawling on all fours. There were many horses at the bottom of ravines that had slipped and fallen over the edge. The Klondiker had not been exaggerating.

Descending from the pass, they reached Lake Bennett, which was still partly frozen, and had a two day wait for a boat to Dawson City. Flora slept in her own tent but went to the log shanty for dinner '*...in the company of four murderers, a man whom they tried to murder, two policemen and a Klondiker...*' She was keen to board the boat.

The small steamer was full, with four small cabins and no sanitary provisions. As Flora was the only woman on board, she shared a cabin with the captain, who worked nights. It took five days and nights to reach Dawson City and despite the conditions, she found her fellow passengers '*a very respectable lot with good humour and kindness.*' On July 23 she disembarked at Dawson City having taken only thirty-one days to travel from London.

Dawson was a sprawling mud-encrusted tent city of about thirty thousand people. Flora camped up on a hill overlooking the town near a fresh spring, next to a young English couple who had come to seek their fortune. She met many chasing their luck, going out to the goldfields, often ankle-deep in mud, and witnessed the harsh conditions and poverty they endured. She quickly realised that most prospectors found nothing. She did meet one pleasant young Englishman who appeared to come from a good background and was dining on wooden packing cases, and in contrast to other speculators, had £3,500 worth of gold in his pouch, but he was the exception. On the first night, Flora asked to be taken to one of the gambling saloons at midnight to see how they played.

There she met Diamond-Tooth Gertie and her husband, Harry. They were two of the first pioneers to open a saloon on the strip. The bar smelt of stale beer, cigars and cheap perfume. It echoed to the sounds of honky-tonk music, drunken conversations and the shouts of the dancing girls ordering more beer for their cheering and befuddled customers. Upstairs the brothel was doing a roaring trade, with heavily-rouged young girls with low-cut dresses and heaving bosoms making as much money as they could, for the minimum of effort. This was not new to Flora. She had seen the brothels in the East End of London - the same exploitation, just a different background, different music and a lot more guns. Shootings and killings were common, and bribery the norm.

Flora was shocked by the amount of corruption she saw. '*The corruption among Canadian officials is a shock to my faith in British Institutions, for which I was not prepared. They sell anything, down to the right to enter a public building, and poor men cannot get their gold claims recorded unless they pay a part-interest to the official.*' She did not shy away from reporting this in her articles, which did not go down well with the Canadian officials, but she stuck to her principles of being honest with her observations, no matter how unpalatable the truth might be.

The final stop was to meet government officials for a large dinner party in Ottawa. Her article on corruption in the Klondike was published in *The Times* that week, and had been published in the Canadian papers under the title, '*The Thunderer has spoken.*' There was already a call for a full inquiry into corruption and the ministers responsible were at the dinner. It was all rather embarrassing, but dressed elegantly for the occasion, Flora charmed her way through the evening, and received a surprisingly warm welcome. She may not have been so popular with the ministers, but businessmen in Yukon welcomed her comments, and Flora was remembered there for many years after.

This was one of the most memorable experiences of her life, and enthralled her nieces and nephews with the tales into her old age.

Flora arrived back in London in the middle of November 1898, and gave popular presentations to the Royal Colonial Institute in London, with articles published in *The New York Times*. She was at the peak of her career.

Back at her desk in Printing House Square, she worked on a variety of articles, with the subject of Africa predominating. South Africa was in crisis and Flora watched with concern, writing frequent articles discussing potential solutions between the Boers and the Uitlanders (foreigners).

In June, negotiations broke down and Chamberlain demanded full voting rights for the Uitlanders residing in the Transvaal, which was rejected. In October, Kruger issued an ultimatum for the British to withdraw their troops, which was refused. On October 11, war was declared. Flora was not surprised. She pressed for a Federation of South African states, but received little support from her editor. She now felt she was losing the support of George Buckle, and felt more and more discontented. This was echoed in her personal life.

Her relationship with Goldie was going nowhere. Lugard had been a most sympathetic and supportive friend, but he was getting ready to sail for the inauguration of Northern Nigeria.

In addition, Flora heard from her elder sister Tommy, that her husband had committed suicide in India, after being denied a promotion. Now penniless with seven children, she desperately needed help from Flora.

Pressures were mounting, and Flora found her work and health beginning to suffer. She considered resigning so she could sort out her private life. She wanted to continue freelance, and with great reluctance, on September 1 1900 she went to Moberly Bell to tender her resignation letter. He fully understood her reasons and accepted it, on the understanding that he could consult her about all the subjects he wanted to discuss. Flora readily agreed.

CHAPTER 16
The race to Borgu

Sir George Dashwood Taubman Goldie was, as his name suggests, a striking figure. He was five feet nine inches tall, lean and gaunt, fair, with a large head, a high brow and an eagle-like hooked nose. He had piercing blue eyes, an Edwardian moustache, an aloof look, and his dynamic, nervous energy completed the picture of a man of action. His biographer, Lady Dorothy Wellesley - the Duchess of Wellington and part of the literary Bloomsbury set - was mesmerised by him. As a child she called him Rameses, after seeing the mummy of the famous pharaoh in the Cairo Museum. Goldie played an important part in the lives of both Frederick Lugard and Flora Shaw.

Goldie was a colourful, complex personality who, at the end of his life, destroyed all his papers and made his children swear never to publish any works about him. This was probably to protect those who experienced his innumerable indiscretions. Queen Victoria banned him from court because of his reputation.

He was born in the Isle of Man in 1846, the fourth son of a Lieutenant Colonel of the Scots Guards and a speaker in the House of Keys. He followed family tradition and trained at the Royal Military Academy at Woolwich. Despite '*being like a gun-powder magazine and blind-drunk at the final exams,*' he passed.

Two years after being commissioned, a relation died leaving him a fortune. '*I was so excited by the freedom that this gave to me, that I bolted without sending in my papers, and leaving all my belongings behind, I went straight to Egypt. There I fell in love with an Arab girl. We lived in the desert for three years - the Garden of Allah! She died of consumption and I returned home to lead a life of idleness and dissipation.*' In 1870 he ran away to France with the family governess Mathilda Elliot, and began a tempestuous love affair. They were caught in the Prussian siege of Paris for four months, and married in London in July 1871. Goldie continued his story to Dorothy, *'All achievements begin with a dream. My dream as a child was to colour the map red. In 1877 I left England (largely to escape from private entanglements) to explore the interior of Nigeria with my brother. He got fever badly when we were half way up the river* [Niger] *and I had to bring him home. On the journey back I conceived the ambition of adding the region of the Niger to the British Empire.'*

At that time Britain only had a few footholds in West Africa; on the coast at Sierra Leone, the Gold Coast and at Lagos, where Britain had taken over from pirates in 1861. The scramble had started between Germany and France to gain control inland. Goldie took hold of one of the ailing trading companies and combined several of the companies on the coast into the National Africa Company which later became the Royal Niger Company. He bought out the last French rival in 1884. He applied for a Royal Charter in 1881 but it was not granted by Gladstone until 1886, (who promptly lost it on a train and a new one had to be hastily drawn up). He was honoured with a knighthood in 1887.

The Royal Niger Company expanded quickly, establishing forty trading-posts on the River Niger, and negotiated four hundred treaties with the chiefs of the lower Niger and Hausa states. In 1885 Goldie sent an experienced explorer, Joseph Thomson, to make a treaty with the Sultan of Sokoto in the north, who dominated the northern Hausa states. The Government had made agreements in 1886 and 1893 with Germany for a British *'sphere of influence'* in the east, and with the French in 1890 agreeing a northern boundary at Lake Chad. The only open boundary was on the west with Dahomey, (now Benin) and the adjacent Borgu state. Although Goldie considered he had made a treaty with Borgu, the French did not recognize it.

Tensions rose between France and England and on July 24 1894 the French mounted a well-equipped expedition under Captain Decoeur bound for Dahomey, aiming to take Borgu. If the British were to have any influence in Borgu, it would require swift action to get there before the French. Goldie saw Lugard as the ideal man to carry this out.

Lugard was reluctant to get involved in West Africa - he still considered himself an East Africa man hoping to return to Uganda. However, he had been so outspoken with his views that he could see there was little chance of returning. Goldie had written to Lugard on April 24, *'You are emphatically and undeniably the man for Uganda; I would not, if I could, take you away so long as there is any chance of an appointment there. Uganda is your own child.'* When the debate was concluded in the House of Commons, Goldie approached him again, more urgently. After discussions with John Kirk, Lugard agreed to lead an expedition, and on June 26 he joined the Royal Niger Company.

Captain Decoeur had left Marseilles heading for Carnotville in Dahomey, where a caravan was to take him to Nikki in Borgu. Lugard sailed from Liverpool four days later on July 28 and took a longer route. He then proceeded by ship 530 miles up the River Niger to Jebba, and then by caravan to Borgu. To complicate matters, there were reports that the Germans were mounting an expedition from the north. The race was on.

The first stop was Sierra Leone. Lugard found the climate more inclement than East Africa, with longer, heavier monsoon rains, more stifling humidity and more disease. He noted, *'The officers in the mess are the colour of a dirty table-cloth. They can't leave the house in this driving rain, and they drink continual cocktails (I believe) and smoke and sleep.'*

Whilst travelling, he read an assortment of books on West Africa by French travellers including Louis G. Binger, the Governor of the Ivory Coast whom he admired. He started learning the Hausa language.

Passing Liberia, the ship stopped at the Gold Coast (now Ghana) where they went ashore to see for himself the appalling underground dungeons of the slave traders. Lugard noted, *'Where in the old days the British crammed thousands of slaves awaiting shipment ...on one side were piled a large number of ready-made coffins ready for the poor devils of white men who die like flies in these parts.'*

On August 19 they arrived at Lagos but could not dock because of a sand bar, as the deep harbour had not yet been built, and continued east to the western tributary of the Niger at Forcados. They stopped off a short way upriver at Warri, at the Niger Coast Protection Station, which later developed into a key terminal for the Southern Nigeria oil fields. The settlement consisted of a group of neatly laid out houses, the base for the Consul, Sir Claude MacDonald and his Vice-Consul, Mr. Crawford. It was a pleasant outpost of shady trees and pristine lawns, with well-trained staff and good food.

Shortly after arriving, Lugard was reminded of the ongoing battle with the slave-traders. He was invited by Crawford to go further upstream in the navy launch *Alecto,* to make a reconnaissance of a position held by a notorious local slave-trader chief called Nana. It was rumoured he held 5,000 slaves in his hell-hole dungeons. Lugard declined as he felt a fever coming on, and decided to rest.

This was fortuitous, for within a short time, the launch returned with its decks blood-stained and covered with dead and injured, including Crawford, who had part of his leg shot away and had to have it amputated. They had been ambushed by slavers and had come under heavy fire from hidden fortified positions, concealing twenty-three heavy cannons.

Lugard attended the funerals of the dead who were wrapped in Union Jacks, and he reflected on the fate of the young men. He thought about his own attitude to fighting. '...*the lust of carnage does not come over me - I do not care to kill men, though I know the strange feeling as one sees them fall, and knows one's hand and eye judgement sent that poor devil to eternity. But to me it remains an act of defence. I have no wish to kill (the enemy) because he is against me — only because I know he is coming to kill me, or because as we are fighting it is necessary to kill in order to win. Strange (it seems to me) that this kind of feeling is I believe altogether an exception. My experience is so. It is (like very much else about me) a woman's character...*'

The next day, Lugard set off in the steamer along the coast to the mouth of the Niger, and to the Royal Niger Company's main coastal station. He was impressed by it. It was well organised, better than that in East Africa. It was purpose-built for the trade of palm oil, allowing ocean steamers to pick up the full barrels from well-built, serviceable wharfs for export to Europe, and had good communications with the upriver stations. On August 30 he transferred onto the river steamer *Nupe* to start the 530-mile journey to Jebba.

The River Niger is one of the great rivers of the world, the third longest in Africa. Its immense volume of rich, muddy water surges about 2,500 miles down a vast waterway from the heart of Africa. As the steamer made its way slowly north, Lugard looked around in wonder, noting the rapidly changing scenery. The mangrove forests with their dark, tangled, exposed roots were replaced with tall, dense, forest trees. These were interspersed with oil palms sweeping down to the banks, intertwined with brilliant scarlet flowers, orchids and a myriad of ferns.

Strange-shaped, continually-changing sediment islands, dotted the river. Fishermen toiled in dug-out canoes, stopping to stare suspiciously as the boat passed by. They lived in numerous, small fishing villages that teemed with busy women carrying wood, cooking and cleaning, and small, naked children playing around smoky fires. At the town of Onitsha he visited the coffee and rubber plantations. He stopped at Asaba to see the modern jail of the Company's Chief Justice. Lugard was reminded of his experiences in Burma, and made some suggestions for the use of elephants in the infant timber trade.

The next stop was Lokoja, situated at the junction of a major tributary of the Niger, the River Benue, which had wound its way from the hills of Cameroons. Lugard watched Hausa troops being drilled. These men were from the northern Moslem Sudanic people and considered better soldiers than those from the south. He chose thirty, plus ten Yoruba from the local area as an escort for his first preliminary expedition from Jebba.

Nine days after leaving the coast they reached their destination, the small but strategic town of Jebba. It is guarded by the mysterious prehistoric Ju-Ju rock rising from the middle of the river, and treated with great reverence by the local people. The river is overlooked by a tall stone monument to the explorer Mungo Park, who must have seen the rock as he drowned near here in 1806 after his canoe was attacked by hostile natives.

Lugard's first impressions of the country were not favourable. It was different to anything he had experienced in East Africa. Besides the climate being oppressive, the people seemed to be more superstitious, even menacing. Tales of this being *the white man's grave* echoed in his thoughts. It chilled his spirits before he had even started his expedition.

Whilst porters were being hired and equipment prepared, Lugard took the opportunity to visit the local king at Bussa. The six-day trek in heavy tropical rain, gave him time to see how his new troops shaped up. He was disappointed with Bussa. The village was squalid and the chief deliberately made him wait for an audience. He reluctantly put on his scarlet tunic with gold lace muttering, *'I detest this mummery.'* He exchanged courtesies and sat by the chief surrounded by goats and naked girls, watching a ceremony that involved long coach horns being sounded in his ear.

The king promised to send letters to the Kings of Kiama and Nikki and provided messengers, but Lugard felt little had been achieved. With a growing sense of urgency he returned to Jebba, sensing the French must be getting close to Nikki.

Lugard's caravan consisted of 320 men, with forty soldiers, two headmen and the rest porters comprising of Hausas, Yurobas, and Nupes. In addition there were three Europeans, including G. N. Mottram, a young doctor who was also carrying out astronomical observations for plotting the maps, and a young inexperienced company man called T. A. Reynolds.

The caravan had been hastily put together. This was hostile country, and Lugard was concerned about the lack of experience and communication problems. He only had two Yoruba interpreters and he missed Dualla. He did not have a good feeling about this trip and for the first time that year, he felt the black dog of depression creeping upon him, and found himself turning inwards.

They set off on September 28 at dawn in torrential rain and headed south down the red laterite track to the Yoruba centre of Ilorin. This was a key town with links to the Moslem north. He noted as he passed through the villages how well-kept the houses were, and how courteous the Yoruba people were towards them.

He quickly found discipline in the caravan a problem. Porters were slipping away at the end of the day to sleep in the local villages, arriving back late the next morning, then fighting each other over the loads. Lugard could only get donkeys, which he knew from previous experience in Uganda would be a problem. He noted in his diary '...*they would be as useless in rain as brown paper.*' They proved as problematic as predicted, struggling on wet tracks and unable to cross the rivers without being unloaded. His two young colleagues went down with fever within days.

From Ilorin they headed north and arrived at Kishi, on the Borgu border. The houses had walled courtyards, the land was well-cultivated, and there were broad, clean roads. The people were formal and courteous, and wore flowing robes dyed in the local dark-blue dye. On meeting Lugard, the king said to him, '*The British have put the country to rights and done great good. Already the Borgu raiders who had been troubling him were beginning to run away at the very news that the white man was coming.*' He invited Lugard to a private meeting.

Lugard went to the king's house with Joseph his interpreter, and met him with a small council. A councellor rose and made a fine speech. '*He thanked God for our coming with great fervour, and said that three days ago you could not have seen a man 300 yards from the town without a bow and arrow; now all went unarmed. The British had introduced law and order into all Yoruba and at last it had come to them. They were on the very frontier of Borgu...they lived in daily dread of them and they raided constantly and carried people off for slaves. They prayed my coming was the beginning of peace; all they desired was peace.*'

Lugard was greatly encouraged and gave a reassuring reply that future peace would lead to prosperity. On behalf of the Royal Niger Company he drew up a treaty which the king signed the next day in front of large, cheering crowds. While he was there, Lugard received letters from the influential Emir of Ilorin, which were to prove most useful later on.

The caravan set off again on October 15, with ominous warnings that the Borgu were planning to attack it. Lugard crossed the border nervously, but as he approached the first town, much to his surprise, he was given another warm reception by the king, who came to meet him dressed in resplendent clothes and accompanied by two naked women, one carrying his sword. Still wary, Lugard camped outside the town erecting a small defensive stockade around his tents.

He had a good feeling about this king, so when invited to meet him secretly that evening, he agreed. Trust was established and the king met at Lugard's camp. *'So I received him there. He was most friendly. Said that now he had seen me he was my lifelong friend.... And I was as safe here in his country as my own – as for him he would like to sleep in my tent to show his confidence in me ...The King said his main object in coming was to ask my destination and purpose of travel. He was afraid he could not allow me to go beyond Nikki (if such was my purpose), as the country was most dangerous, in fact he had come to warn me that the Nikki people were very bad and in especial very treacherous...We parted in great good fellowship. Learning that I am by profession a soldier, and by practice for seventeen years a hunter, he was delighted. I like the manly tone and bearing of this king - he has good features – a thin hard wiry-looking man.'*

The meeting had gone well, mutual dignity and respect shown, and some useful local knowledge gleaned, especially the bizarre warning by the king telling him not to trust his own people.

During the journey, Lugard had developed a painful cyst in his mouth which he had to self-cauterize regularly. Worse for him, he was unable to smoke his pipe in the evening – vital to keep the insects at bay. He also had an eye infection which developed into opthalmia, making writing extremely painful under lamplight. Despite this, he went to the king the next morning *'doing the peacock in my scarlet coat,'* to further resounding trumpet fanfares, to explain the treaty and get it agreed. It was signed two days later.

Before parting the king gave him a further warning of a hostile village ahead preparing to ambush him with about 400 men and 60 horsemen, and that they would have spears and poisoned arrows. He seriously considered turning back. His soldiers had turned out to be almost untrained and not even capable of building a bridge or stockade. The 300 porters were undisciplined, and he did not relish the prospect of being attacked by a large force with poisoned arrows. He discussed it with the other Europeans and the head men; surprisingly they all wanted to go on, not wishing to return empty-handed.

Lugard felt that the best way to prepare was by further training for the soldiers. He instigated harsher discipline and ordered thirty lashes if a porter dropped his load, misused the cloth they were carrying (the most important exchange currency for food) or stole from local villages, *'...much as I abhor flogging, but the only way to improve discipline.'* He studied the poisons that were known to be used and tried to find antidotes.

The caravan continued towards Nikki, but was in a sorry state. All the Europeans were down with fever, only fourteen donkeys were alive out of the thirty-four that left Jebba, and the few horses remaining were covered in sores and emaciated. Lugard's solution for his fever was '*10 grains of antipyrine and 13 miles marching in a blazing sun, in a perfect bath of perspiration put me right!'* The soldiers and porters were holding out well under Lugard's guidance, and thankfully, with no sign of the enemy, they walked right up to the walls of Nikki.

Lugard learned that the old king in Nikki had been told by his medicine man that if he came in contact with white men he would die within three months. After three days, with various messages being sent and a public flogging of one of his porters who had stolen cloth, he arranged a meeting with the Moslem missionary, known as *The Liman*, at the court. The King sent a message saying '*...he was quite astonished and said that it was indeed true that Europeans were quite different in their methods from other people and it was wrong to keep people waiting.'* The King sent princes with gifts and water, and Lugard offered some of his rapidly decreasing stock of cloth.

A meeting was held with the counsellors and after long discussions, the treaty was agreed, signed and presented to the King seated behind a screen. Lugard noted '*...He was very cordial, and said that never before had Europeans entered Borgu. Now he thanked God that it was in his lifetime that they had first come, and even if he died tomorrow that fact and honour would remain. Now that we had made a treaty of friendship, and from North and South and East and West, whichever direction we wished to go in at any time, the country was open to us and we were welcome.'*

The treaty at Nikki was particularly important, as it became a point of international controversy later on. Unlike treaties made in Uganda, the eagerness of the Borgu and Yoruba chiefs to sign could be explained by their desire to have insurance for protection against their enemies in the Moslem north and pagan east, rather than a desire to be part of the expanding British Empire.

On November 12, Lugard sent a copy of the treaty to George Goldie and headed south. Captain Decouer and his French caravan arrived in Nikki sixteen days later only to find Lugard had won this particular race.

The borders of Borgu and Dahomey were not well-defined, so Lugard decided to visit the border villages on his way carrying a letter from the King and announcing the agreement. He took note of the trading that was taking place in the villages, seeing kola nuts, horses, linseed, tobacco, gunpowder and slaves all being exchanged.

On November 9, after a long march to the village of Neshi, he was told by his guide that an attack from nearby villages was imminent, and that it was the younger war-chiefs and princes who were behind it, resenting the white intruders. Lugard issued instructions for extra vigilance but everyone was so tired from the march they fell asleep. He stayed up and kept guard all night, sounding the reveille half an hour before dawn.

The caravan set off early and after crossing a stream, climbed a slope towards a village in the distance. Suddenly, a large group of several hundred men armed mostly with spears, bows and arrows, appeared at the crest of the slope. With their leaders on horseback, they started advancing towards the caravan across a tobacco field.

Lugard refused to open fire first. The following was his own account of the ensuing battle. '*I was unwilling, as I am always, to fire the first shot and waited to see. Perhaps it was a pity, for I think I could have dropped one of the horsemen with my own rifle, and as it was, their bowmen crept up in the long grass on each side and fired many arrows before I was aware and gave the order to fire. The soldiers were a mere excited rabble – they blazed off their guns as fast as they could stick in cartridges, firing from the hip or anywhere – vaguely into the sky. A steady advance was impossible – the shouting, yelling and firing was deafening. As I advanced the men rushed forward, and the mass of porters huddled behind the firing line, and would not keep back despite threats, curses or blows. Joseph, my only form of communication, was rushing around like a pea in a drum, off his head with excitement.*'

Lugard took the lead and tried to straighten the line of his soldiers when suddenly he felt something strike him upon the back of the head. As gunfire was continuing wildly all around, he concluded it was a graze from a bullet fired from one of his own men. He tried to remove his pith helmet, but it appeared caught on something. Mottram rushed over and said he had been struck by an arrow, which had gone right through the cork and pierced his skull.

One of the Hausas tried to wrench the helmet off, unsuccessfully, and it was finally Lugard's hunter, Mallum Yaki, an expert in jungle craft, who managed to cut off the helmet, but was still unable to remove the arrow from Lugard's head. By now Lugard had sunk to the ground, with Mallum trying with increasing force to remove the arrow. At one point, Lugard was being dragged along the ground by Mallum in a desperate attempt to remove it. Finally, Mallum put his foot against his master's head and gave one mighty tug. This time he was successful, but to his horror he found a piece of skull also attached to the arrowhead. The only consolation for Lugard was that it was not barbed, but the iron tip had penetrated his skull by twenty millimetres; far worse it was poisoned, and they had no idea what the poison was.

Mottram found one antidote he had been given which looked like sawdust and applied it to the wound. Mallum gave him another by chewing on a lump of something and stuffing it into the hole. Another hunter came up with a piece of root which Lugard chewed as the glutinous paste turned his saliva to jelly.

All this time the fighting was still raging, and Lugard was shouting instructions to keep going forward. Wrapping a cloth around his head, he struggled to his feet and ordered his men to advance.

Eventually the attackers were forced back into the village. He gave the order to cease fire and to keep the caravan moving. Out of this chaos, Bio, his trusty guide appeared, most agitated, and produced several more antidotes of equally repellent taste, which Lugard agreed to take. He halted Bio swiftly when he started chanting various long-winded, magical incantations!

They had to retreat from this hostile area as quickly as possible, and marched another thirteen miles in stifling humidity before setting up camp, exhausted. Lugard collapsed onto his bed and immediately fell into a deep sleep.

To everyone's amazement, he awoke the next morning refreshed, with no ill effects from the wound and more astounding, none from the antidotes, one of which must have saved him.

He had been completely outnumbered that day, but the enemy did not have rifles. When they saw him rise after being hit, they must have thought he had magical powers on his side. They were probably right. He suffered no fatalities, whilst the assailants lost thirty, but Lugard was not pleased. At the height of the battle his soldiers had been in a complete panic, and were a shambles, highlighting their lack of training. They had been extremely lucky.

He needed to get back into Yorubaland as quickly as possible, and headed for Ilesha, where he heard the French had intervened in fighting between Dahomey and Borgu. The Royal Niger Company had wanted him to go further west, but he knew the enemy were still near and he was running short on supplies. He sent decoy guides to the west, and headed south through the spear grass towards Saki, a major Yoruba town, avoiding another ambush.

The King of Saki had a broad road cleared between his camp and the palace so that Lugard should not 'tread on dirt.' There were further rumours of attacks and the King was keen to sign a treaty to protect his people from the Borgu.

Mottram was sick and his interpreter Joseph was giving cause for concern by getting drunk frequently. When Lugard went down with a bad bout of fever himself, he again felt in low spirits. *'It was not till late I got the first burst of fever over, and I had a weary night. It is mere purgatory to be down with bad fever when you are in a tight place, and it all depends on yourself. Then things begin to look hopelessly bad, and in one's fever nightmare one dreams and fancies all kind of disasters; and the long hours seem to move up, as though each minute were an hour, and one gets nervous and at last by the mere strain on the nerves one begins to fancy every noise in the night to be the premonitory sounds of an attack! And one wonders how on earth one will see it thro' when one's head is bursting and one's strength all gone…All today I kept off a relapse by piling on waterproof sheets and blankets and closing my tent tho' the temperature must be close on 100 deg (F) or more at midday…'*

This still did not deter him from carrying out night patrols of his camp, sometimes in heavy fog, to watch for any Borgu surprise attacks. The king asked him to go south and see the Alafin of Oyo and report his journey to him. He offered an escort of five hundred Yoruba warriors, which was readily accepted. They were well-armed and included a troop of cavalry with high-built saddles, and magnificent robes which accentuated Lugard's rather shabby state of dress. He was grateful for their services, especially when they passed a spot where a French traveller had perished the year before at the hands of Borgu bandits.

On December 8 he came to Iseyhin, a walled town with 60,000 inhabitants, nestled in a fertile agriculture area, rich in oil palms. He was well received, and met some native Methodist missionaries for the first time who had established a Christian mission. Three days later he arrived at the important religious centre of Oyo, and donned his scarlet jacket, white trousers and sword to make a good impression for the influential Alafin of Oyo. *'The king, seated under a kind of straw dome which formed part of the verandah, was got up in the height of his magnificence, but in the dark background it was hard to gauge all the splendour of his presence and belongings — we could only distinguish outlines of gold and velvet and plush draperies, and a hatting which was unique. Its gold and parti-coloured fringes drooped over the royal countenance and hid its lustre from the vulgar gaze…in front of the king, sitting alone and bolt upright like a Hindu idol was — I presume — a princess of the blood royal.…a scarlet cloth was laid, and between it and the [royal] presence were men bearing gigantic umbrellas of crimson and plush, and velvet with fringed and tasseled edges — the things being some eight feet across and eight feet high. Around the space was a dense mass of humanity. All the sightseers who had been gazing open-mouthed had now flocked in thro' the big gate. They formed a dense ring of very orderly folk and seven umbrella holders stood on each side. I came forward and was asked to stop just short of the scarlet cloth – my chair was placed and a man with an umbrella summoned to shield me from the sun.'*

The Alafin complimented Lugard on reaching Oyo without being attacked. He said he had warned the Borgu chiefs that their actions were affecting peace and trade. He requested that Lugard help him in negotiations with a Captain Bower, an official of the Lagos Government. Bower was in Oyo to mark out a demarcation frontier between Ilorin and Ibadan to the south, and was causing a lot of friction between the chiefs.

As Lugard left Oyo on December 16, he met Bower and his caravan riding towards him. He found his manner high-handed to start with, but after a few frank exchanges Bower agreed to have Lugard along with him for a week to assist in completing the boundary survey. This developed into a cordial relationship and on Christmas Day he insisted Lugard dine with him at his camp. Lugard was a little hesitant as he was rarely away from his men, but on his return he was given a warm welcome from them, which he found most touching. *'…They are queer devils – they fear me, I know, but I am equally sure they like me, for I don't think I am ever hard on a man without a good cause.'*

The boundary survey and maps were completed in early January, and Lugard continued north to Jebba, visiting a large number of Yoruba towns on the way. He had marched 700 miles in 107 days. By the time he arrived at Jebba on January 13 1895, Mottram and Reynolds were in a bad state. Lugard was in a remarkable condition considering his fevers, his extraordinary wound and unknown antidotes, and his continual eye problem. He paid the men off and wrote *'…they came to bid me farewell and declare their eagerness to follow us anywhere if we should return to travel elsewhere in Africa…'* He caught the boat at Lokoja and had finished his reports by the time he reached Akassa.

One further incident occurred at the end of this remarkable expedition. He had been waiting for further instructions, and due to the delay and the heat and humidity of Akassa, decided at the last minute to catch the boat back to Lokoja to wait there. Fate was with him. The next morning at dawn, a large number of the local Nembe, led by King Koko attacked the Company station.

There had been increasing resentment of the way the Royal Niger Company was monopolizing the market and denying access to the local traders. After renouncing Christianity, King Koko formed alliances with chiefs in Bonny and Okopma. Armed with heavy guns, he led one thousand warriors in fifty canoes and stormed Akassa. There was a fierce battle; twenty-four employees were killed, and warehouses and machinery destroyed. The acting agent and some staff escaped but Koko captured sixty staff and held them hostage. The King sent a letter demanding changes by the Company. His demands were rejected. In a horrific drug-induced massacre, forty-three African hostages were mutilated and eaten in a ceremonial feast.

There was an outcry in Britain, and on February 20 the Navy retaliated with a heavy-handed counterattack, in which King Koko's city of Nembe was razed to the ground. Three hundred inhabitants were slaughtered, and the King fled into exile.

Lugard heard about the attack whilst at Lokoja and was appalled at the way the negotiations were handled. It would reflect badly on the Company and lead to an inevitable inquiry.

He had to sit it out for a further two months in Lokoja before catching a boat to Liverpool, arriving on May 9, the first vivid memories of West Africa still fresh in his mind.

CHAPTER 17
Looking south

Lugard returned to London to find himself in the midst of a diplomatic war between the French and British. His signed treaty had taken so long to reach London that the French had claimed they got to Borgu first, and that Lugard had never met the King, or even signed a treaty.

Goldie had sent a letter to *The Times* on March 1 confirming the treaty was in the agreed form. The letter backed Lugard unreservedly. It was soon apparent that the King of Borgu had also signed a treaty with the French, when Decoeur eventually reached Nikki. Lugard noted in a letter to his brother, '*It's very funny, and the way they blackguard me is absurd...Of course Nikki made a treaty and swore anything they wanted in the face of an expedition of 300 or more soldiers armed with magazine rifles, followed by a second, presumably of greater strength...*'

The French papers got hold of the story and described it as '*a veritable steeplechase,*' to which Lugard retorted, '*Had the Editor changed places for one day with Mr. Mottram and the donkeys, he would have modified his metaphors!*'

Decoeur's expedition had run into heavy fighting shortly after Nikki and he was badly wounded, forcing him to return to France. The French sent further expeditions into Borgu in 1895, one travelling down the Niger from Dahomey to establish a new town north of Jebba, called Arenburg. This unsettled the Foreign Office, so they increased support to Goldie who, since the destruction of his base at Akassa, and a subsequent inquiry, was coming under fire from all sides. The Germans had also mounted a successful expedition to the area further west. This was enough for the French to tone down their outburst against the British; they needed an ally in the developing complex scene in Europe.

Lugard was being pulled into this cauldron of European politics, and was able to exchange views with his newly-acquired ally and friend

Joseph Chamberlain, whom he had got to know well the previous year. Chamberlain was about to be appointed Colonial Secretary and Lugard wrote to him in June 1895, '*The intervention of the French, especially on the Niger seems a matter for grave anxiety. If they do not care, they will someday go too far and find themselves forced to retreat or go to war. I am convinced they do not mean the latter, but they have a way of bluffing which is very dangerous and which may easily lead to serious trouble.*'

Lugard's relationship with Goldie continued to deepen, constantly exchanging ideas and proposals, and this developed into a warm and trusting friendship. Lugard continued lobbying various politicians and, with Goldie's approval, sent a constant stream of letters to *The Times,* dispatched a flurry of articles for the monthlies, and made further rounds of presentations and speeches. He still did not enjoy the oratory, but he attracted a lot of interest which helped the sales of his book.

London in 1895 was a bustling, vibrant, international city. It was slowly being lit by electricity, the first cars started to appear on the streets, and the underground railway network was rapidly expanding. There was a vibrant Arts scene, and the public were mesmerized by the Oscar Wilde trial and his downfall. Lugard's work and contacts were all concentrated here, so he took lodgings at 63, Jermyn Street, just off Piccadilly, and close to the centre of power. He shared his lodging with a Doctor Cross, who he had met on the Niger and with whom he had developed a good rapport. They enjoyed evenings exchanging views on Africa and discussing each other's philosophy of life. One such discussion included the two bachelors mulling over what attracted women to men, and the challenge for the quieter man on how to attract a wife. It could well have been a scene from a Sherlock Holmes story in Baker Street, whose tales had captivated the Victorian public since 1887.

The Liberal government under Rosebery was fracturing, and in the General Election in June 1895 it was defeated. This ushered in ten years of Conservative rule led by Lord Salisbury. He appointed Joseph Chamberlain as Colonial Secretary, who had a new vision for imperial expansion in the colonies. Lugard knew he was going to be part of that exciting development. He had been staying with Chamberlain at Highbury during the election and wrote to Ned a month later, '*...A gigantic majority for the Unionists, and out of it all, Mr. Chamberlain emerged as one of the strongest and most influential men in the country. Now you may know that I had a great deal to do with him, and perhaps I am not wrong in saying that the very prominent part he has taken in Africa questions, and the intimate knowledge he has shewn regarding them, is due in very large measure to myself.*'

Lugard added, '*I was staying at Highbury at the time of the elections, and he asked me where I would like to go, and what I would do if I were sent there – what scheme I would put forward for the practical working of the thing etc. At the same time he warned me that he had no power as regards East Africa. It is under the F.O., and no-one except the Foreign Minister and the Prime Minister could touch it....To be frank my view is that the Foreign Office is a monument of incompetency. As Moberly Bell said, there is not a single official in it who is up to the standard of a second-rate or third-rate appointment in The Times. The heads of department (re Africa at any rate) are men who strike you as absolute fools, even in the first five minutes of conversation. The Colonial Service I have always heard is much abler... What the spring may produce – goodness knows. I must do <u>something</u>, for I am living at present mainly on savings plus a few occasional dollars for magazine articles.*'

Flora Shaw, as Colonial Editor of *The Times*, had been meeting with all the main players on the foreign stage at that time, and now had enough influence to open any ministerial door. She immediately saw the implications of Chamberlain's appointment, writing, '*The change at the Colonial Office was marvellous, it was a total transformation; the sleeping city awakened by a touch. Everyone in the* [Times] *department felt it, and presently everyone in the Colonial Office felt it to the furthest corners and the loneliest outposts of the Queen's Dominions.*'

Flora had already fallen in love with George Goldie. She had first interviewed him when working for the *Manchester Guardian* in 1893, and their affair had been ongoing intermittently for over a year.

Lugard must also have known of the philandering reputation of Goldie as their friendship developed, but it did not appear to affect their relationship at this time. Lugard's mind was still on Catherine.

Catherine was now a widow, after her husband Colonel Gambier drowned at sea on a journey from India in August 1894. She lived in London with her daughter Kitty, now aged five. Catherine pursued Lugard and the correspondence started flowing once again. In a memorandum to Ned in 1941 he wrote, '*We met* [in 1895] *and my infatuation again mastered me. We resumed our old relations until I returned to Africa (Ngami) in February 1896, and while absent we exchanged letters on the old terms.*' He knew he was living a delusion, but the fading image of the ideal woman he had built up in his mind was still there. Catherine had fallen into impecunious circumstances after the death of her husband, and Lugard felt compelled to support her and Kitty. He provided her with a home in London and an allowance, causing immense angst and consternation with Ned. He needed to get away.

As the government machine moved slowly through the transition, it looked increasingly unlikely that Lugard would get the diplomatic appointment he wanted in East Africa. He was offered various military positions in Uganda but as that was not the direction he wanted to pursue, he declined. Goldie was still pushing for Lugard and assured him of his faith, and writing to him in August he said, '...*much that surprises me after our comparatively short friendship, but I have unlimited confidence in your straightness, capacity and friendly feelings to myself. I can number on my fingers - almost on one hand – the number of men whom I really trust after nearly half a century of life – hundreds whose honesty I trust but not their discretion.*'

By September 1895, it was clear the position in East Africa was not available. However, another door opened from an unexpected direction.

The offer came from the British West Charterland Company, formed in 1895 by a group of wealthy city men to prospect for gold and diamonds in Ngamiland (now Botswana) in the Kalahari Desert. They had been attracted by the success of the diamond fields of Kimberley and were looking further north, to the mineral-bearing strata in this vast and inhospitable region.

Concessions had already been bought, but they needed someone capable of negotiating with the tribes, the British South Africa Company (Cecil Rhodes) and the Colonial Office. They considered Lugard the perfect man for their needs. The British West Charterland Company offered him the post of managing director in Africa on an extremely generous salary of £6,000 per year. He was given a free rein to run the company, could take on his brother as second-in-command, also on a good salary, and have complete financial control. They would give him their total backing. He was also assured he could resign immediately if he were offered a government post that he was still interested in.

Lugard was taken aback with the generosity of the offer and wrote to Flora Shaw to get her opinion. He told her of the '...*absurdly liberal offer... and that the gold-mining venture doesn't appeal to me in any way, except of course, that I am quite poor.*'

He had further discussions with another of the company directors, Oakley Maund. Lugard was impressed with his views. It was not just the money the Company could make, but they wanted imperial success as well, and the profits would be invested in the development of the country.

Finally, he knew he had to get away from Catherine, and the thought of having Ned working by his side and sharing this new adventure with him was all that he needed to sign the contract on December 7 1895.

CHAPTER 18
Chasing the diamonds

In 1895 Ngamiland, a region in the north part of Bechuanaland (now Botswana), larger than England and Wales combined, had only twenty policemen based in the little town of Ghanzi. The British formed it as a Protectorate in 1886 and the Resident commissioner stayed comfortably installed in Mafeking (now Mahikeng), just across the border.

To the south was the Cape Colony, with its booming diamond mines. It was surrounded by the Dutch to the east and the Germans to the north and west, and dominated by a single figure - Cecil Rhodes. He ran the powerful British South Africa Company (BSAC) and was determined to get charters to push a railway line north from Vryburg to Mafeking and on to Bulawayo as part of his Cape to Cairo dream. Rhodes had a Charter to go through the east of Ngamiland but he had to recognise any existing treaties.

Lugard thought his first task would be to start negotiations with a man for whom he and Goldie had a strong dislike. The feeling was probably mutual. Lugard had asked Rhodes to delegate power of administrative control of the region to him, but Rhodes was not interested. He wanted his own people in charge.

Flora Shaw was a keen admirer of Rhodes, so Lugard had sought her opinion whilst in London. He wrote to her in November 1895, '*I am strongly opposed to serving under the BSAC. I know you think very highly of Rhodes and his subordinates, so far, at any rate I do not ...because men I trust (and whose opinion would carry far more weight with you than mine) all seem to mistrust (him)...Under these circumstances I naturally prefer that Ngamiland should be wholly free of Charter and Rhodes influence and I even feel that, if placed under his control, I would very greatly dislike to go out.*'

Flora was still supporting Rhodes, and closely involved with the events leading up to the Jameson rebellion only one month later, which would have a major impact on her life. She replied:

'Dear Capt. Lugard,
    ...I think you will have to work in friendly relations with the BSAC if anything is to be achieved. I feel the force of all you say and the weight of the opinion which you quote. I cannot help thinking however, that if you were brought into personal touch with Mr. Rhodes and could realise, as I do, the absolute unsordid and unselfish nature of the devotion which he gives to the Imperial cause that you would recognize the ennobling influence of a great conception and much of your prejudice would disappear....He appears to me to seek nothing for himself. He cares neither for money, nor place, nor power, except in so far as they are a necessity for the accomplishment of the national ideal for which he lives...' She ended the letter asking if she could arrange a meeting for him with Rhodes to help him make a decision.

Lugard was not convinced and forwarded her letter to Goldie to get his opinion. Goldie replied in his distinct style and, considering that at that time he was still intimately involved with Flora, its coldness was a little strange.

'My Dear Lugard,
    ....I now return you Miss Shaw's letter which, as you say, is remarkable.
    I fully believe in her view that 'The God in the Car' cares nothing for money except as a means to an end. What man of sense can, provided he has wholesome food, warm clothes, shelter from the weather, a few favourite books and a pipe? Women, as a rule, still love luxury, ostentation and rivalry. It is a fault of their education and useful vice for the progress of civilization. As to love of power, no man in a civilized community has any power worth exercising. Men in power today are slaves of work and of the public, and not masters — even of themselves.
    So far I can go, but no further; yet I strongly advise you to accept Miss Shaw's offer. I have always told you that your Ngami people must, in the end, arrange with the Company; why not at once?
    Yours very truly,
    George Taubman Goldie'

After the failure of the Jameson fiasco in December 1895, Rhodes had fallen from power, so it was no longer necessary to get any concessions from him. Lugard was now able to get Ned seconded quickly from his regiment in India to act as his second-in-command, and who would also act as the expedition botanist, to collect specimens for Kew Gardens. The War Office allowed an extension of his own secondment, and was able to get the BSAC to agree for Sir John Kirk to join the board, strengthening his own position by having one of his most trusted friends as a director.

Lugard acquired some basic equipment of tents, rifles and survey equipment from the Royal Geographical Society, photographic equipment, the all-important drugs, and a collapsible boat. The remainder he intended to procure locally when he arrived. He finalised his team by enlisting an enthusiastic, newly-qualified doctor called Spon, a Royal Engineer sergeant surveyor, and a colourful American mining engineer called Colorado Browne from the mid-west. They sailed on *The Tantallan Castle* on February 22 1896, just as Jameson was arriving in England for his trial.

Lugard spent the journey studying all aspects of South Africa, writing letters, and reviewing mining regulations with the engineer and Ned. On March 9 they were greeted by the impressive sight of Table Mountain.

On arrival in Cape Town, Lugard went with Ned to present a letter of introduction from the Colonial Secretary to the High Commissioner, Sir Hercules Robinson (also caught up in the Jameson fiasco), the Commander-in-Chief, General Goodenough, and Admiral Rawson. He was briefed and also made aware of some of the serious environmental problems currently ravaging the region.

A devastating outbreak of rinderpest was working its way across Africa from Uganda, and had spread south across Bechuanaland, killing thousands of cattle. A chronic drought had also struck the area, drying up many wells, and an unprecedented plague of locusts was decimating the north-west, working south and eating everything green in their path. Added to that, the Second Matabele War had just begun and first reports of settlers being massacred were starting to come in.

Lugard had not expected this to be an easy expedition, but the word '*impossible*' was starting to be used in his diary.

Lugard and Ned caught the train from Cape Town to Kimberley and had time for a quick stopover to visit a diamond mine. It had been opened in 1871, was over 1200 feet deep and they were most impressed to find that it was lit by electricity. From there they travelled by train to Mafeking, 647 miles from Cape Town, taking a mere thirty hours. They had decided Mafeking would be a better starting point than Kimberley, as prices were escalating due to the Matabele War.

The traditional method of transport in South Africa was to use twelve to sixteen trek-oxen. The alternative was mules, which needed more food and water, or donkeys, which had given him many problems in Nigeria. Lugard decided on a mixture of four light wagons drawn by a dozen mules each, and half a dozen lighter wagons drawn by donkeys. He had concerns about the twenty-seven local drivers as they were only used to driving oxen. He was also worried about the amount of food required for the mules, so arranged a smaller expedition to follow on later with additional supplies.

In Mafeking he met Earl Grey, the newly-appointed administrator of Rhodesia who had taken over from Jameson. The two men had encountered each other briefly in London, and Grey immediately tried to persuade him to abandon the expedition and help with the Matabele rebellion. Lugard thought about it and decided that, as there was no immediate danger to European life, especially to women and children, he was not going to get involved. There was also the realisation that he no longer craved the excitement of battle. '... *I regret the mad soldier's ambition which has gone from me, but so it is... Courage is an affair of age, and of the liver and of various other things prosaic... 'Tis pity 'tis true and pity 'tis, 'tis true.'*

He knew he had not lost his courage, but that he had brought it under control by reason. He also picked up more information on the Jameson Raid and was not impressed. He noted in the diary, '...*I believe Dr. Jameson to have been a single-hearted honourable man above lucre and personal gain, but surely England will begin to doubt if he was the Heaven-born Administrator he was boomed to be ...from all I hear it seems the general opinion that Jameson and Rhodes hatched this plot against the Transvaal deliberately for months – well, we shall see.'*

He continued following Flora's articles in *The Times* and was still concerned at what Perham calls her '*blind enthusiasm for Rhodes and Jameson,*' worried that her emotions were dominating her intellect on this matter.

He was also having concerns about his new mining engineer, Colorado Browne, a key player on the expedition. In character he was the opposite to Lugard, describing him as '*a good fellow, but sketchy to a degree,*' whilst Browne accused Lugard of trying to deal with everything down to the smallest detail, and not letting him get on with his job. It was a justified criticism, and Lugard admitted in his diary that Browne could well be right. '*I know this to be a fault of mine and I lose much of the important issues of life by over-attention to detail. For instance I never read the important books of the day which I long to read, because I simply cannot skim through my Times and I lose the valuable for the ephemeral.*'

Ned could see the problem and by acting as a mediator helped him overcome the difficulties, but Lugard still noted, '*I would rather take a wagon-load of Bengal tigers to Ngamiland than this man!*'

With all these concerns on his mind, the expedition headed out of Mafeking on May 4 1896 with ten Europeans, twenty-seven local drivers, twelve wagons and carts, and sixty mules and donkeys hauling around seventeen tons of supplies and equipment. They followed the track that Livingstone had explored forty-seven years earlier in 1849. Before they left, Hercules Robinson made Ned a JP, to administer any justice that may be required in the outback.

They marched along the Marico River, and within a few miles they saw the ravages of the dreadful disease rinderpest. Thousands of dead oxen lay bloated in the scorching sun. The wretched animals had tried to get to the water holes and died in them, contaminating the water. Everyone was continually engulfed in clouds of black flies covering every inch of the wagons.

Colorado Browne had overloaded his wagon with his mining equipment and after ten days the axle broke and his driver deserted. He then declared he was seriously ill and, much to Lugard's relief, returned to Mafeking.

Gaberones (renamed Gaberone in 1969, the capital of Botswana) was the first stop, and there Lugard cabled the directors of the BSAC to send a replacement mining engineer. Lugard heard that north of Bulawayo there were 4,000 wagons stranded and 64,000 oxen dead. He noted everything he saw and heard of the rinderpest, and sent the observations back to London to contribute to understanding this little-known disease.

On June 1 the team arrived at Palapye, the residence of Chief Khama, a highly-respected leader of the Ngwata people, who was a Christian and a constructive and modern-thinking statesman. He had already made trips to England, where he met Chamberlain and Queen Victoria. He had banned alcohol and expelled any traders who refused to obey the law.

Lugard requested a meeting, and Khama came to see him. There was an immediate rapport between the two men. They had lunch several times and the question of boundaries with his rival chief, Sekgoma, was settled, adding he would not object if the prospectors strayed over the lines at times. Lugard looked at the tall grey-headed chief and was most impressed with his statesmanship and dignity, despite having lost his entire herd of 10,000 cattle to disease, leaving him almost ruined. He noted, *'He is such a gentleman - so unobtrusive and yet so thoroughly well-bred and at his ease…he is proud of being a black man and he is most anxious not to ape a white man. For this reason he lives in a native hut and in all ways is one of his own people.'*

The Chief also assisted him with six drivers and offered runners to Cape Town to assist with communications. Lugard set off again on June 15 across an even more hazardous part of the Kalahari Desert. Soon the wagons had sunk up to their axles in hills of loose sand. The animals floundered in agony. Sharp thorns ripped the hands and the sun beat unmercifully down. They limped only a few miles a day.

The old wound from Nyasa started giving him trouble again, and at night, after completing another meticulous entry in his diary, he would still be picking out pieces of bone that had finally come to the surface of his arm, whilst trying to keep warm in the freezing desert nights.

They reached a small halt called Lotlhakane, situated in a salt-pan that was so bright that Lugard could not bear to open his eyes for more than a few moments at a time. He recalled what had happened to another Boer expedition in the same area in 1878. '*This is the fateful place where the Boer trek of 1878 suffered so fearfully from thirst. The maddened oxen rushed down and fell into the pits, and could not be got out and were cut up and taken out piecemeal, and the blood and water and filth left in the pit was doled out. Women kept their children alive with blood and vinegar. A wretched remnant only escaped.*'

The caravan reached Chief Sekgoma's homeland in early August, with a third of the mules and nearly all the horses dead. The rest were a bag of bones. Here they reached the wonderful sight of the broad and deep River Botletle, which has no outlet to the sea, but mysteriously disappears into the depths of the salt-pans. They were at last able to use the collapsible boat, so that evening it was time to relax, and he and Ned went out sculling! '*I have launched my boat and sculled on the Botletle! It is brilliant success, and last night took Ned out at sunset and returned by the full moon for an hour's enjoyment. Ned could hardly contain himself for pleasure. The contrast of the placid flowing river from the deep sand and thorns we have lived in, is like another world. I christened her 'The Kitty,' the first white man's boat which has ever been on the waters of the Botletle …and we drank a little toast to its success in its new career.*'

One day he heard the sweet song of a sedge warbler near the river, giving a much-needed soothing distraction that set him thinking of the different songbirds he had heard. '*…the sedge warbler is always one which to me conveys (more than the song of any other bird I know) an impression as though the songster was a brimful of happiness…the nightingale is proverbially sad – the robin reminds me of dark and depressing November days and I hate it – it is a pugnacious song. The blackbird and the thrush sing of the country and are charming, their song is didactic and though beautiful, lacks pathos. It is what narrative poetry is to lyrical. But the blackcap, the sedge warbler and the nightingale are the lyrical songs par excellence.*'

The idyllic muse did not last long. Water brought its own problems, with lions and hyenas attracted to the camp at night. Mosquitoes joined the flies to bite and torment. The men were now at the limit of their endurance. They held a meeting and after hours of debate, gave notice and walked off.

They held nothing against Lugard, only the terrible conditions. Two days later, whether it was out of loyalty or the protection of Lugard's rifle, they returned, much to the relief of all.

They had marched 670 miles from Mafeking, averaging just over four miles per day. Around thirty per cent of his transport animals had been lost. This led Lugard to thinking of the rapid improvements in motorised technology, and the plethora of new methods of transport that were being invented at that time. He noted, *'I observe that there is a movement for the adoption in England of 'motorcars' or self-propelled vehicles. If such vehicles could be procured, capable of burning wood as fuel, they would be invaluable. Wood abounds and such vehicles would be independent of forage, of water (except at long intervals) and of lions.'* It would be many decades before there was a vehicle capable of dealing with this extreme terrain, let alone propelled by wood.

Lugard was relieved that the runners were still getting through with the mail. He received one letter from Joseph Chamberlain, concerned that Lugard had failed to get into the country, followed by another that he and his brother had been reported missing - a regular occurrence in Lugard's career !

He was now only one hundred miles from Nakalechwe, the headquarters of Chief Sekgoma, with whom he needed to negotiate to be able to start drilling. He decided to leave most of his men at the camp by the river with Ned in charge, and just take his interpreter, Hicks, and a couple of porters and ride ahead.

It was another hard journey. They had to cut through thick bush, and reached a dried lake composed of burnt reeds. This had been described by Livingstone as *'a fine-looking sheet of water, seventy miles in circumference!'* They camped by the remains of the lake having to endure bitterly cold nights, which created ghostly crimson fogs in the mornings.

On arrival at Nakalechwe, he found to his surprise two Europeans, a German trader called Muller and a young Englishman who was acting as a doctor for the village, even though unqualified. This was fortunate for Hicks because had become so sick he was unable to walk, and was now having to be carried on the back of a cart.

Lugard had heard tales about Sekgoma from Chief Khama, and also from the missionaries who had called him a monster. He decided to put on his best outfit of a ragged coat, white flannels and flapping boots for the occasion, and was surprised to meet, not a monster, but a little man (even by Lugard's standards), well-educated, better dressed, obstinate, suspicious and a cunning negotiator. It took eight days going backwards and forwards to reach an agreement.

Lugard, well-used to this ritual, tried to appear indifferent, smoking cigar after cigar, sometimes through his nose to relieve the boredom of waiting. He got just three concessions, including a lump-sum payment instead of a percentage if minerals were found, but it was enough and the agreement was signed in triplicate.

Sekgoma presented the agreement to his people before signing to get a democratic consensus. They had already seen the impact of diamond mining on Kimberley, which had transformed the town beyond recognition in only a few years, destroying the local tribes' rural life forever, so were naturally nervous about their future.

Hicks had made a remarkable recovery under the care of the young doctor and was now able to make the strenuous trip back to the camp, but Lugard went down with dysentery, and all the others suffered from severe sunstroke. It was an almost lifeless band of souls that drifted into the camp from the mists of the desert.

They set up a more permanent camp near the hills of Kgwebe, building some houses, stores and huts, and finding some ancient bore holes for water that had been hand-dug many decades before. The heat was intense. Violent dust storms drove the sand into every crevice leaving them choking and gasping on the hot air.

Many of the transport animals died of heat exhaustion. One of the Europeans died. The predicted clouds of locusts followed, sweeping down from the north, smothering everything and devouring every green shoot in sight. It seemed a biblical torment, that caused despair among the men, and it was only Lugard's iron determination, and Ned's support that pulled them through.

The rains came in the middle of November and immediately the desert burst into life; trees and bushes pushed out green shoots, carpets of small, colourful flowers including lilies appeared across the desert floor, and insects emerged from their life-saving bunkers in the sand. Birds came back to sing and brighten the days with their songs. Ned was especially delighted, at last able to get out his notebook, making meticulous observations and taking botanical samples which he sent off to Kew.

With the rains, disease returned, with the mules, horses and goats all dying. Surprisingly, it was the hardy, small donkeys that survived. All the Europeans were sick at some time and even the porters and servants went down with fever.

Lugard sent Ned to Cape Town to purchase new stock and equipment, and missed his company immediately. He had been an enormous support to him on this expedition, both physically and emotionally. *'Ned starts in a few days and I am oppressed by the thought of losing him. He is my 'alter ego' – and my right hand. How I am to live quite alone without him I don't know – how I am to get through the work without him I don't know. It is a depressing thought, for he is the apple of my eye. I am, I know, irritable, imperious and difficult, especially when I am 'not quite myself' or overworked, but Ned has the patience and the self-negation, and unselfishness of a woman and an angel. There was never anyone like Ned. He has every good point that partial critics can discover or invent in me doublefold, and he lacks all my <u>many</u> and most serious and palpable faults, and his love for me is like David and Jonathan.'*

It was an extraordinary relationship between the two brothers. Ned was seven years younger than Fred and had been constantly separated from him when young. He followed in his older brother's footsteps to the same school at Rossall, went to Canada for a short spell and then joined the Army. It was not until Ned was twenty years old that Fred started corresponding with him, advising, supporting and helping him where he could. Ned gave the affection and loyalty that Fred needed, and that brotherly love continued to the end of Lugard's life.

A series of incidents then occurred which tested Lugard's spirits to the limit. First, in a mining accident, an African was blinded by a blast fragment. Then the weekly mail run stopped coming through. It was the highlight of the week for all the Europeans, the link to their families and the outside world, and a major morale booster. After eight weeks silence they heard that that a six-man mail team had died on the road and another man had been eaten by a lion, so Chief Khama had stopped sending the mail.

The final incident occurred with a new German mining engineer, Otto Passarge, who had been recommended by Sir John Kirk. He had just arrived with an overseer after a particularly difficult and gruelling journey. That evening, a dinner was held to welcome the new arrivals. The overseer appeared in particularly good spirits, keeping everybody entertained and all seemed well, but a few hours later, in the middle of the night, Lugard was called out by a guard to find the young man lying in a bush with his throat cut *'in a most decisive manner.'* The young man had apparently been in an agitated state during the journey. He had been agonising over his work, and a love affair he had been having with his cousin. The nightmare conditions of the journey must have been the last straw, taking him over the edge into mental despair. Lugard was deeply shaken by this incident, and after burying him in a deep grave under a tree he wrote, *'God forgive him his deed – I at least have no fears on that score.'*

Lugard sensed the effect of this tragedy on the camp, so to boost morale he started a programme of building better quarters, constructing roads, and sinking more wells, to improve the quality of life. He linked up the road with Sebetwanes Drift which connected to Palapye, which was waiting for Rhodes' railway to connect the town with the outside world.

He insisted on a fair but disciplined regime with the black workers. He forbade any white man to take the law into his own hands and strike a native, and if there was any punishment, it had to be agreed by him after a full investigation. He had to come down hard on the German mining engineer Passarge, who insisted *discipline must be upheld* in a brutal fashion, that resulted in many of his men leaving, creating difficulty in finding new labour.

He also recorded his distress and anger when he heard that, during the suppression of the Matabele rebellion the British deliberately left packets of dynamite scattered around the veldt to kill or maim, and of rebels being shot. Lugard believed that it was the white man's injustice, started by the appointment of bad administrators that often led to such uprisings. He noted, *'The way some of our Boy-Administrators are (thinking) they are all very good because they are <u>British</u> – and because they are mostly told by themselves! I am a trifle bitter, perhaps, but it is enough to make a man bitter who has any sense of right feeling and justice. Africa seems to rub off all the angularities of justice and tone it down to convenience and even to the right of might. And the secret of it all is that the wrong class of man is often pitchforked into a place where he has infinite power of doing harm.'*

The little settlement lead a simple life. They converted some of the huts from an abandoned mission, and made tables out of packing cases. At dusk, Lugard lit up a cigar and watched the sun go down across the plains studded with large boulders, vast expanses of acacia thorns and the strange shapes of the baobab trees.

Because the servants were often sick, Lugard did his own household jobs, sewing his tattered clothes and (after sieving out the weevils) baking his own bread. He started a competition, where his bread was voted the best in the camp.

One day the police officer who represented this vast area paid a visit to find Lugard ill. Despite the protests of the policeman, he got up, cooked the dinner himself comprising of soup, mince, compressed vegetables and dried apples. He served his guests and promptly returned to bed to continue his recovery.

After a few months Ned returned from Cape Town and brought with him his wife Nell and their young son Cyril, who was only two years old.

They had only been married three years, and as Nell had already spent some time in India, and was also a botanist and an artist, Ned was ready to risk bringing her out to Africa. Lugard was delighted to see them back. He got on well with Nell, and gave up his small house to make them as comfortable as possible. He wanted to give the family time together, and although living nearby, would only eat with them once a week.

The results of the drilling in the Kgwebe hills by the mining team had not been good or even promising. They had worked out a methodical pattern for the drilling, radiating from the camp, but they found that most of the volcanic rocks were felstone-porphyrite, which rarely contain gold. Some of the rocks and slates associated with diamonds had been found but these too were not favourable. For the first time Lugard was facing complete failure, even though it was totally out of his hands.

He found some consolation in knowing that, although Sir John Kirk had always been doubtful, the other directors had been excessively optimistic. At least he had kept the costs of the expedition down to the minimum, and despite all the hardships he looked back on the experience as an extraordinary achievement. He wrote in July 1897, *'I have always in my own mind looked upon it as a marvellous and most curious undertaking. To exploit a country like this till lately 750 miles from the nearest railway point…with an almost impassable desert intervening, with no food and little local labour available…with above all this vast deep coating of flying sand, this absence of water, this climate which has proved so fatal…'* The same day he continued in a pragmatic tone, *'Inshallah (if Allah wills it) we may find these blessed diamonds! It would make one's work appear successful, though as a matter of fact the finding or not finding is no part of the success of my work, which is the organization and control of the means to an end – simply that.'*

He felt that his days in the Kalahari were coming to an end, and was still holding out hope that he would get an offer from Salisbury for an administrative post in East Africa, for which he longed. He became more frustrated with his involvement with commerce and could not wait to get back into government.

The more he thought about it, the more bad-tempered he became. This started affecting his relationship with Ned, who told him straight that *'his manner is unbearable.'* That resolved it. The following day, on his thirty-ninth birthday on January 21 1897, he sent a letter of resignation to the BSAC.

Two days later, when having dinner with Ned and Nell, a runner arrived carrying an official letter with an embossed 'S' seal in red wax. He immediately knew it was from Salisbury. He opened it nervously, but was not prepared for its contents. He was thanked by Lord Salisbury for his willingness *'to give up your present lucrative employment'* and continued *'that a somewhat costly scheme for strengthening the British Administration of East Africa has been abandoned and there was now no call for your services.'*

This was a bitter blow, but knowing he had upset various powerful people with his forthright views in London, not entirely unexpected. His support from Chamberlain and Kirk was not enough. Lugard promptly sent a letter withdrawing his letter of resignation and went back to work drilling for gold.

One Sunday in August another letter arrived, this time from the Colonial Office. Lugard had joined Ned and his family for dinner, and Nell had somehow conjured up a meal of several courses, and had even found some china that a passing missionary had left them, plus a real luxury - a table cloth. Lugard looked at the letter which was stamped with large seals and marked 'Secret'. Inside was a cable to the British High Commissioner in South Africa with an offer to him. It was dated July 30 1897. *'It is the intention of HM Government to raise without delay a West African force of 2,000 or 3,000 men to occupy important places on the Hinterland of the Gold Coast and Niger territories, which are within the British sphere of influence and which may otherwise be occupied by the French. Forward this information by letter in the most sure and secret manner if possible in cypher, to Major Lugard, and in the name of HM Government offer him the command of this force at a salary of 1500 pounds and with the title of Commissioner and Commandant of the forces with the local rank of Lieut. Colonel. If he accepts he must immediately come home to receive instruction. In any case he must keep the matter absolutely secret.'*

It was not what he expected. A military role was not what he wanted, and he did not want to return to West Africa. Disappointed again, he felt he had neither the will nor the competence for the job. After a long talk with Ned that night, he knew that, despite abhorrence for the task, he must accept. He also felt that this would have been the advice from his wise Uncle Edward.

There were conflicting emotions. Although this had been his toughest assignment yet, both physically and emotionally, it had in many ways been the happiest. He had complete autonomy at his little settlement, the real pleasure of Ned by his side, with Nell and little Cyril, who had shown the true spirit of early settlers. Nell had found it a hard but memorable experience, and wrote later that with Fred there *'there was a feeling of someone so strong behind.'* Ned and Nell stayed there for another two years before the camp was finally closed down. Ned was then recalled to the Army to go to South Africa for the start of the Boer War.

Preparations started immediately to hand control over to Ned. Lugard headed back with only 300 pounds of luggage, two boys, one mule and one horse to maximise speed. It was another gruelling trek through the deep, hot sand, harassed by lions, stung by bot-flies and drinking contaminated water which brought on more dysentery. It was hell, close to killing them all, and it was a tremendous relief to see a team of eight mules sent out by Chief Khama to escort them into Palapye.

Khama was delighted to see him again but shocked at his emaciated state. Lugard was also pleased to see his old friend, and had been impressed by reports that he had received of the generous and courteous treatment of his men. At Palapye, he cabled his directors again with his resignation, and accepted the offer from Chamberlain before hurrying on to Cape Town.

At Cape Town he entered another world. He was a guest at Government House attended by two ADCs who had been with him at Sandhurst. Table Mountain was the backdrop and the house was surrounded by exquisite gardens running with streams, and filled with roses, violets and hedges of plumbago.

An added pleasure for Lugard was meeting his old friend Sir Alfred Milner again. '*The same charming, utterly unaffected and shrewd and able man I have always known.*' Milner was especially pleased with the infrastructure works that had been started, and Lugard was able to get across his views on Bechuanaland and the administration of a company operating there.

Lugard sailed to London on October 6. On board he met the German Governor of South-West Africa to whom he took an immediate dislike. '*… the most repulsive evil face it is possible to conceive.*' This man had endorsed a cruel and brutal regime in that state being carried out by many German employers that was hated by the local people. Lugard refused to speak to him for the entirety of the voyage, and he decided '*to slack*' which, for him, must have been quite a novel experience.

On arrival at Southampton he found that his new military mission in West Africa was no longer secret, and the French had found out about British intentions in the Niger. They had already sent five hundred Senegalese troops to Nikki. This was now going to be a much more difficult task.

He noted with foreboding, '*The task before me is one from which I shrink and which I detest.*'

CHAPTER 19
Chessboard games

While Lugard had been in the Kalahari, the situation in the Niger Basin had deteriorated sharply. The slave-trading Emirs of Bida and Ilorin had started slaving expeditions once again, and Goldie decided to strike back. He wanted to eradicate slave trading and extend his trading area to the north, where cotton and tobacco were being grown.

In February 1897 he led a force of 513 men and thirty-two Europeans, with six Maxim guns and seven artillery pieces to attack and take the capital Bida against 30,000 Fullah horsemen and followers. It took two days to rout the enemy. Because of the ruthless efficiency of the Maxim gun, thousands were killed, with the loss of only eight of the Royal Niger Company. Goldie ordered part of the city to be set alight as he marched into Bida, and immediately appointed his own Emir.

After setting up a new administration, he returned to Ilorin, where there was another smaller but decisive battle. He drew up a new agreement with the Emir of Ilorin. By March 1 Goldie was back at Lokoja and sent a telegraph to the Prime Minister saying that the expedition had been a total success, and slave-trading had been dealt a substantial blow.

Meanwhile, the French were making excursions further north, aiming to take over Bussa completely. Indeed the situation throughout Africa was becoming more complex; Britain had returned to Sudan to take on the Mahdists, fighting had broken out again in East Africa, the trial arising from the Jameson debacle in South Africa was ongoing, and the battle to control West Africa was continuing. It was a game in which there was no umpire and the rules were continually changing. It could only lead to inevitable conflicts.

In West Africa there were two main areas being contested, the hinterland of the Gold Coast and the Niger area that Goldie was operating in. The

French thought the British had now overstretched themselves in Africa, and saw this as an ideal time to take advantage.

Joseph Chamberlain anticipated their moves, and began to formulate his own plan to create a West African force of 2,000 soldiers with Lugard in charge. After lengthy, and often discordant discussions with Goldie, who was wary that the power of his company was being whittled away, a letter was sent to Lugard in the Kalahari offering him the post of Commissioner and Commandant of the West Africa Force.

When Lugard landed in Liverpool on October 12, his first call was on Chamberlain. He was handed a mountain of documents to study, to bring him up to date with the latest events. It took him a month to read them, and on November 12 he was again summoned to the Colonial Office.

Chamberlain was seated at his desk looking dapper, an orchid in his button-hole and his trademark monocle in place. He stared unnervingly across the table. Lugard recalled later, '*When he screwed his eyeglass, you felt as you were going to be sifted to the marrow.*'

After formalities, Chamberlain asked Lugard when he could go out to West Africa. '*Whenever I am ordered,*' he answered diplomatically, and added, '*but I hardly know yet what I am to do.*' Chamberlain explained his plan for the West Africa Force and his overall chessboard strategy. Lugard had already heard about this from Goldie, and had not been impressed. It involved going into an area the French occupied, infiltrate and isolate them, but on no account attack. They were not to be seen as aggressors.

Lugard was still not impressed, and as Chamberlain became more domineering, he became more obstinate and reserved. It was a frustrating meeting. Lugard insisted he set up the base at Lokoja (where he would be out of the jurisdiction of the Governor in Lagos) and there he would train three hundred local troops to start the risky harassment of the French. Chamberlain reluctantly agreed.

After the meeting, Lugard mulled it over again, but was still not happy with the role being offered. He only resisted resigning after a further session with Goldie, later writing in his diary, '*I am certain of his upmost support, and he is a legion in himself and will lead others or compel them.*'

There were to be two battalions in the new force. To Lugard's annoyance, the War Office had already appointed officers. He found out that the Colonel recruited had never seen active service, and seemed more interested in the design of the uniforms than the choice of men. He was also suggesting setting up the transport system with elephants. Lugard had rarely been complimentary about the War Office but was now convinced '*The War Office is the most incompetent department in the Empire.*'

The arguments started immediately. Lugard insisted he wasn't going to accept men that had been rejected from other posts, and demanded he have his old transport chief from India and Burma, Colonel (later General Sir) James Willcocks. He wanted to appoint him as his second-in-command, knowing that good transport was essential. He chose a Colonel Fitzgerald as commander of the second battalion, and further insisted that all the men undergo a rigorous medical examination. This included the doctors.

Lugard then turned his attention to the artillery. He chose his weapons carefully; the heaviest component was not to weigh more than 150lb, and wanted six of the latest 75mm guns, with Maxim Nordenfeld guns as reserve artillery. To accommodate the men, he requested portable huts for the Europeans. When told they would cost twenty thousand pounds, he found another company himself and had them delivered in two weeks for less than half the price.

Lugard built up a substantial force, with each battalion consisting of about 1,200 men, with twenty-nine British officers and forty-four NCOs. These battalions were backed by Royal Engineers, a signal company and two batteries of artillery. In addition he had two gunboats on the Niger River. Within one month of starting the preparations, the first battalion was sent to Lokoja to start recruiting and training local soldiers.

Despite the long hours Lugard was putting into organizing the force, he was still regularly meeting up with his close friend and ally Goldie, and deepening his friendship with Flora Shaw. The time in the Kalahari had finally allowed him to exorcise his obsession with Catherine. In 1941 he wrote, '*I arrived in England in October 1897, to find that her love was (and indeed had long been) dead. I then determined that I would compel myself to accept this final decision, and hence forth be only a friend and protector.*' He continued to write and support her, but there is no record of him seeing Catherine again.

He admired the way Flora had handled the Jameson trial, and complimented her on the erudite series of articles she was now writing on West Africa in *The Times*. She had traced its long history going back to the old Muslim Emirate. She pointed out that Kano had been founded when William the Conqueror arrived in England, over a thousand years before. He was impressed by her knowledge of the development of the people of West Africa and their problems.

It was Flora who proposed that the new Protectorate should be called Nigeria. The original proposal put forward was Goldesia but Goldie refused his name to be used. He had no desire to be remembered. He maintained this stance to the end of his life, when he destroyed as many papers as possible, and made his children swear they would never go into print about him or he would curse them! It was not until 1900 that the name Nigeria was eventually adopted, when Northern Nigeria became a Protectorate.

Another woman Lugard had come into contact with at this time was Mary Kingsley, also an ardent admirer of Goldie. A charismatic traveller and writer, still in her thirties and single, she was famous for travelling down the Niger and across forests and swamps in long Victorian skirts and bonnets. She lived amongst the native tribes and gave popular public speeches and talks on her visits to England. They were entertaining, melodramatic and not necessarily accurate. This irritated Flora, and she avoided Mary if they were invited to the same functions. Another reason could have been that Goldie was attracted to both charismatic women.

Mary wrote a book in 1899 entitled *West African Studies,* in which she said, '...*how great England can be when she is incarnate in a great man, for the Royal Niger Company is so far Sir George Taubman Goldie. For nearly twenty years the natives under the Company have had the firm, wise, sympathetic friendship of a great Englishman who knew them personally.*'

One topic on which Mary disagreed with Goldie, Lugard and Flora Shaw was the actions of Liverpool traders who were selling liquor to the West Coast. She supported the traders, and said she saw no evidence that the liquor trade had brought drunkenness to the West Coast. She blamed the prejudice of the missionaries and the zealousness of the temperance movement for the hysteria.

It was a point which Lugard thought about later when he was tackling the opium problem in Hong Kong. Mary Kingsley died of typhoid in 1900 aged only thirty-seven, nursing the Boers in the camps in South Africa during the Second Boer War. When Goldie heard of her death he wrote, '*She had the brain of a man, and the heart of a woman.*'

After the uneasy interview with Chamberlain, Lugard was still struggling with his decision. He was not convinced of the chessboard policy, and yet had agreed to carry it out. He consulted Goldie again, who reassured him that he would continue to fight against it through the press and Parliament. This was enough reassurance to convince Lugard he should continue. Chamberlain still tried to persuade him to locate the base in Lagos, worried about the influence of Goldie, and the greater difficulties with communications, but Lugard was adamant, and Chamberlain finally agreed.

Meanwhile, events on the international front were causing concern. The French had put down an uprising in Borgu, reoccupied Nikki and detained the King. They were questioning Lugard's treaty again. In response the British sent two gunboats up the Niger and occupied Okuta to block any French advancement south.

During February 1898 the situation became increasingly tense, with daily articles in the papers on both sides, and reports that the French had sent a force to Sokoto. Goldie sent some of his troops north, but did not attack and created a stand-off. There was genuine concern that this could escalate to all-out war with France.

Flora wrote in *The Times* on February 21, '*The peace of the world ought not to rest on the ability and inclination of a number of youthful officers to control their native troops.*'

The French denied troops had been sent to Sokoto, and blamed the Royal Niger Company for inflaming the situation. On February 24, Chamberlain went to the House of Commons to get approval for the West Africa Frontier Force and the appointment of Lugard. He was attacked by the anti-imperialists for risking war with France. Chamberlain argued that the Force would be required whether the French were there or not. The cabinet was absolutely united. Flora reported in *The Times* the next day, '*The whole nation, with the exception of a few cranks, supported the government's policy.*'

Lugard now felt he not only had the support of the press, but of Parliament as well, and went for a last meeting with Chamberlain. The meeting was much more cordial this time, with Chamberlain confirming the initial objectives and not pushing the chessboard policy. Lugard noted, '*…the conversation was very social and friendly and he was his old self entirely, with the personality which I like and admire. For him, when he is natural, I have great admiration, and would do much, but his hectoring role did not come off with me and only made me hesitate on the verge of resignation.*'

With recent developments in mind Chamberlain then asked, '*Now suppose it came to war, what would you do?*' continuing, '*Would you consider withdrawal of all troops from Borgu and attack Dahomey itself?*' Lugard confirmed this would be his action but that a gunship must anchor off Porto Novo and prevent reinforcements coming into Dahomey. This was agreed, and Chamberlain added that he gave him permission to write to him unofficially, and tell him everything more freely and fully than could be done in an official capacity. With that they shook hands and Chamberlain wished him luck.

When Lugard passed this remark on to Goldie he was delighted and commented, '*Coming from Joe it was a very high mark of confidence and friendship.*'

Two days later, on March 12 1898, Lugard and Willcocks boarded the *SS Benin* at Liverpool to set sail to Lagos, with much on their minds.

CHAPTER 20
Cat and mouse

As the ship sailed out of Liverpool heading down to the Azores, Lugard reflected in his diary on the importance of his family to him. His half-sister Emma was happily married to the Reverend Robert Brayne, a parson living in Norfolk. She was bringing up six sons all destined to go to Cambridge, and needed monetary help, which he willingly gave. His elder sister Agnes had been recently widowed after a short marriage and liked to send him practical presents (including a robust air-tight box to keep his cigars dry when travelling). He had managed to see his elderly father who was nearly ninety years old, frail and nearing the end of his life. Ned was still in the Kalahari with Nell, and he envied the happy family life they had created. Watching the family growing up around him made Lugard think again about marriage.

He was free from Catherine, and had a desire to have a home he could return to. His savings had amounted to a reasonable sum from the last expedition, and he considered a house near Haslemere, in the Surrey Downs near to friends and family. He just needed the right person to share his complicated life.

It was a tedious, uncomfortable boat ride to Lagos, the old steamer piled high with coal and baggage, even in the lifeboats. There were brief stopovers at Accra and Kotonou in Dahomey, where Willcocks decided to go ashore and have a look around. He was most upset when the French tried to charge him fifteen francs for the privilege.

At Lagos they found the Governor had travelled north and left the residence undergoing decoration. Lugard felt this snub was deliberate and that there was going to be no love lost between them whilst the army was being assembled. The Governor sent a polite invitation to Lugard to meet him in Ibadan. Lugard noted in his diary, '*He wants to make it appear, I suppose, that I am his puppet who is to dance to his tune.'* Lugard politely declined saying that it was urgent he reach Lokoja to get the housing erected before the wet season started.

The boat left Lagos on April 4 1898, and at Forcados they transferred to the company launch to start the journey up the Niger. This was Willcocks' first trip on the mighty river, but it was memorable for all the wrong reasons; it rained heavily, was unseasonably cold, needing blankets to keep them warm, Lugard had toothache, and finally the boat was struck by a rare tornado. It lifted the twin screws clean out of the surging water, the propellers spun violently in the air sending metallic spasms through the boat, before plunging back down into the water. Finally, because the boat was so heavily loaded, it ran aground on one of the shifting mud banks, needing an enormous effort to refloat. It was a relief to all when they arrived at Lokoja on April 16.

Lugard found that the 1st Battalion already numbered 1,070 men, and were halfway through their training. He was not happy with the inexperienced Colonel making his first priority to build a large parade ground. Lugard quickly organised the building of the living quarters, and arranged the administration according to his own orderly methods.

He was not interested in the spit and polish side of military rules, but demanded discipline and high standards from his men. He wanted the new recruits to be led by example, not fear. He wrote in his instructions on March 31 1898, *'The continual exhibition of patience, tact and firmness combined with kindness and justice will assuredly produce the best results possible.'* He demanded that his men *'...avoid causes of offence to the native population and to treat them in a courteous manner.'* This applied especially to troops on the march, who were to avoid looting, stealing of crops and violation of women. He continued, *'It has been our pride that British expeditions, in respect of their treatment of the native populations, have borne a character throughout Africa which has contrasted greatly with those of other nations, and we are to uphold British traditions.'*

Colonel Willcocks had recently arrived from India, and the first impressions of his Hausa and Yoruba troops did not give him confidence. This changed when he witnessed them in action later. Many died thousands of miles from their homeland, and Willcocks wrote in his memoirs, *'... if I had my choice once more, nowhere would I sooner serve than my faithful Hausas and Yorubas, whom I learnt to admire, and whose reputation is very precious to me.'*

The 2nd Battalion had been recruited in Ilorin by Colonel Fitzgerald, and was marching to Lokoja. New telegraph lines were being erected from Lagos to Jebba to improve communications. Goldie's three hundred troops from the Niger Company were also transferred under Lugard's command. They were led by (later Sir) William Wallace, the Agent-General, and Major A. J. Arnold, a regular officer on loan. Lugard could now turn his attention to the French, and the chessboard policy he despised.

After consulting with Willcocks, Lugard decided to split the troops into three groups. The first was to operate south of Lokoja under Wallace and Arnold, the second based at Fort Goldie at the northern end of the British territory, and the last group was to march to the French outposts to the west of Fort Goldie under Willcocks, and take the town of Ilo. This would then form a south-west arc through the towns of Bugasi and Ibasoro to squeeze out the French posts.

Soon after arriving at Lokoja, Lugard went down with a high fever from reoccurring malaria and had to take to his bed. From underneath a pile of blankets he continued to dictate letters and issue a battery of instructions and orders. These varied from advice to Willcocks on stores and transport, to scolding the bureaucrats in Lagos for stopping the erection of the tele-graph line to Jebba. He noted, '*One earns one's pay, I think, in West Africa.*'

On April 24 Willcocks set off to Fort Goldie, and Lugard tried to imple-ment further improvements for the running of Lokoja, despite only having one clerk. He was already having problems with his new European staff; one had committed suicide and many were getting sick, despite building a hospital and bringing three brave pioneering nurses from England. They did an excellent job in difficult conditions and later received decorations for their work. He was also having difficulty sourcing enough nutritious food locally, until he found an enthusiastic young Guards officer called the Hon. Richard Somerset. He set up a farm on Jebba Island underneath the Ju-Ju rock, and supplied fresh vegetables and meat to the camp, which undoubtedly saved many lives.

Willcocks had been carefully briefed by Lugard on the strategy of the chessboard policy, despite not believing in it himself, and the game started. The first town that Willcocks headed for was Kishi. By the time he reached Fort Goldie, the French had already quit, so he had an easy start. He moved on to two more villages where the French tricolour was flying. The French retreated with no resistance. It appeared they were playing the same game as the British, avoiding any confrontation, and just sent letters of warning that they were on French territory.

At Kiama, where Lugard had obtained a treaty in 1897, the French made their stand. Willcocks occupied the village of Betikuta, two miles from Kiama and raised the Union Jack, waiting for a French reaction.

Two days later, a smartly-dressed French sergeant was escorted by twelve Senegalese soldiers carrying a tricolour, and raised it on an adjacent flag-pole and saluted. Willcocks did the same with his Union Jack, saluted and then saluted the tricolour. Pleasantries were exchanged, but the proceedings were suddenly interrupted by the arrival of the King of Kiama.

Lugard had met the King on his previous expedition and the two men had got on well. The King was bemused at what he saw, and made a speech saying that a few years previously, he had met and made friends with a great white man who had made promises to him and then gone away, and he had heard no more of him. Willcocks was able to reply, '*That great man has now returned and is not far away.*'

The argument continued, with the French sergeant accusing Willcocks of violating the law of nations by forcing his way into a country over which the French flag was flying. Willcocks retorted that the French flag had no right flying there, to which the angry reply was, '*You have insulted our flag. The history of Borgu shows how England has overridden all treaties,*' and proceeded to produce a large bundle of manuscripts in French purporting to be the history of Borgu.

By this time Willcocks was having difficulty keeping a straight face, and replied that, as it had not yet been translated, the British were unaware of it. At this the Frenchman laughed and decided he was '*a thorough gentleman with a nice way of putting things.*' The situation was defused. Willcocks called on the King, assured him that there would be no war between the white men in his country, and left with the sound of booming drums echoing in his ears.

The cat and mouse games continued with the French, with flags going up and down around the villages to the entertainment of the local chiefs, but not a shot was fired.

By this time the wet season had started, and travelling was becoming far more difficult, so Willcocks decided this was a good opportunity to pay a quick visit to Lugard, who was now in Jebba, and report back on his progress. Lugard had not recovered, still suffering from the effects of malaria and was delighted to see his old friend. A message had just been received from Chamberlain authorising Lugard to occupy a position on the Niger between Bussa and Ilo, but he was in no hurry to carry it out.

Lugard still considered the French had serious intentions of staying in Borgu and that if he pushed towards Bussa they would stir up the northern states of Sokoto and Gandu against the British. Intense negotiations were now going on between the French and British governments in Paris to get a convention agreed, and Chamberlain wanted a fallback position in case they collapsed.

On May 24 it was the Queen's 79th birthday, and it was decided to have a small celebration. A parade of the 2nd Battalion was held, which had arrived with Colonel Fitzgerald, but events were unfortunately overshadowed by the deaths of two young Navy officers who had drowned while swimming in the river.

Willcocks had been shocked at the physical appearance of Lugard on his return. He was seriously worried about the state of health of his chief, and with the amount of work he was taking on. He did not tell him directly and kept a cheery face, which Lugard appreciated. '*Dear old Willcocks was as full of almost boyish good spirits as ever and he pleased me by his keen appreciation of my work.*' However, before Willcocks returned to Betikuta, he wrote a letter to Lord Antrobus at the Colonial Office in London expressing his concerns and fears that Lugard would not survive if he continued with his present punishing regime.

The little village of Betikuta was now becoming the focus of world attention, with newspapers in London and Paris reporting this feud could be the spark that starts a war between Britain and France. Chamberlain inflamed the ill-feeling to force an agreement. He was willing to concede Nikki but he was not going to back down on Kiama or the real aim - Sokoto.

Willcocks built a small palisade for protection to allow for the worst, but was praying for a swift agreement on the treaty. He sent out Major Arnold with a company of infantry to Kiama to scout out the French defences, making sure they got no nearer than 400 metres from the town gate. He saw new tricolours flying, increased security, with some of the sentries posted in the trees, and defences being built. Meanwhile, Lugard has sent a telegram on June 7 that there was an acute danger of fighting breaking out. He immediately received a reply from Chamberlain telling him to avoid conflict at all costs.

On June 14 1898, to everyone's relief, the convention was signed in Paris, without a shot being fired. Chamberlain's hard-fought negotiations with the French ensured a good deal had been struck. The British lost Nikki, but they got Kiama, and a vast northern arc taking in Sokoto through to Lake Chad. After further lengthy discussions the treaty was ratified in 1899.

By this time Egypt had become the centre of attention, with Kitchener fighting his way south against the Mahdists culminating in a bloody victory at the Battle of Omdurman on September 2 1898. The news of the Niger Treaty was quickly bumped off the front pages.

For Lugard it was a hollow victory. He had achieved all that was asked of him, getting an army trained up and positioned in the right place at the right time, without causing a conflict. This new force was to play an even more important part in the future, when world war broke out and it became an international force. He had transformed Jebba, built houses, a hospital, offices and a training ground, and set up a farm, all completed in six months. But the cost to his health had been heavy.

He spent two more months at Lokoja completing his reports and paperwork, and handed over to his now good friend James Willcocks. He was leaving it in good hands. Willcocks rebuilt bridges with the French from the start. He entertained the French officers in his camp and delayed marching into Kiama for two hours after the French evacuated. He gained the trust of the local chiefs, who were recovering from the high-handed and oppressive methods of the French, which had been heavily criticized by Lugard.

Willcocks described in his memoirs how on one occasion, when approaching a village, the inhabitants fled into the bush at the appearance of a white man. He hoisted a Union Jack and at once the people emerged from the forest and returned. On another occasion he saw a Muslim trader's slaver caravan, and as soon as the slaves saw the Union Jack, they rushed over to claim liberation. Lugard had begun to lay down his legacy for Nigeria.

He was tired and weary when he boarded the boat to London in August 1898.

CHAPTER 21
Birth of an administrator

The return from Lagos to London in August 1898 was different from all the other journeys Lugard had made. It was not just the sheer exhaustion, the lingering fever, or the guilty feelings of leaving his loyal comrades at such a critical time. Lugard had gone out as a commandant of a military force still being formed. He returned as an administrator in charge of an annexed slice of Africa.

Military games and success were now of little interest to him. His second-in-command Colonel Willcocks could handle that aspect. The real challenge to him was the creation of a Protectorate which would be safe, prosperous and healthy, one that benefited the inhabitants, as well as the British Empire. But he wanted to do it his way.

After a brief break seeing his family, friends and regaining his strength, Lugard went to stay with Joseph Chamberlain, still Secretary of State for the Colonies, at his home at Highbury. The discussions were wide-ranging from the various international tensions between the European states, to the future of Niger. Chamberlain was concerned about the French, and that Africa continued to be fraught with violent tensions. He was considering the scenario if war ensued.

Chamberlain wanted to buy out the Royal Niger Company from Goldie. He proposed to form a Protectorate consisting of the Hausa states - Bornu, Borgu, Ilorin, and the Benue districts, administered under a new Governor. In an almost casual fashion, he offered Lugard the post. In an equally casual fashion, considering it was going to transform his life, Lugard accepted. It was also agreed that Colonel Willcocks would take over command of the West Africa Frontier Force (WAFF).

Lugard returned to London elated, and threw himself into the task with a new lease of life. His priority was to complete the setting-up of the WAFF and persuade the War Office, the Colonial Office and the Crown Agents to provide enough staff, provisions and facilities to function efficiently.

He liked to interview prospective staff himself, even the office clerks, needing to be confident they could cope with conditions in West Africa, not just impress him with how many people they knew. He insisted all staff had medical examinations, including the doctors. He did not trust the government departments to get good deals with contractors and negotiated with them himself, spending the money saved on other essentials.

His next objective was to achieve a smooth transition when Goldie's company was bought by the Government. It was a long process which had been put under the management of a departmental committee headed by the Under-Secretary of State for the Colonies, Lord Selborne. The committee included Goldie and the Governors of Lagos and the Niger State Coast Protectorate. They favoured two governments, one in the north and another in the south, although three were considered for a while, and optimistically aimed for the transfer of administration in a year by January 1 1899.

Lugard spent the first three months in 1899 with Goldie agreeing what land, buildings, equipment, military stores and other plant the Government should take over from the Royal Niger Company, and at what price. He then worked out the revenue and expenditure, customs, liquor control, mineral rights and many other domestic matters. The final stage of the process to create the Protectorate was the formal revocation of the Royal Niger Company's charter, and the acceptance by Parliament of the new acquisition and the value of the compensation.

On July 3, an agreement was reached with the Chancellor of the Exchequer to pay the Royal Niger Company 865,000 pounds. After a long debate in the House, it was begrudgingly passed on July 27 by the opposition led by Sir Henry Campbell-Bannerman.

Parliament had been swayed by Chamberlain. He stood up and announced that Lugard would govern the new Protectorate which was to be called Northern Nigeria. Slavery would be abolished, there would be an absolute prohibition of spirits (except in a neutral zone where they could be sold but not stored) and a railway line would be built from Kano to the River Niger to enable the passage of trade from the north to the south. He concluded, '*I do not think that even as a pecuniary bargain this country will have any reason to regret the change they are asked to assent to.*'

The one outstanding dissenter was the Irish politician, John Dillon, the leader of the Irish Parliamentary Party. He gave a passionate speech saying, '*…I refuse to recognise as a great gift to this country an addition of thirty-five million of unknown people. It is out of the power of this country and still more* *out of the power of this House, to discharge to these helpless, silent, inarticulate races those moral duties which are entailed in the government of a great empire. In the years to come, crimes may be committed in our name, and slaughter may be perpetrated which it may be impossible for the already overburdened Ministers of the Empire to investigate, and nobody can forecast the extent of the evil that may result from this great accession to the territory of the British Empire.'* Lugard listened to the debate in the gallery, and had little time for Dillon's views. (He was later suspended from Parliament in 1901 for using violent language towards Chamberlain).

For Goldie, over twenty years of dedicated work had come to an end. He had built the Royal Niger Company from nothing, and at the age of fifty-two, had no desire to continue as part of the new Protectorate. This would have been unacceptable anyway due to the financial settlement agreed. His whole life was changing. The previous year, in 1898, his wife Mathilda had died, and his relationship with Flora Shaw had cooled, (his affections had transferred to Mary Kingsley). Goldie had reached a watershed in his life.

His close relationship with Lugard was also coming to an end. During the negotiations, Goldie would go down to Hazelmere, and the two men would take long walks or cycle rides down the Surrey lanes putting the world to rights. These were their last days together, and they were destined to go their separate ways. Goldie wanted something new, and after the Company had been sold, he went on a long journey to China to consider his future.

Lugard's health had much improved, but mentally, the intermittent black spells returned, together with the doubts. He missed the companionship of Ned, who was about to be transferred from the Kalahari to South Africa for the Second Boer War, but Nell was back in England. She was one of the few people with whom he would share his confidences.

After an Easter visit Nell wrote to Ned, expressing her concerns over Lugard's lack of faith. *'His health is again superlative; he walks immense distances, but is so indifferent about time and food – would he not drive a wife wild?'* She was a devout Christian and on asking Lugard what he thought the difference between Paradise and Heaven was, he gave the jaunty answer, *'You will know when you get there.'* Then added wistfully, *'I don't suppose I shall ever get to either.'* He feared his family considered him a hopeless atheist and noted *'...they are not far wrong.'*

Nell continued in her letter, *'Poor old Fred...he seems to have found all false in life where falsehood should not have been. He has no faith in <u>anything</u>... it's too sad. Ned darling, you must try to bring faith and love and happiness and peace to dear old Fred. <u>You can</u>. I know he would be greatly biased by* *what he sees you believe. I can only pray for him.'* This was brave of Nell, for she knew she could lose some of Ned's love and attention because of his intense loyalty and love for his brother.

Flora Shaw was getting restless at *The Times* after a successful trip reporting on the Klondike goldfields in America, and was considering a journey from the Cape to Cairo to report on Rhodes' dream. Goldie had already advised against it as being too dangerous, but she wanted Lugard's opinion. Valuing her expertise on colonial matters and her intense interest in Africa, Lugard had sought out her views on his plans and aspirations for Nigeria. He wrote a letter to her on February 23 1899.

'Dear Miss Shaw,

Your letter only reached me yesterday, and I was out all day and so dead-tired on my return that I could not manage to reply in time to catch the early country post. I am extremely sorry to hear of your projected journey from North to South of Africa.

Sir George was quite right – I am quite sure you will succeed, and achieve more information and see more than anyone else has done; but any brainless and energetic person can travel – whereas you are very urgently required for far more difficult and important work. I shall be delighted to call at the first leisure moment I can secure, and more than pleased to be of any use I can to you.'

Flora cancelled the trip, and before Lugard returned to Northern Nigeria she wrote, *'I look upon it as part of my personal work to endeavour to bring all the influences which I believe to be working for the good in Africa into harmony with each other.'* Once in Northern Nigeria, Lugard wrote to her almost every day and their friendship deepened.

When the Second Boer War broke out in October 1899, Lugard's departure to Nigeria was delayed as the Army considered which officers of the WAFF would be transferred to the battlefront, some never to return. He received his Commission of Appointment after he had sailed, and he was promoted to Brigadier-General (*'a silly title I did not want'*) as head of his little army. His knighthood followed in 1901, which was of little consequence to him.

He sailed with (later Sir) Henry Cowper Gollan, his private secretary, on December 4 so he could arrive at Lokoja precisely on December 31 1899, ready for the ceremony to be held symbolically on the first day of the new millennium.

Henry Gollan and the Chaplain to the WAFF gave their accounts of the simple ceremony in their memoirs. It was conducted with military formality on the parade ground of the Lokoja camp on the banks of the Niger River where the major tributary, the Benue River surges to meet it. A square had been formed with the 2nd Battalion of the WAFF, a battery of guns and the Royal Niger Constabulary. It was observed by a small group of European civilians and local spectators.

At 7am precisely, Lugard walked onto the parade ground with his skeleton band of staff, stepped onto a small podium, and in a clear and impressive voice read out the Queen's proclamation. In the corner of the square was a flagstaff with the Royal Niger Company flag flying in the breeze. This was slowly lowered and the Union Jack raised with the African military band playing the national anthem. The guns fired a salute, and the local troops gave three cheers for their new, and considerably distant, Queen Victoria.

It was an historic occasion for Nigeria, the first step towards unification with the south which followed in 1914, then complete independence in 1960; the majority of the population completely unaware they were now part of the British Empire, or even who Queen Victoria was.

The three Colonels in charge of the WAFF – James Willcocks, Thomas Morland and (later Brig.Gen.) Arthur Lowry Cole stepped forward and Lugard read the Royal Warrant of his Appointment, with Willcocks administering the oath of allegiance. The troops were inspected, marching proudly past the podium, and Lugard formally took over the Company's Constabulary as part of the Frontier Force. The Company's Agent-General, William Wallace was inducted as a Resident in the new Government. Finally, the Queen's Proclamation was read out to the troops in the local languages of Hausa and Nupe to complete the formalities. This was followed with two days of sports, which was of far more interest to the local spectators, who joined in enthusiastically.

That evening a dinner was held for the fifty British Europeans in the WAFF mess that had been hastily built the previous month. After a toast to Queen Victoria, Lugard gave a speech praising the work of Goldie and the achievements of the Royal Niger Company saying, '*Thus far, Gentlemen, The Royal Niger Company has laboured and we have entered into their labours.*' He praised Goldie for his genius, his marvellous foresight, his courage in the field and for his public spirit, saying, '*Though a man of wealth whom lay no necessity for work, he has for many years worked longer hours than city men do for gain.*'

Compliments flowed for the hard work of Joseph Flint, who succeeded Goldie as head of the Royal Niger Company, and for William Wallace who was joining them. Finally, he thanked his close friend, Colonel James Willcocks, who had been summoned from India to work with him in creating the Frontier Force and was heading up its first operations. He concluded by saying, '*We drink to the success of Northern Nigeria – that success is not a thing which will grow of itself…it is in the hands of each one of us; it is we who are selected to mould the young beginnings, to set the precedents and set the tone and, in short, to make or mar this work…Gentlemen I do assure you that I enter on this task with a deep sense of responsibility, and of doubt of my worthiness for it, and though (as our greatest Poet has said) it is not in us to command success, I shall at least endeavour to deserve it. In the words of the oath I swore this morning – words which recall those of the Preacher of old, 'I will endeavour to do right to all manner of people, without fear or favour, affection or ill-will' and I trust that when the time comes for me to 'hand in my cheques' and look back on my tenure of office, it may be said of me, that to the extent of my ability I did my duty – not sparing myself…'* The toasts and celebrations continued late into the evening.

Early next morning, Lugard went straight to his office, sat at a make-shift desk, eager to start his first day of governing. It was an awesome task. Northern Nigeria covered nearly 300,000 square miles, with a population of over eight million people, (the actual figure was unknown when he took over). Only a fraction of the country was occupied in the south and west and the remainder not even explored.

There had been a handful of expeditions before Joseph Thomson, the genial Scots explorer who reached Sokoto in 1885 on behalf of the Royal Niger Company. (His motto had been, '*He who goes gently, goes safely; he who goes safely, goes far,*' and was the inspiration for Rider Haggard's hero in his novel *King Solomon's Mines*). None of the expeditions that survived had explored more than fifty miles from the banks of the great rivers, and were unaware of some of the most highly-developed and civilised Muslim states of tropical Africa, with high, red-walled cities and armies of horsemen.

Seldom can a Governor have been appointed to a territory where so little was known about it, or even been viewed.

Lugard laid out a faded map of Nigeria on his table. On it he had marked in pencil the agreed external 1899 treaty boundaries, and lines of the known provinces. He knew about the Yoruba states, starting from the tropical coast at Lagos, north through the major cities of Ibadan and Oyo to the temperate forests of Ilorin, but knew little of Borgu to the east. He had encountered the hostile slaving states of the Nupe centred at Bida and Kontagora, but still had much to learn of the important and historical Hausa states which stretched right up to the borders of the Sahara Desert.

These included the ancient Muslim cities of Kano, Sokoto, Zaria, Daura, Gobir and Katsina that had flourished since the eleventh century. They had grown with the spread of people migrating with camel caravan trains from the north, bringing influences from Egypt, Iraq and Syria. There were also the Fulani people, who mostly followed a nomadic pastoral life, travelling with their cattle with impunity, crossing borders from Senegal to Sudan in search of fresh pastures. Many had also settled in the towns. Often fair skinned, their features showed they were descendants from North Africa. They were mostly Moslem and usually led a peaceful existence.

However, in 1804, as continually happens in Islam's history, a Fulani holy man called Shehu Usuman Dan Fodio, from Gobir, led a puritan revival and called for a return to Islamic fundamentalism. He demanded the faithful expel all heretics. He raised a Fulani army and threw out many of the old Hausa rulers, replacing them with Fulani. This extended their new empire right down to Ilorin, and throughout Northern Nigeria. Usuman died in 1817 and his son, Bello, chose Sokoto as his new capital, and made his brother the Emir of Gwandu.

The early explorer Hugh Clapperton (1788-1827), another intrepid Scot, was the first European Bello met in Sokoto in 1827. He died of malaria and dysentary whilst he was there, but there are accounts left by his servant, Richard Lander, who survived the journey. Clapperton and Bello had wide-ranging discussions, from the signs of the zodiac, to Bello enquiring of Clapperton if he was a Nestorian or Socinian Christian. Many rebellions followed, led by the deposed Hausa chieftains, and over those fractious years the Fulani Empire declined.

By the time Lugard arrived in Nigeria, there were flourishing political and cultural communities with crowded mosques, busy markets where skilled metal and leather artisans sold their wares, and farmers produced food using advanced agriculture methods. But there was still a flourishing slave trade.

In the first few months Lugard set to work constructing housing, appointing magistrates, establishing a police force, starting a postal service, and organizing hospitals, schools, transport, public works and marine departments. In addition he set up an Anglo-French boundary commission and customs service controlling liquor imports. All this while he had '...*a double-barrelled attack of fever and have been laid up for some time with most painful boils (on my stern, so most painful sitting), but neither have stopped me working.*'

He used a house in Lokoja as his temporary headquarters. He wanted to establish another headquarters further north at Zungeru, away from the fever-infested river, and nearer to where the future action was going to be. He had asked for a ludicrously small budget of 134,000 pounds, with only104 civilian staff, 200 British officers and NCOs and two to three thousand African soldiers. This was, as usual, cut by the Colonial Office to 88,000 pounds, and Lugard managed by filling the posts late or not at all. He had no properly-trained office staff and no printing machine, so all laws and edicts had to be typed.

Lugard had clear ideas on how he wanted to implement the law. He wished to develop a humanitarian side to the imperial policy that had been hitherto lacking. From his experiences in India and Uganda, and discussions with Goldie, he wanted to rule 'indirectly' using native institutions as much as possible, and not administer the people directly. He wanted to use the ruling Fulani laws, and consequently issued a Natives Court Proclamation setting up native courts to try the local people according to native laws and customs. Cruel punishments and methods repugnant to natural justice and English law were forbidden. This relieved the workload on the Supreme Court but imposed more responsibility on the Residents. He deliberately called the chief administrators 'Residents' to show they were advisors rather than executives.

Lugard's most important law, and an issue dear to his heart, was the Slavery Proclamation. He had gained much experience in East Africa and had discussed the problem at length with his close friend Sir John Kirk, a leading expert in Britain, and with Goldie. It was a complex issue, as seen from the after-effects of the abolition of slavery in the USA in 1865, only thirty-five years previously. If he simply abolished slavery, the law would either be ignored or economic chaos, mass unemployment and riots would ensue. He had to find another way to end the trade.

Lugard therefore introduced the abolition of the legal status of slavery. This meant that no new slaves could be introduced after April 1 1901, and no owner could restrain or recapture a slave after that date. This would enable gradual freedom for existing slaves and freedom for all new-born children. It allowed all slaves who were treated well by their owners, and who were actually prospering, to remain if they wished. He deplored the savagery and waste of life and resources of slave-trading and wrote in his first annual report in 1900-1901, '...the worst forms of slave-trading still exist to so terrible extent, and the slave-traders are not even provident of their hunting grounds, for those who are useless as slaves are killed in large numbers, villages burnt and the fugitives left to starve in the bush. In Kabba hundreds of ruins attest the former existence of a population and a prosperity that has gone... the Fulani and Nupe began early in the year to ravage the districts nearer home and with Kontagora the 'Gwamachi' (The Destroyer) ...laid waste the country from the Niger banks on the west and south to the eastern highlands, and to the *north as far as the borders of Sokoto and Zaria…and the two armies raided for slaves almost to the banks of the Niger and close to Jebba.'*

The Fulani slave-trading tribes were pushing south, testing the British who were trying to expand north. It was inevitable there were going to be military engagements. For the present, with his limited resources, there was not much Lugard could do. Further complications arose when, after only three months, another Ashanti War broke out in the Gold Coast (now Ghana), and Lugard was forced to send Willcocks with 1,200 men, and fifty officers and NCOs. Fighting the slavers was delayed until the troops returned in December 1900. The men distinguished themselves in the heavy fighting in Ghana and Colonel Willcocks returned delighted with their performance, saying, *'I have never served with finer fellows. How I love them. Always cheerful, plucky, brave and uncomplaining…'*

Lugard had been sending out small patrols, which had been attacked by Kontagora horsemen. Once Willcocks returned, he sent out a stronger force from Lokoja and took Kontagora easily – the horsemen were no match for machine guns. When the old Emir was eventually captured after fleeing to Zaria and admonished for his slave-trading practices, he retorted, *'Can a cat be stopped from mousing?'* and declared, *'I will die with a slave in my mouth.'*

Lugard's next military objective was to retake Bida, a strategic town, which had been reoccupied by Emir Abu Bakri after Goldie's siege in 1897. Lugard led the troops himself, and on finding the Emir had fled, marched straight into the centre of the town. His troops formed a large square and Lugard assured the chiefs that not a shot would be fired unless attacked. No shots were fired, and he reinstalled the old Emir Markum (even though he was not that impressed with him), and announced a new era for Bida, where people would not be carried off as slaves. He was keen to depose the rulers but to keep the Fulani chiefs. He wrote in his first report to London, *'I am anxious to show no hostility to them, and show them good government and justice, and I am anxious to utilise, if possible, their wonderful intelligence, for they are born rulers…'*

Before Lugard took his first leave in April 1901, he briefed Colonel Morland for an expedition to Yola, the capital of Adamawa state. It was over five hundred miles east of Lokoja, and adjacent to the Kamerun border. The Fulani Emir was running a large slave-trading centre, plundering the aborigine tribes who lived simple lives in the surrounding forests.

The Emir's palace was on the River Benue, with easy access by boat. In August 1901, after all conciliatory talks were rejected, Morland took 365 men and attacked the town. The Emir inflicted a few casualties on his troops, then fled across the border and a new Emir was installed in the palace. This was another blow against slavery and a chance to extend British influence right to the eastern border of Nigeria.

Lugard saw the completion of his new headquarters at Zungeru, and the building of a new railway link to the Kaduna River as a priority. All the building materials were ferried up the Niger and Kaduna rivers to Wushishi, and transferred to porters who carried them to the site. His Director of Public Works (later Sir) John Eaglesome, drew up plans for the route of the railway, and the earthworks commenced before he left.

After a lot of opposition from London, the project was approved. Later that year he wrote to Ned, '*In May, the final sanction for the line was given, and the rails were rolled in Leeds, and the first steps for the location were made in Africa, and before Christmas the first train steamed into Zungeru. My little railway is in working order, with two trains per diem...*'

By April 1901, Lugard had been in office fifteen months and had established all his basic plans for the administrative framework and infrastructure for the Protectorate. It was a good time to take a well-earned break in England.

It was a summer he would never forget.

CHAPTER 22
Coming together

In October 1900, Flora closed down the house in Cambridge Street, and moved back to the cottage in Abinger with her sister Lulu.

It was a relaxing time but only lasted a few months. One day in December Lulu arrived back at the cottage smiling radiantly, with a handsome young Irishman called Jack Bagwell on her arm. She announced they were to be married in January, and wanted it to be held in Abinger. Flora agreed, and helped organise a happy occasion, with many relations coming over from Ireland and France, the cottage bursting with chatter and laughter.

When they had all gone, Flora was once again on her own, and quickly felt her depression returning. Her sisters were concerned, and after discussing various options, suggested to Flora that her niece Hilda Brackenbury, the daughter of her deceased sister Mimi, should come and live with her. Flora agreed, and found Hilda a delight. She was a perfect confidante and just the daughter she would have wanted.

Shortly afterwards, her longtime admirer, the newly-knighted Sir Frederick Lugard, returned on leave and knocked on her door.

So began the beautiful summer of 1901.

When Lugard returned to London in April 1901 he found the country in mourning. Queen Victoria had died on January 22 at the age of eighty-one, after sixty-four years on the throne. The Victorian age with its righteousness, high morals, and dominated by the Empire had come to an end literally, and entered a transition phase leading into the Edwardian age, which heralded a more relaxed attitude to life, and a gradual waning of enthusiasm for Britain's imperial policy.

A new era of technology had arrived. Marconi had sent his first trans-atlantic wireless message to Newfoundland. More and more cars were appearing noisily on the streets. The Aero Club of the UK had been established with a race on for the first powered aircraft. H.G. Wells had just published *First Men in the Moon,* Rudyard Kipling was writing a bestseller called *Kim,* and the first cinema was about to open in Islington, in north London.

Lugard felt more relaxed than he had been for a long time. He worked relentlessly, but now he saw a clear purpose. In his personal life, Catherine was in the past. He was confident enough to keep her as a friend and continued to support her and Kitty. Catherine responded to his help by sending melancholic poems, bemoaning her plight. He needed someone new to share his life.

He was forty-four years old, still an eligible bachelor, freshly knighted and well-known. His sisters tried to play matchmaker with him, arranging occasional meetings with those whom they considered suitable. He enjoyed the company of young ladies, but had little interest in light banter and none of the girls had the depth he was looking for. Margery Perham records that on one occasion he made a half-hearted proposal to a most eligible young lady but she refused, most likely to Lugard's relief and gratitude.

Flora Shaw always attracted him. He was delighted when, shortly after returning from Nigeria, she invited him to her cottage at Abinger. She was pleased to see her old friend again, and keen to hear the latest news from Nigeria. He knew that the affair with Goldie had finished, and he quickly sensed in her a sadness. He recognised the pain she was going through, and felt an overwhelming desire to help, and to comfort. That meeting was the start of frequent visits to her little cottage in the Surrey Hills in the following months.

The first two weeks of April were unusually warm, giving luxuriant spring blossoms, and a thick layer of bluebells carpeted the woods around Leith Hill. The good weather continued to August and spilled over into September. Lugard told Margery Perham later, '*We walked here up and down the azaleas, we talked of her work and my work. It was wonderful. I could never tire of hearing of her work, it was unique. And, she really, I believe, admired my work.*'

They took long walks over Leith Hill and across the Downs, talking for hours on wide-ranging subjects. Her company brought Lugard a closeness he thought he would never feel again. He was falling in love. He loved her beauty, intelligence, wit and charm, and knew he wanted to marry her.

He also knew he would have to return to Nigeria imminently, and on October 12 after another idyllic day, he proposed to her. He wrote to Nell that evening after returning to London, '*I have asked Miss Shaw to be my* *wife. She has refused — but not <u>I think</u> in terms which preclude hope. She has had a blow which has broken her down mentally and physically, and I think from what I hear, that she has barely escaped brain fever. Hence she could answer in no other way. I go to see her tomorrow. I feel sure you will like me to tell you this — and perhaps it will account a little for my silences and abstraction. Matters in this connection have been ceaselessly in my thoughts of late.'*

His instincts were right, and a few days later Flora accepted his offer of marriage. She felt an overwhelming excitement, yet at the same time had many concerns. This was not the passion of young love. She was still in her prime, and had retained her good looks, but she was five years older than Lugard, and both of them had plenty of emotional baggage from their previous relationships. Flora was also concerned how the marriage would affect her work. How could two such independent and emotionally vulnerable people make it work?

It was an immense step, but they were determined to make it a success.

CHAPTER 23
Marriage and adjustment

After Flora had accepted Lugard's marriage proposal, they only had a few days before he returned to Nigeria. It was a hectic time. They decided they would marry quietly in Madeira the following June. It was a convenient stop between England and Nigeria, and a perfect location away from any media attention.

They quickly agreed Little Parkhurst would be their home, but the cottage needed a substantial extension to incorporate their new lifestyle. Flora set about organising the work enthusiastically. She chose a London architect, Edmond Friker, and was involved with every detail of the planning, from the layout of the rooms to the design of the oak staircase and finer details around the doors and fireplaces. The new brickwork was carefully matched with that of the cottage, and the windows were arranged to give a pleasing, balanced, symmetrical look.

The final design was an impressive mansion, with the cottage blending in perfectly. The ground floor, dominated by a grand reception hall and a decorated oak staircase ensured an impressive welcome to the many visitors that would come from all corners of the globe. The reception hall led to a generous, light, drawing room with a large, welcoming fireplace. The dining room was to the right of the hall with ample space to seat twenty people at the dining table. Flora knew that Fred would be spending a lot of time in the study, so she made it spacious with bow windows overlooking the rear garden. A door from the study led to an expansive lawn to cater for summer teas they would enjoy with guests and family.

The Second Boer War was entering its third year and Flora was following events closely. She had been corresponding with her widowed sister-in-law Jenny who was living in the Cape Colony (Flora's brother, Robert, had been killed in a mining accident). When the war started on October 11 1899, the British thought it would be over swiftly. They totally underestimated the Boers capability, who employed effective hit-and-run guerilla tactics, extending the British forces to their limit.

Lord Roberts, the Commander-In-Chief, instigated a 'scorched-earth' policy and deliberately destroyed the houses of the Boers. He set up sixty concentration camps to house over 100,000 homeless Boer women and children. The appalling living conditions resulted in thousands of deaths, and the politicians and press alike condemned the barbarity and inhumanity of the camp system.

Flora despaired at the cruelty and futile loss of life. She wanted to visit the camps to assess the situation herself, and assist with a process of mediation or reconciliation with some of the Dutch leaders. She consulted Charles Moberly Bell and he quickly agreed for Flora to go out for a visit and write an article for *The Times*.

Flora had already discussed her plans with Lugard before he had set off to Nigeria. He was concerned about the idea, especially the risk to her health, knowing the many diseases that were endemic in the area. He knew he could not stop her if she had made up her mind, so insisted a maid should accompany her this time, to which she had no objection.

She left England in early December in high spirits. When she landed in Cape Town, she received a predictably cool reception from the Governor, but her main task was to gauge and report back on the public opinion of both sides - the British and the Dutch.

All of South Africa was under Martial Law at that time. It was disliked intensely by the Dutch, who considered it unjust and repressive. Flora was also surprised to hear that despite the Jameson Raid fiasco in 1895, there was still support for Rhodes in the Cape, although it was divided. She set out to interview as many of the Dutch leaders and settlers as possible in the Cape and the Orange Free State. She wanted them to consider an honourable surrender, which would involve no backlash or punishment. Depressingly, she found little sympathy for the idea, even though the Dutch knew that the Boers had no chance of winning.

Flora visited the concentration camp at Bloemfontein to see for herself the desperate conditions that were being so strongly condemned in the British press. It was a tent city for 7,000 family members whose men were known to be fighting, and whose houses and crops had been destroyed in the 'scorched-earth' policy. The camp commander showed Flora around and allowed her to speak to selected families. The women were extremely vitriolic of the British, blaming them for a barbaric war against women and children.

Emily Hobhouse, an outspoken humanitarian, had visited South Africa six months earlier, and had been extremely critical of the camps. She had highlighted the many deaths, especially of children, due to poor sanitary conditions, bad nutrition, and woeful medical care, and had called for the camps' immediate closure.

Improvements had been made by the time Flora visited, but in her reports she failed to mention the plight of the tens of thousands of black internees who were interred in separate camps suffering even worse conditions, and the many who had died of disease, malnutrition and exposure. It was a frustrating time for her. Flora had concentrated on trying to find solutions to stop the war altogether, but because the visit was short, her research was not as comprehensive as she would have liked.

Whilst in Cape Town, Flora wrote to Lugard frequently. She wanted to honestly express her feelings, and her desires for their future. They had both been completely open to each other about their previous relationships, but she knew that the past was not quite behind them. Lugard had told her about Catherine and, although she believed the affair was over, she knew there was still a tie through Kitty. At the end of December she wrote, '*I hope you look upon our marriage as I look upon it – and I think you do – that is, as a loyal friendship made absolute for life by the public tie with which we bind it. Such a friendship is among the great good things in life...*' continuing a few days later, '*You once said that you would win my love. I, too, hope to win yours ...we cannot force it. Let us not try on either side, but let us be content to marry as friends.*'

It was a strange start for a marriage, but theirs was not a traditional relationship. They knew the dangers of rushing into a marriage, but time was against them, and they had the willingness to let the love and trust in each other grow.

In Johannesburg she met with Lugard's old friend Lord Alfred Milner. The war had taken its toll on him, and he looked tired and had aged noticeably. Flora raised her ideas again, that once peace had been established and some sort of unity achieved, this beautiful country would be perfect for emigrants from Britain to escape the poverty of the English cities. He held similar Positive Imperialism views and agreed. He was already looking at ways of unifying the British and Dutch after the war was over. He wanted to create peace and stability. The Treaty of Vereeniging was eventually signed on May 31 1902, and Lord Milner became the first Governor of Transvaal and the Orange River Colony.

This was Flora's last assignment as Flora Shaw, and it must have left her feeling very discontented.

During the conflict nearly 22,000 British and imperial soldiers died, 7,894 in combat, 13,250 from disease, 934 were missing and 22,828 wounded. In the sixty-six black concentration camps housing over 115,000 men, at least 20,000 died. Of the 116,000 interred in the white concentration camps, the vast majority women, 27,927 died including 22,074 children.

Shortly after Flora returned to England, she heard that Cecil Rhodes had died on March 26 at his seaside cottage at Muizenberg. He had been suffering from heart and lung problems and his death had been expected. It brought closure to Flora's involvement with South Africa.

She returned to Abinger in March 1902 and prepared to travel to Madeira. There was much to do. She completed reports for *The Times*, finalised preparations for the wedding, and assembled her luggage, an impressive forty-six trunks and cases, for her life in Nigeria. Flora set sail in May looking forward to a few relaxing weeks before Lugard arrived.

After six months in Nigeria, Lugard was finding the sheer volume of work daunting and stressful. He was continually asking for more resources and had only 104 staff to govern the entire region; this included doctors, police, engineers, marine department and public works managers, accountants, telegraphists, storemen and clerks. A significant percentage were sick with fever or on leave at any one time, so he was always understaffed. He was responsible for thirteen provinces, thousands of miles of frontier with only two battalions, and Sokoto and Kano threatening to go to war.

Without Ned to restrain him, it was no surprise he was overworked. His health suffered, and he felt the black cloud descending on him. He was sinking into one of his *'three-cornered moods.'* (A Victorian expression for someone that has a dark, reclusive side nobody can reach), and became critical of his ability to solve the enormous problems in Nigeria. This was reflected in the letters Flora received in England.

They increasingly disturbed her and she wrote to her niece Hilda, *'I don't recognise him in his letters of the last eight months. I feel sometimes as if I were in a strange nightmare of being married to a stranger, but what fortunately remains always solid and unshaken is my trust in his goodness ... When we meet, I think all will be well... I am planning to give him a really pleasant little holiday, and shall try to do his health good and to make him happy first of all.'*

Madeira proved to be exactly the tonic Flora needed. From her balcony suite in the famous Reid's Hotel she could see the glistening blue sea, and smell the scent of a proliferation of flowers drifting in on the light summer breeze. It had been a long time since she had been able to relax like this, walking in the villages, talking to local people, reading, and writing to her close family and friends. The stress of the visit to South Africa, and the completion of the house was temporarily forgotten.

Madeira was a popular stopping point for ships on their way out east, and one unexpected visitor was Dr. Jameson. She was delighted to see him. He had completed his short prison sentence and was on his way back to South Africa for a more successful period in his life. Flora described him as '...*like Sir Frederick in being real and good... but it is one of the saddest faces I know.*'

As she relaxed, Flora started to feel and look younger than her forty-nine years. Her striking blue eyes contrasted beautifully with her thick brown hair. Her figure was still svelte, and she looked and felt good in the white dresses that she now enjoyed wearing. Her time dressed in black was over; she was looking forward to the days ahead.

Lugard sailed from Lagos at the end of May. As he stood on the deck looking over the ship's rails smoking a cigar and watching seabirds following in the wake of the ship, he was nervously thinking of the days ahead. He was now forty-four years old, his gaunt body punished by years of sun and fever, giving his skin a dark-yellow complexion. His cheeks were hollowed and his keen, hazel eyes sunken. He still kept his trademark moustache, but his hair was receding like an ebbing tide from his precipitous forehead. He was a striking figure, who could instil fear if required, but he had a disarming gentleness that only his closest friends and family knew. It was this side he wanted to show Flora, and was eager to give her his deepest love.

He had opened his heart to Flora, and told her the history of Catherine. When Catherine heard of the engagement, he received a torrent of abuse, concocting a story that he described later as '*an hallucination.*' He continued, '...*when she heard of my engagement to be married, she wrote letters of such bitter, stinging reproach and self-justification, as to throw a shadow over my marriage.*' All these mixed thoughts were going through his mind as he headed towards the woman he loved.

He arrived in Madeira on June 3, and Flora welcomed him warmly with a kiss. The suite was decked out with flowers, books and cushions, which she had carefully prepared. Warm Atlantic sunshine poured in through the balcony windows, the scent of the flowers was intoxicating. They spent the next happy week together strolling through the villages, basking in the sun and relaxing, before getting married. They chose June 11 for the special day and arranged a civil service at the Consulate. '*He had his frock coat and top hat, and I wore white with my white feather hat.*' It was deliberately a private, simple ceremony with only a few local witnesses, followed by a blessing in the church at Funchal by Archdeacon Linden. On returning to the hotel in a horse-drawn carriage, they were touched to find that '*the locals had arranged exquisite baskets of beautifully arranged flowers and a special lunch in the suite.*'

Ned was still in South Africa and wrote a heartfelt letter to Flora just before the marriage. He gave his full support to her and his wishes for their every happiness. Flora knew how close the bond was between the brothers, and how much Ned's blessing would mean to Fred. The letter meant a lot to her and she wrote back on the eve of the wedding,

'*My dear Ned,*

We are to be married tomorrow and I must write you one line today to thank you for the kind and reassuring letter which has just reached me. You 'know' that I shall make him happy you say. I trust with all my heart it may be so, for I have not the slightest doubt that he will add to my happiness in a way which, only one who knows as you do the chivalrous generosity of his nature, can understand. I believe there is nobody else in the world who knows him as you do, and for you to think that I shall be able to make him happy gives me confidence and encouragement. You may be sure that I shall do my very best for he is well worth making happy. He has been tenderness and kindness itself to me since he arrived here just a week ago. We have one more week here before we start together for Nigeria. In the life that lies before us, there is no-one, after Fred, to whose help in doing what I want to do for him I look forward more confidently and more affectionately, than to yours.'

A friend lent them a little house called *Camacha,* hidden up in the hills behind Fuchal, where they spent their honeymoon. The wave of emotion and peace that swept through Flora that day rendered her almost immobile, with Fred taking delight in looking after her every need. On June 13, she wrote to Hilda, '*I can hardly tell you how entirely at rest I felt - and feel… Nothing could exceed his kindness and tenderness to me nor the gentle care with which he is surrounding me …it all seems all dreamlike still, and I find myself from time to time looking at my wedding ring with a kind of surprised remembrance that it is there for life and that this new companionship is not to fade away, but to grow I hope clearer and more real as life goes on… I never thought before what a comfort the taking of hands is in the marriage-service… From the moment that we took each other's hands to plight our troth I had no feeling but of perfect peace in the service.*'

Letters of congratulation came pouring in from around the world. As well as from their families in England, Ireland, South Africa and India, there were warm wishes from George Buckle and Charles Moberly Bell, their close friend Lord Scarborough, Lady Kirk, wishing joy to her husband's greatest friend, and even from Flora's adversary at the Jameson enquiry, Labouchère There was a jaunty note from Lord Curzon, the Viceroy of India, saying, '*If it be the Flora Shaw I congratulate you. If it be another may she be equally brilliant and not less charming.*'

The marriage could not have started off on a happier note. After another nine days of bliss, they set off in good spirits on the *SS Jebba* on June 20, sailing to West Africa to start a new chapter, their lives now entwined.

CHAPTER 24
Nigeria – uniting the north

The balmy days in Madeira were soon replaced with busy preparations for the return to Nigeria. Lugard and Flora sailed to Lagos, and transferred to the river steamer *Empire* to navigate up the Niger to the new government capital at Zungeru.

As they wound their way upriver from the coast, past the palms and creeks, watching the crocodiles and hippos basking in the sun, Lugard nervously observed his wife's first reactions to this unforgiving country. It was Flora's first visit to Nigeria, and she was taking in the new sights, sounds and smells with the eye of an experienced foreign journalist. It was the beginning of the rainy season, but this year the rains were late and the mighty river was much lower than normal. This meant they had to stop at Lokoja, to wait for the monsoon rains.

Flora was pleasantly surprised by the deserted government house at Lokoja. It was perched on a hill overlooking the junction of the two rivers. Many rooms were empty, but it was still functional. The days were hot and uncomfortable. The turgid humidity sucked the energy from the body. It was cooler in the early evenings and Flora liked to sit quietly on the verandah watching the sun set over the distant misty hills.

They stayed at Lokoja for a month, with Lugard getting back to a frantic regime. He rose by six o'clock, greeted with a cup of tea by Flora, then walked the short distance to his office to work through a mountain of files until 6pm. If it was not raining, they went for a brisk walk to get some exercise, inevitably getting soaked in perspiration, before changing for dinner. This would be followed by a relaxing hour on the verandah, and bed between ten and eleven. It was a constant routine, with little variety, seven days a week.

Shortly after arriving at Lokoja, Flora arranged a dinner party for twenty guests to celebrate the coronation of Edward VII on August 9 1902. It needed some resourcefulness as all the ingredients had to be sourced locally. There was a brief panic in the kitchen when a hyena paid a visit during preparations, attracted by the cooking of the chickens. Flora borrowed some crockery from the mess, decorated the table with roses, and was able to offer the guests a few bottles of wine that she had brought from England. It all went well, with the King being toasted and the national anthem playing in the background.

All the guests were young English officers, well-educated and about to be sent into remote parts of the country, some over 1000 miles distant with no railway or telegraph communications. Many would die of fever, some during hostilities and a few from wild animal attacks. Flora looked at the eager faces and felt proud of them, at what they were aiming to achieve. They were trying to do their best for the country, the Empire, and for Lugard.

By August the rains came and river levels rose quickly. They moved up to Zungeru, but Flora found herself even more isolated in a small town that was expanding quickly. She wrote to Hilda, '...*Everything is much further away from civilization than I expected. Zungeru is a little town looking rather like a pretty English suburb, with white houses nestling among the trees, and in the distance hills rising to an occasional mountain in the sky. The pace at which Fred works is really wonderful and under his stimulus the place is rushing up like a crop of mushrooms ...Every day new houses appear and new roads are cut. The electric light plant is getting in order ...Everyone is now asking me about bringing their wives out and there is a general set towards civilization.*'

Flora watched her husband working unceasingly, and quickly appreciated just how much he had taken on. She wrote to Moberly Bell, '*I am beginning to realise the really big work which is involved in the administration.....Every office is under-manned and the extra work has to be got through somehow by expedients ...Sir Frederick is fortunately immersed in it all, and is content to work hard every day from six in the morning til night falls. Sundays are the same as week-days and except at meals I rarely see him ...I was astonished at Lokoja, which far from being a mere trading settlement under the Niger Company has become a considerable town ... The pace at which the country is being civilized is not realised at home. But a great deal more money is needed to do what might be done ...Sokoto and Kano are now writing that there can be nothing between us but war. These are the two most distant provinces which are still not annexed. Near us, the people are realizing all the value of peace...*'

A little later Flora wrote to a friend, '*We are at Zungeru ...little more than a year ago this spot was undiscovered jungle where hartebeest fed on the wild luxuriant grass and lions fed on the hartebeest...Sir Frederick has been ill lately and has been ordered, on pain of their resignation, to take an overland trip into the higher air of one of the interior provinces. It will be a 12 days ride and to reconcile him to spending the time, the Resident of the Province has just represented to him that there are two Kings to put on the thrones, and one to depose, which he might do en passant!'*

Flora had plenty of time on her hands and wrote long letters to Joseph Chamberlain giving a full account of Lugard's work in Northern Nigeria. She told him how Lugard was operating on tiny resources and how his health had suffered because of it, with the doctors urging him to seek employment at home. Finally she asked Chamberlain to come and visit Nigeria, to see the problems and progress for himself. With the war in South Africa still occupying his time, he politely but firmly declined. It was a frustrating time for Flora. She could see the problems that her husband was facing, but could only see him a few hours a day, and felt impotent in her desire to help whilst she was in Nigeria.

It was only a matter of time before she went down with one of the many fevers rife in that area. Lugard was always worried about her health and knew well the dangers of a fever. He wrote to Ned, '*The doctors peremptorily ordered her home and I insisted too and she has, with the utmost reluctance, consented – agreeing that it is beyond doubt, best. She is devoted to you, says she could tell you alone of anyone in the world all that she feels, for she knows you are my alter ego and says you understand me.*'

Once Flora returned to Abinger she recovered quickly, able to breathe again away from the suffocation of remote colonial life. After spending only five months together, this separation would have strained many marriages. For this unusual couple, there was an understanding and openness between them, a determination to protect the deep emotional bond they had. They were determined to work on the love that had kindled, combined with a dedicated sense of purpose.

Flora was convinced she could help Lugard more in London, and get him out of Africa before it killed him. Shortly after she returned to Abinger, Flora wrote the following letter on November 27 1902, '*...I am glad to have been in Nigeria, glad to have seen your work, and to have realised conditions which nothing but personal acquaintance with them could have enabled me to understand and I am glad too, dear, to be able to feel deepened respect and admiration for the character of the man whom I have chosen for a husband. Whether it is for joy or for pain I can feel as I felt when I promised to marry you that yours is one of the simple, sweet, heroic souls with whom it is an honour to be associated. I grieve to be separated* *from you but to have the hope of being able to win you to happiness in the future is well worth while...'*

Meanwhile war was looming in Sokoto, and Lugard knew he had to solve this problem before he could return home. In May 1902, before he had arrived in Madeira, he had received a brief, chilling message from the Sultan of Sokoto that stated his case clearly. *'From us to you. I do not consent that any one from you should ever dwell with us. I will never agree with you. I will have nothing ever to do with you. Between us and you there are no dealings except as between Mussulmans and Unbelievers, War, as God Almighty has enjoined on us. There is no power or strength save in God on high.'*

War was inevitable. The Sultan was not only the leader of one of the most powerful states in Nigeria, which had been so since the Caliphate was formed in the Fulani wars of 1804, but he was also the spiritual leader of over one million Muslims. Sokoto also had control of over two million slaves, the largest number outside the southern states of America. As long as the Sultan defied British rule, slave-trading would continue and there would be increasing trouble with many of the other Emirs.

In May 1902 the Second Boer War came to an end. The British people were tired of conflict. Jingoism was gone and they wanted peace. The last thing the country needed was another war in Africa, and this was signalled to Lugard by the politicians in the Colonial Office.

However, tensions were building in the north, and came to a head when a Resident, Captain Moloney, was murdered in the palace at Keffi in Zaria. The chief fled to Kano and was warmly greeted by the Emir, who rode in state with him. This was open defiance, being the second murder within a year. The lives of other Residents in the north were greatly at risk.

Exchanges went back and forth to the Colonial Office until December, when Lugard decided he could wait no longer. He announced his plans to mount a military expedition to Kano. The Colonial Office was not going to stop him, but neither did it like to have plans forced on it. Sir Montague Ommaney recorded at the time, *'I do not suppose that HMG will desire to forbid the responsible man on the spot to undertake an expedition that he holds to be absolutely necessary.'*

The Government felt it needed someone to keep an eye on Lugard, so General Kemball was sent from Lagos to Kano. On January 17 Lugard gave orders to Colonel Morland to advance to Kano before General Kemball arrived. Lugard had complete confidence in Morland, and wanted his own man in charge. It was a calculated risk and he wrote to Ned later, *'If we'd messed it, I should have been broke.'*

Colonel Morland marched from Zaria to Kano with 722 men,

twenty-four officers, twelve NCOs, four guns and four Maxims. Lugard followed on from Zungeru on February 2 with a small band of selected officers to survey, to look at potential railway routes, and to draw up political settlements as Morland advanced.

After Colonel Morland crossed the border of the Kano Emirate, he passed through a series of walled towns leading to Kano. He had sent ahead Captain George Abadie to act as a political officer with a small band of troops. The first small hostile town Abadie came across was called Bebiji, and he found the gates shut. He talked with the defenders, trying to persuade them to open the gates and not to fight. They refused, saying they were threatened with death if they opened the gates. The young captain fired a warning shell through the gate and killed the chief standing behind it and several headmen. The Bebiji panicked and Morland's men quickly secured the town.

Word soon spread to following towns, who all opened their gates to Colonel Morland and the chiefs fled to Kano. There was no looting or destruction and no harming of non-combatants. Lugard wrote later, 'Contrary to all their own experience and custom in warfare, the British troops did not harm them, and they remained quietly in their towns and brought ample supplies of food and water for the troops. These were duly paid for as though no war was being waged, for indeed, we had no war against the people of Hausaland, only their Fulani rulers.'

Colonel Morland's next objective was the ancient city of Kano. It looked a formidable obstacle that few Europeans had seen since Clapperton discovered it in 1824. The city housed over 30,000 inhabitants, and was surrounded by eleven miles of glistening red laterite mud walls varying from thirty to fifty feet thick, forty feet high, and interspersed with thirteen gates. These were made of wood or thick layers of cow hide. There were also double ditches in front of the walls and castellated fortifications behind, which had deterred centuries of invaders.

On closer inspection, some gates were in better condition than others, so Morland started shelling to test them out. The Zaria gate stood firm but the second was breached, and with bugles sounding, the troops charged in with ladders and axes. The startled defenders let out a burst of inaccurate fire and fled - as Lugard had predicted.

When Morland and his men passed through the gate, they were amazed to find a wide expanse still a mile and a half from the city with the Kano garrison of 800 horsemen and 5,000 foot soldiers fleeing. Morland pursued them inflicting 200 casualties, with no losses to his men. The small column of British troops pressed on and took the Emir's palace unopposed. They found a massive inner citadel covering thirty-three acres, with walls up to thirty feet high. One of the gates dated back to the fifteenth century.

The inhabitants were drifting around '*in a strange way looking on as if the matter did not intimately concern them…*' Morland discovered that the lack of resistance had been due to the absence of their leader, the Emir of Kano who had fled to Sokoto. The fight was by no means finished.

The Emir of Kano was called Aliu, and had a harsh and cruel reputation. He had fallen back to Sokoto with all the Fulani leaders and the bulk of his army, consulting with his councils. He knew that Lugard would want to depose him, and appoint the nearest heir as his successor. They were by no means united; Aliu had therefore taken every possible claimant with him and threatened them with death if they sided with Lugard. Three had already perished.

Morland put Captain Abadie in charge of the city, quickly set up headmen in the fourteen main quarters, and the markets were swiftly reopened. The slave market was already closed. He gave strict orders to the troops that there was to be no pillaging and the local people were to be treated civilly.

Lugard was delighted when he heard of Morland's success, and hurried to Zaria arriving on February 11. It took him five days to negotiate an agreement with the new Emir, after which he pushed on to Kano, battling against a hot harmattan wind blowing down from the Sahara. It took him three days to march to Kano arriving on February 21.

Lugard was impressed by the size of the city, the construction of the houses and the fortifications. He had never seen anything like this in Africa. He installed himself in the palace in a private audience chamber and wrote a letter to Flora. '*…It is a marvellous place. 18 feet square- walls of mud very thick. At each corner about 8 feet from the ground runs a curved arch of mud, but excellently finished, to the opposite corner…tapering to the centre of the roof…walls about 18 feet thick and centre of dome say 24 feet …the whole wall is covered in all kinds of quaint designs and shapes in white, black, pale blue and yellow, the latter being made up of ground up mica which glitters. The door is carved, and great quantities of Arabic writing have been found, and interesting correspondence with Sokoto. The arsenal contained enormous quantities of every conceivable kind of ammunition and even, I am told, some of home manufacture…*'

He toured the town and saw the grim evidence of a major slave centre. He went to visit the gaol. '*I visited the dungeon myself. A small doorway 2 feet 6 inches by 1 foot 6 inches gives access into it. The interior is divided (by a thick wall with a similar hole through it) into two compartments, each 17 feet by 7 feet and 11 feet high. This wall was pierced by holes at its base through which legs of those sentenced to death were thrust up to the thigh, and they were left to be trodden on by the mass of other prisoners till they died of thirst and starvation... The total space is 2,618 cubic feet and at the time we took Kano, 135 human beings were being confined here each night... there was not even standing room ...victims were crushed to death every night and their corpses hauled out every morning...it was empty and even when I myself went in three weeks later the effluvium was unbearable for more than a few seconds...One of the great pools in the City is marked where men's heads were cut off; another near the great market is the site where limbs were amputated almost daily.'*

The Emir started to mass his substantial cavalry and troops outside Sokoto, even though he was not confident of their loyalty.

By this time General Kemball and the Northern Nigeria Regiment had arrived from Lagos and took over from Colonel Morland. He left Kano with a force of six hundred men to march towards Sokoto. After one hundred miles they came to a thick belt of waterless scrub where they knew the Emir of Kano's forces were camped nearby.

Kemball sent a small scouting party of mounted cavalry led by twenty-eight-year-old Captain Wallace Wright to recce a detour to the south. Unbeknown to him, Aliu had panicked during the night, and had slipped away to the border disguised as a salt trader. His brother, the Waziri, had taken over and had set out with a large force towards Kemball.

The Waziri unexpectedly came upon Wright and his scouting party, and shots were exchanged. The young captain, who had only been in Nigeria a few months, could have retreated, but instead fell back and formed a traditional square with his well-drilled troops. He quickly gathered mimosa thorns as a protective barrier (as Lugard himself had done at Tofrek all those years before). The total force was forty-five men of the Northern Nigeria Regiment and one other white officer, with no artillery.

The Waziri had 1,000 horsemen, and 2,000 footmen armed with spears and some guns. The army lined up confidently dressed in flowing robes and high turbans. The horses were covered in quilted armoured cloth. For the forty-five men it would have been a terrifying sight. The Waziri spurred his men on and led the charge with his chiefs, shouting praise to Allah in a state of religious fervour, straight at the small square of soldiers.

Wright held his nerve and waited until they were within fifty yards to open fire. The leading horsemen fell in their dozens. The Waziri regrouped his troops and they bravely charged another ten times, firing wildly with the same disastrous results. Dead men and horses piled up in front of the square, some dead and dying only fifteen feet away. The attack lasted for two hours, and stopped only when the Waziri and seven of his principle chiefs were dead.

Captain Wright had one man wounded and lost three horses. It was an incredible feat of courage, supported by the discipline of his men, and the reliability of the latest rifles. For his action, Captain Wright was awarded the Victoria Cross and received it personally from King Edward VII in London the following November. He was to serve Lugard again ten years later in the war in Cameroons, and served on the Western Front in 1916. He ended his career as Brigadier-General, retiring in 1940 to live in Surrey, close to Lugard.

Wright followed the remnants of the Kano army, and was startled to see the Kano cavalry firing at its own retreating foot soldiers, punishing them for their inadequate performance. The small-walled villages shut their gates to the Waziri forces, which Lugard had predicted. They had made their decision; they preferred to have the rule of the British, rather than the cruelty of the old Emir. The Kano cavalry melted into the night.

Later that day, Lugard heard from another brother of the defeated Emir, called the Wombai, who sought peace with him. The Wombai asked if he could bring the many refugees who had fled, and the soldiers back to Kano. Lugard agreed, and sent out an Agent to bring the refugees to within six miles, and to escort the Wombai for talks.

The Wombai came nervously with his chiefs. After a long meeting, trust was established and the future of Kano was agreed. Slavery was abolished, freedom of religion was guaranteed, and the Wombai would be the new Emir after reaching agreement with the Sultan of Sokoto. Mohammedan law would prevail as long as it did not contravene British law, and existing rulers would be kept, but the High Commissioner would retain a veto. A new fairer tax system was agreed, along with land and mineral rights.

That day about 4,000 horsemen and around 6,000 people filed back into the city giving up their firearms. They were allowed to keep their spears, swords and mail shirts. The following day Lugard received a telegram from Joseph Chamberlain, '*Congratulations on successful occupation of Kano, by which a large number of people have been released from tyrannical oppression.*'

Lugard was deeply relieved. Not only was it a military success, but it vindicated his policy. He wrote to Flora that day, asking her to follow this up in the Colonial Office and *The Times*, to mute the criticism he knew he would receive. He would miss the boat to London, but now he needed to get to Sokoto as soon as possible to finalise the agreement with the Sultan.

The next day on March 7, Lugard rode out of Kano on a camel with seventy Yoruba soldiers. He was escorted to the gates by the Wombai and a squadron of horsemen who saluted their new leader. General Kemball and Colonel Morland with his 700 troops were about a week ahead of him. Seven days later Lugard reached the outskirts of Sokoto.

In front of the massive red walls of the city was a plateau and on the open slopes was an army of 15,000 horsemen and 3,000 footmen. Morland advanced slowly with his troops, four guns and a Maxim. It was soon obvious that only a small number of the Sokoto horsemen were going to fight. These came in small harrying groups and were easily repulsed. Morland overcame another group defending the standard, and with that the remaining Sokoto army scattered.

The British had lost one man, with around one hundred killed from the Sultan's army. There was no will to fight. The Sultan and the Magai (Emir) of Keffi fled from the battlefield to the borders of Bornu. A few months later both of them were killed in a fierce engagement at Burmi.

Lugard reached Sokoto on March 19 in a weak and disheveled state. The water they were carrying had contained soda and potash, and in the intense heat he had suffered chronic stomach pains, hardly able to eat. At the city walls he put on a clean coat, pinned on his medals to look more like a High Commissioner, and went to meet the Waziri of Sokoto.

The Waziri was a blind old man, (the previous Waziri had been killed in a skirmish) and was accompanied by his senior chiefs. Lugard gave them assurances that the fighting was over, and the option of bringing back the old Sultan or electing a new one. The chiefs quickly chose a new Sultan called Atahiru, who had chosen not to fight the British, and to whom Lugard took an immediate liking.

This appointment was crucial. The Sultan was the Suzerain of the Moslem rulers of Northern Nigeria, and exerted immense influence. At a further meeting with the chiefs, Lugard explained that the old treaties with the Royal Niger Company had become void, and that they were now under the authority of the British Government. He added, '*You need have no fear regarding British Rule, it is our wish to learn your customs and fashion, just as you must learn ours. I have little fear that we shall agree, for you have always heard that British Rule is just and fair, and people under our King are satisfied. You must not fear to tell the Resident everything and he will help and advise you.*' There was a murmuring of approval. The installation of the Sultan was held the following day, followed by a prayer recited aloud by the mullahs.

The next day Lugard left in high spirits, riding out with an escort of sixty mounted infantry heading east for Katsina, another important city famous as a centre of Islamic study from the fourteenth century. He covered 167 miles in six days, a record even for him.

The thought of seeing Flora again was spurring him on. He wrote to her, '*Your description of the bird sounds at Abinger, of your walks in the brisk, keen, spring morning are like a mental draught as one plods along the scorching track…the garden and early bulbs must now be growing interestingly. I wish I were there to see them, but I have, and I know you will have, a satisfaction in knowing that my task is being well done, and fully done before I leave.*'

There was still an outside chance of being attacked on the way to Katsina, as the Katsina people were divided on whether they should fight this infidel. It was not until thirty years later, when the Emir, who was a senior chief in 1903, was visiting Abinger, Lugard heard the full story. He told Lugard that the chiefs had debated whether to ambush the vulnerable little group as they travelled. Luckily they did not, and allowed Lugard to enter the city in peace.

Lugard confirmed the appointment of the Emir and complimented him on his city of learning. His successor, Emir Muhammadu Dikko CBE, visited Abinger many years later and afterwards placed a bronze tablet at the Yakada gate in 1939 to commemorate Lugard's entry there on March 28 1903.

Lugard fully recovered from his stomach ailments, and made good progress back to Kano to install the new Emir. He was met by the Emir-elect, a thousand horsemen, and throngs of people cheering him back to his new Residency. He followed the tradition in the installation by having a sword and a dagger fastened on him, and opening a state umbrella. Five days later Lugard reached Zaria and installed another new Emir recommended by the Sultan of Sokoto.

By April 17 he was back in Zungeru having covered eight hundred miles in an extraordinary thirty-eight days with new rulers agreed and installed in Sokoto, Katsina, Kano and Zaria. All Lugard wanted to do now was to get back to Abinger to be with Flora.

He caught the boat from Lagos on May 5. Three weeks later he was walking with Flora through the bluebell woods adjoining their new house, Little Parkhurst.

CHAPTER 25
Consolidation and change

Lugard could not wait to get back to Little Parkhurst and Flora, and to recuperate after his punishing tour. Work on the house had progressed slowly, so they rented a furnished house in Cadogan Place in London, convenient for his numerous visits to the Colonial Office, and for Flora to receive the increasing number of visitors for dinners and receptions. They made frequent visits to Abinger, for meetings with the architect to finalise details at the house, and for Flora to design the garden.

By October, they could wait no longer and with the builders still working around them, they moved in. There is a photograph showing Flora standing proudly at the front door with the new Lugard coat of arms and date of 1903 engraved in the stone lintel above them. Flora was eager to begin entertaining, with Rudyard Kipling and his wife Carrie being early visitors. They had just moved into their new house, Bateman's in East Sussex, and drove across in a new car or 'fire-chariot' as Kipling called it. It was an enjoyable and no doubt entertaining night, as recorded in a letter Kipling sent to Lugard in his own inimitable style following the dinner.

Bateman's   *Sep 30 1903*
Burwash,   *In the Month of Truce*
Sussex

In the Name of God, the Fashioner of Miracles, the Dispenser of Dominions; the Apportioner of the Yoke to be Borne

To

The Emir of the Emirs of Nigeria in his house under the trees over against the hills to the North.

I have read that which you gave me to be read, and it is sent to you again as promised. I send it by the accepted post of this country according to the customs of this country – as though it were dried figs or a parcel of tobacco; none the less I who am no more than a humble student of the Alphabet regard it in value as equal to thrice its weight in gold. By the perusal of that writing I have gained comprehension. Allah has enlarged the skirts of my understanding and I have bowed the forehead of reverence upon the carpet of wonder thrice.

For it is, under permission of the Most High, no smaller thing than the making of a Kingdom which I have read – a going out of giants and shahada – martyrs and witnesses to our Faith.

It is true that Allah-al-Bari has bestowed upon this unworthy one a gift of imagining the deeds of men in very far places but I testify that all I have imagined (and sold for bread) there is not in the whole of it one tenth part anything so wonderful as those things - and notably the going up and coming down of the little armies - which are set down, accomplished, in your writings.

This Emir is from the heart.

I desire therefore that, when the writings now returned are all set in order and made public (though that public is as a Pig before whom the pearls of the Red Sea are less acceptable than the straw of the Stye) I desire, remembering your promise, that one such book may be given for my own to put among my books. For it is well written.

"When a gold mine is shown to such an one, shall he not desire to camp by the side of it with mattocks and spades; and when learning is unrolled each man of right heart desires to sit long upon the carpet of wisdom"

And also I desire hereafter, one by one, as they may be written, all the little books that come out of your Kingdom which touch upon the customs and the manners and the fashioning of the Kingdom; of the making and breaking of the Emirs, the ordering of Justice and the discomforting of evil doers and mad mullahs.

If it is acceptable to you I will send you a little book in two days – a book of verses.

We arrived with speed and expedition at our house within four hours after that we had left your house. Extolled be the Beneficence of Allah Who hath caused men to make so commodious fire-chariots. We slew none upon the road, either going or coming- not even a sheep or a dog, nor did the messengers of the Cadi – the feraches of the Courts – in any way molest us.

We send salutations, I and my household – (having eaten your salt) to you and to your household and especially to the Lady Zobeide in her garden.

And we commend you to Allah al Malik, al Hakim-al Wasi- or Rascid-or Sabur-Who is the King, The Comprehensive, The Director, The Patient, Who has created men and Kingdoms.

Follows my seal
  Rudyard Kipling'

There followed a long and enjoyable friendship with Kipling over the next thirty years.

Lugard kept in constant touch with Zungeru whilst on leave. He still struggled to get more money for staff and the expanding infrastructure, especially to extend the railway, but he did manage to get agreement for his brother to be transferred from India. For Ned to be approved, Lugard had to confer on him the grand title of Chief Clerk, Office of the High Commissioner. Ned was vital to Lugard, delegating and mediating, and helping him through his black spells.

In October Lugard was asked to give an address to the Royal Geographical Society in London on Nigeria. A few days before the presentation he received an unexpected letter from George Goldie, who wanted to attend and give Lugard an introduction and eulogy. However, Goldie had been sent a copy of Lugard's address and took umbrage at a section he had written about the Royal Niger Company. He asked for a meeting to discuss its withdrawal.

Lugard's relationship with Goldie had cooled substantially since getting married, especially having heard the full story of his callous treatment of Flora. Lugard declined a meeting and wrote a curt reply agreeing to withdraw the section, adding, *'There is nothing in this passage which so far as my information goes is not in accordance with fact...'* He added, *'It is kind of you to have at first intended to eulogise me, but I am sure you will not misunderstand me when I ask you in no event to do so.'*

Goldie replied in conciliatory terms, anxious not to lose Lugard's friendship, but it was too late. He sent a letter the next day saying he would be unable to attend because of the death of an aunt, and a letter to the President extolling Lugard's achievements and virtues. Their long and deep friendship was finished, and although they saw each other a few times over the following years, it was rare for Lugard to speak of him again.

Shortly before his address, another significant event happened. He heard that Catherine had died from cancer in September 1904 at a home in Parkstone, Dorset. All Lugard's letters to her were returned and he burnt them all. She died a bitter and sad woman. This ghost was finally laid to rest.

The address to the Royal Geographical Society was given on November 4 to a packed house. The content was mostly political with the references to Goldie, brief and factual, and was well received. One of the tributes was given by Sir Harry Johnson, who had completed the work that Lugard had started in Uganda. He added with great warmth and generosity that 'Uganda certainly owes its incorporation in the British Empire to the really remarkable efforts of Sir Frederick Lugard.'

Lugard returned to Nigeria later in November and was not to return to England for seventeen months. During this time Flora wrote her own book, *A Tropical Dependency – An Outline of the Ancient History of the Western Sudan with an Account of the Modern Settlement of Northern Nigeria*. It was the first in-depth study of African history showing how far back sophisticated forms of government had been present in Africa, and focused on the reasons why slavery became so important, and not on its evils. It was published in 1905 under the name of Flora L. Shaw (Lady Lugard), to great acclaim, and it became compulsory reading for many of the new African leaders of the independence movements in the twentieth century. Lugard was immensely proud of her.

When Lugard returned to Northern Nigeria it was a fragile Kingdom. The Emirs were watching his every move for signs of weakness and indecision. Lugard needed to introduce a new tax system to raise funds and he plunged back into the administration of the fourteen provinces. There was an urgent need to visit each of them personally, to support the Emirs and explain to them the aims and methods of British colonial rule. He undertook a tour of 2,000 miles by land and 1,000 miles by water, a long and arduous journey, but ultimately rewarding.

He met old enemies such as the Emir of Kontagura (Ibrahim 'the Destroyer') who had threatened Lugard in Jebba, but had been reinstated as he still carried great influence. Because Ibrahim's base was only twenty miles away, Lugard decided to walk there. He marched with Ned and a small band of officials on narrow paths through the bush, led by an orderly carrying a Union Jack, much to the astonishment of the local people, and arrived covered in dust. In contrast the Emir was sitting on a fine black horse with a double-pommelled saddle, wearing a high indigo turban and greeted him in impressive style. His absolute command over his people was obvious, and his cooperation essential.

Lugard took Ned up the Niger River by canoe to the Ju-Ju rock at Jebba, and showed him the shell of the first house-station, which the jungle had reclaimed. They continued into Yorubaland, were carried across the Oyo River to Ilorin, where over 10,000 people thronged to see him. Forty-eight crowned Kings and four hundred chiefs assembled that day, dressed in a variety of traditional headdresses, gold crowns and plush robes.

Despite a Christian or Moslem veneer, the old pagan religions still dominated here. Many believed in the spirit world, and at night they heard the drums beating hypnotically out across the villages to announce strange, ancient rituals. This is one of the regions where the voodoo religion originated.

Lugard and Ned sailed up the Benue River in the government steam yacht *Corona* to Yola, an old slave trading centre, to install another Emir. After the ceremony, Lugard was presented with a royal black horse, some oxen, and hundreds of eggs. From Yola, they marched another 300 miles to the ancient Kanuri kingdom of Bornu.

In the capital Kukawa, they were met enthusiastically by the Shehu (King) and had long discussions about the new conditions of colonial government. The Shehu took an oath of allegiance in front of thousands of his people. Lugard wrote to Flora, '*Thirteen months ago there were sixty residents here and the vast ruins were full of leopards, hyenas and wild beasts. Today there are at least 20,000 to 30,000 in a growing city, in which houses and walls are being repaired in every direction...*'

They travelled to the smaller emirates of Gummel, Katagum and Hadeija. The first two had welcomed the British, but Hadeija had not. They had a reputation in their heavily fortified city for good fighting men and a fine breed of horses. The Emir was a tall, proud, strong man. He refused to stoop to enter a doorway – if it was too low they would have to knock the wall down for him to enter.

The Emir rode with his retinue to Katagum, and Lugard noted that the Emirs of Gummel and Katagum stayed on and formed a giant crescent around Lugard with their 1,000 riders, as if to protect him. The ceremony went off without incident but he had been warned by his Resident to be wary, which proved good advice.

Lugard enjoyed his return to Katsina, where he experienced another elaborate ceremony for the installation of the Emir, and sent a full description to Flora. The Emir carried out full ablutions before swearing on the Koran, and approached in a dirty white gown and filthy turban to indicate humility. He was presented with a new gown and a snow white turban wrapped around his head. Having taken the oath, the Emir was invested with a sword in a silver scabbard covered in Arabic inscriptions. A chief then beat a drum slowly twelve times, the signal for accession, and would not be beaten again until the next accession. It was the first time the drum had been beaten for eighteen years.

The Emir of Kano came forward alone, and Lugard presented him with installation presents from the Government - a fine saddle, a sword and a Persian carpet. The Emir was delighted. There was a blast from the long ceremonial trumpets, and the Katsina people rushed forward to carry their new popular King. Lugard mounted his fine black horse and inspected the assembled ranks of artillery, infantry and mounted infantry.

Various dignitaries visited Zungeru. The Sultan of Sokoto sent envoys to herald Lugard's return, with presents of horses, cattle and saddlery. They were shown round Government House and marvelled at the electric lights, plumbing and furniture. The Emir of Kano paid a visit to Zungeru and Ned was intrigued to see they followed the Fulani custom, where the eldest son of the King must never look upon his father's unveiled face.

A few days later, the King of Kiama arrived with a small entourage. He was a simple chief of the Bariba tribe from the eastern borders of Nigeria, an old friend who brought lion and leopard skins and guinea fowl as presents, and was delighted when Lugard welcomed him with full honours. Ned was impressed with the old man saying, '...*a first rate ruler, a fine type of native chief, a good horseman and a brave man...I was introduced to him personally and he literally stroked me down with delight at finding I was F's own brother!*'

Lugard sent a flood of letters to Flora describing his travels; the colourful characters, descriptions of the ceremonies and the beautiful vistas. Lugard shared his deeper thoughts late at night, contemplating the frailty and impermanence of empires. He was constantly grateful that Flora had married him, and by the end of the tour in May 1905, Lugard was impatient to be reunited with her and see their completed home.

It was another glorious summer at Little Parkhurst. The Visitors Book shows they entertained many visitors, including the Chamberlains, the Scarboroughs, the Kirks and Alfred and Neville Lyttleton both for business and pleasure. Flora had nearly finished her book and its publication was eagerly awaited. After that happy summer, the thought of another long separation for both of them was too much, and they had lengthy discussions on the options for their future.

The African colonies were expanding quicker than the Colonial Office could handle. Its cumbersome structure needed reorganising, and both Lugard and Flora thought a new department for African or tropical affairs should be opened, with an experienced Under-Secretary of its own. They called it 'The Scheme for Continuous Administration'. Lugard would remain the Governor, spending half the year in Nigeria and half at the Colonial Office. He had the utmost confidence in his staff in Nigeria, local rulers were now in place, and he could concentrate on policy and development.

Flora had already set about lobbying Parliament before Lugard had returned home, and throughout the summer they continued to push the Scheme. Flora targeted every relevant minister in the Balfour government with meetings, receptions and dinners, with mixed success. The Government was fracturing and becoming increasingly unpopular with the public. Horrific stories continued to emerge about the concentration camps in South Africa.

In November, Lugard reluctantly returned to Nigeria with nothing decided. By December, Balfour had resigned and called for a general election, which was held on January 12 1906. It was a landslide victory for the Liberals and the government under Henry Campbell-Bannerman came sweeping in with a host of new faces.

Flora scanned the names and was not impressed. Lord Elgin had become Colonial Secretary and a young upstart called Winston Churchill, his Under-Secretary. Elgin was not well-known at that time. An undistinguished Indian Viceroy, he was the son of a Viceroy, a family man of a shy and serious disposition, and likely to be inaccessible.

Churchill was entirely different. Still only thirty-one, he had served in four military campaigns, was a hugely successful writer and an eloquent speaker. He entered Parliament as a Conservative, castigated his own side for its incompetence and then defected to the Liberals. Lugard wrote to Flora when he heard, calling it 'bad news'.

Flora went to see Churchill the next day, marching into his office without an appointment. He sat at his desk surrounded by piles of files and looked up intently at this formidable woman. Flora came straight to the point. She had heard many good things about him from the Colonial Office but was concerned that he was not in favour of the Lugard Scheme.

Churchill reassured Flora that he had great admiration for what Lugard had achieved in Africa, but wanted him back in the summer to discuss his ideas first. He was not going to give any commitment to the Scheme.

He had read Lugard's memorandum making his case, and had also read the arguments of the mandarins who were alarmed at his proposals. Churchill sided with the latter. His concern was that having people such as Lugard in the Colonial Office, who had been powerful in their kingdoms and had extensive local knowledge, would only cause problems and delays for the Secretary of State.

Flora suggested a trial period of a year for the Scheme, but Churchill rebuffed it, saying the decision would have to be made by Elgin. Flora expanded her ideas on the development of a metropolitan economy in the colonies, with new products, communications and use of labour. Churchill was most interested in this aspect, and they parted on cordial terms, but Flora was not impressed by him. She wrote to Lugard, '...*it must seem ridiculous that a boy of his age and experience should have the power and influence that he has...*'

Meanwhile, Lugard was facing a crisis in Nigeria with a major incident in Benue state. At a small trading post in Abinsi on Benue River, a minor argument between a Hausa trader and a Jukun buyer from the local tribe had escalated and the Jukun man was stabbed. Violence erupted quickly and the locals slaughtered all the Hausa men, drowned their wives and children, and burned down the trading post.

As the trading post was on the main trade route to north-east Nigeria Lugard immediately dispatched one hundred men from Lokoja to check out the situation. He informed London that he needed to dispatch another six hundred troops as a backup force to stabilise the area.

The new government was determined to avoid any more unnecessary bloodshed, and ordered Lugard to cancel the backup force. Churchill especially held strong views on retaliatory punitive measures leading to massacres; he had fought at the Battle of Omdurman in 1898, and seen the bloody, excessive retribution carried out against the Mahdi. He was firmly set against further punitive expeditions intended to impress the tribes of the advantages of British rule.

Lugard's opinion was that if a strong response was not made, there would be further disturbances leading to even more bloodshed. He went ahead anyway and did not wait for a reply. When the troops arrived at Abinsi they found the store razed to the ground and the area strewn with headless corpses.

Two weeks later Lord Scarborough went to Nigeria and paid a visit to Lugard. They got on well, and as the new head of the Royal Niger Company, Scarborough came to make an inspection. Lugard had not heard back from the further expedition he had sent to Abinsi, but as they were sitting down for dinner, he received a disturbing telegram from Ambrusa, near Sokoto.

A company of seventy mounted infantry, with three British officers, had been annihilated and a Maxim gun had been captured at a small town called Satiru. They had been attacked by a new Mahdi called Mallum Isa and his followers.

The timing could not have been worse. Lugard's main force was over five hundred miles away at Abinsi, and only twenty-five native infantry were available. In addition, most of the Residents were on leave or sick, and the highly experienced Resident at Sokoto was travelling and exposed to danger.

They waited nervously for a week to see if any of the Emirs would join the rebels, and tried to get reinforcements from the Governor in Lagos whilst the troops in Abinsi were marching back. The Resident of Sokoto, Major (later Sir) John Burdon managed to get back to see the Sultan, who was relieved to see him unharmed.

A council of war was called by the Sultan of Sokoto, and they came out firmly on the side of Lugard. The Sultan immediately began assembling a force to attack the Mahdi at Satiru, which triggered a wave of telegrams from other Emirs pledging their support and troops to Sokoto.

On March 10, Lugard sent 573 rifles and several Maxim guns to Sokoto. Joined by several Sokoto chiefs they marched on Satiru. Two thousand rebels were waiting for them. They charged hysterically at the British troops waving axes and gardening tools, and the troops opened fire. When the smoke cleared there was no one left alive on the rebel front line. The remainder scattered. The troops then entered the town to continue the slaughter on further rebel suicide charges in the narrow streets. It was carnage. As they went through the town they found the bodies of the three British officers who had been killed, and buried them with full military honours.

The Mahdi, Mallum Isa, was killed and the main instigator and other ring-leaders were captured and tried by the native court. They were executed and their heads set up on spears. It was estimated that 1,500 rebels died that day. The final misery for the people of this doomed town came when the Sultan summoned the population of Sokoto to raze Satiru to the ground, and pronounced a curse on anyone who should rebuild its walls or till its fields.

Lugard's decision to condone this slaughter is inconceivable today, and raised many questions about his judgement at the time. In his eyes his actions were justified - he saw the massacre as a legitimate retribution that would prevent further bloodshed in the event of another uprising by a dominant Muslim group. He knew he had the full support of the other Emirs, and believed in the need for a show of strength. At the same time he regretted the medieval methods and barbarity used, that he had spent so long trying to eliminate. He knew his actions would cause a storm of outrage with the politicians in London, and the British people.

Lugard wrote to Flora a few days later, '...*the slaughter of these poor wretches has been terrible - but in the face of the death of three British officers I could hardly order to treat them with mercy and had to leave it to those on the spot. They fought very bravely indeed. The execution which our weapons can do will have a great moral effect...'*

The news of the massacre at Satiru caused uproar and disgust within the Liberal Party, and had major repercussions for Lugard. Prime Minister Campbell-Bannerman called it *'imperialist methods of barbarity'*. In a follow-up debate in the House of Commons, Churchill endorsed his view. *'Most certainly the Government wish to discourage these and all forms of military operations in West Africa and all other parts of the British Empire under the authority of the Imperial Government'.*

Ultimately Lugard's lack of control to prevent the carnage at Satiru cost him his job, and tarnished his reputation, and even questioned his place in African history. He was ordered to return to London for consultation. Shortly afterwards he received confirmation that his proposed Scheme was rejected by Lord Elgin.

He knew his days in Nigeria were numbered, so he swiftly carried out two more operations before he returned. First he exiled the Emir of Gwandu, who had been a thorn in his side. Then he dealt with Hadeija, which had been openly defiant, and had required the stationing of 250 soldiers in the town to keep order. After turning down several peaceful settlements, a small force marched on Hadeija. Five hours of street fighting resulted in the Emir, his three sons and many cavalry riders being killed. Six British troops were wounded. The next day the people returned to the city, the markets were reopened and a new Emir appointed. There was at last a fragile peace throughout Northern Nigeria.

These incidents led to some of Lugard's trusted Residents to question whether the people were being unnecessarily oppressed because of Lugard's methods. Charles Orr (later Sir), who as a friend, and with great respect for Lugard, wrote a few years later, *'In this state of civilization the big prey upon the small. Obviously the whole situation is hopeless unless one can trust the Emir...if he is using me to suppress the people, how must we feel towards the government? An alien race, different in colour, ideas, character, habits , religion backing up the other alien race in oppression – what must they feel ?... If I am merely an instrument of injustice and oppression – what is the use of me working myself to death in an unhealthy climate amid intense discomfort and in exile from home and friends ?...Of course there is only one thing to do, namely go on probing and probing and trying to get to the truth, knowing that one is doing one's utmost to replace injustice by justice.'*

The Satiru massacre raised many moral questions, and is still a contentious subject in Nigeria. Today's politicians struggle with just the same dilemmas arising out of modern conflict.

In May 1906 Flora was invited to stay with the Duke of Marlborough at Blenheim Palace. He had served as Under Secretary of State for Colonial Affairs from 1903 to 1905 and was impressed by her breadth and depth of knowledge on colonial matters. Whilst discussing the expansion of the railways in Nigeria, in which the Duke had a particular interest, his nephew Winston Churchill strode in and joined the conversation.

The discussion moved on to the future of Nigeria. Flora was taken aback when, after speaking of his high regard for Lugard, Churchill suggested, '*Abolish the West Africa Frontier Force! Give up the greater part of Nigeria, which is far too big for us to hold! Put an end to the whole system of punitive expeditions and be content with the peaceful administration of a small part of the whole.*' He added that he had not yet come to a firm opinion and would discuss it with Lugard.

Flora was astounded at the naivety of his statement and came out with all guns blazing. '*The Manchester electorate (Churchill's constituency) might think that 250 white men can govern some 12 to 20 million coloureds, and put down slavery, and open the country to trade without any military or police force, without an administrative organisation and without any expenditure on railways and other public works, but we who have the intelligence and experience know that they are quite wrong... How can you expect an Empire to prosper if these are to be your methods?*'

Churchill reeled under the attack, retreating on some of his points, but insisted that punitive expeditions were expensive and unnecessary. She came back with, '*Remember that in England, which has been settled for upwards of a thousand years we still have military and police forces without which would have been impossible to maintain a good government. All civilization rests on force as a background. I assure you there is nobody in the world less military than my husband; his government is essentially one of peace, but he has made it so by knowing how to repress disorder.*'

The debate continued back and forth, with the Duke of Marlborough listening with great interest, enjoying the verbal sparring, his preference for Flora's views. Churchill did listen to Flora, and respected her knowledge on colonial matters, and at dinner later that evening he approached her to continue the discussion, this time more tactfully. He turned on his charm to get her views on South Africa, where there had been a recent Zulu uprising in Natal.

Churchill looked tired dealing with continuous problems from the colonies, and irritated by questions in the House. Flora felt some sympathy for him, and warmed to him further when the next day she found comments in *The Times* in which he referred to Lugard as '*that distinguished soldier and administrator*,' and that '*he was coming home to confer with the Colonial Office about many things.*'

Shortly after Lugard returned from Nigeria on June 12 1906, Flora invited Churchill to visit Little Parkhurst before he was about to embark on a tour of East Africa. Churchill replied '*I would like nothing better.*' It was an enjoyable visit, the first of several. Churchill kept in contact and consulted with Lugard for many years.

When Lugard returned to England with Ned, he knew that it was unlikely he would be asked to return to Northern Nigeria. He had the consolation of knowing that he had left the Protectorate in a relatively peaceful state, a basic government administration system in place, and plans ongoing for an orderly development. On returning to London, he completed his final reports and continued discussions about the railway system and plans for growing cotton.

He enjoyed some of his happiest times with Flora, and they resolved not to be parted again. Lugard soon found that he had little in common with Lord Elgin. Lugard found him cold and unapproachable, and had no interest in discussing his ideas with him. His relationship with Churchill was far more cordial, but Churchill was not yet in a position of power.

In July Lugard handed in his resignation to Lord Elgin, who did not seem at all perturbed. He headed to Little Parkhurst for the most relaxing summer he had ever experienced.

It was short-lived. Flora's time lobbying in the Colonial Office and at dinners and receptions had made an impression on those that mattered.

The situation in China was deteriorating and a new Governor was needed in Hong Kong.

CHAPTER 26
Heading east

The offer of the post Governor of Hong Kong was a surprise, received only a few months after his resignation. The thought of governing a small, well-established outpost on the tip of China, of which he had little knowledge, did not inspire him. It intrigued him, but there was no excitement.

Flora saw it entirely differently. She saw it as an opportunity to explore and experience a new continent, and to learn about its ancient history and cultures. En route they could revisit America and Canada; she was eager to show her husband the places she had visited during her Klondike assignment nine years earlier, in 1898.

Also the climate in Hong Kong was better than in West Africa, and they could be together. This did attract Lugard, and besides, he was too young to retire. He accepted the job.

Flora's favourite niece, Hilda Brackenbury, accompanied them. She was in her early twenties, had almost become a daughter to them, and was travelling out to marry Lugard's aide-de camp, Captain Mitchell Taylor, who had been serving in the cavalry in India.

They followed Flora's previous route. They sailed to New York, then went by train across Canada via Ottawa and Winnipeg to Vancouver and the Pacific coast, enjoying the breathtaking views of the Rockies from the train window. They caught a boat to Japan and arrived at Yokohama near Tokyo, a busy, bustling commercial centre, the largest port in Japan, later destroyed in the Great Kanto earthquake of 1923. As they travelled south-west to Kyoto with its beautiful temples, Flora was fascinated by Japanese culture and traditions, and collected prints for Little Parkhurst. They continued west to Nagasaki and caught the boat to China.

They crossed the Pacific to Shanghai, a thriving international city with companies from Europe, Russia and Japan furiously competing for business, while the revolutionaries plotted to overthrow Empress Dowager Cixi. The final leg of the journey took them down the east coast of China by boat to Hong Kong. Lugard noted, *'Flora is simply and enthusiastically interested in a new place and a new environment and asks as many and as simple and embarrassing questions as a child of six.'*

As the boat approached Hong Kong, Lugard's mood became darker. He wrote to Ned, *'The day after tomorrow we reach Hong Kong and to you I will confess that as I look back over my life, I do not know that I can easily recall any task upon which I have entered ...for which I feel less aptitude, and from which I shrink more than the one that begins tomorrow.'*

Lugard arrived in Hong Kong on July 28 1907 full of trepidation. It was a hot, humid day. He had struggled into the Governor's uniform which consisted of a heavy, braided coat and a feathered hat and breeches that had cost him a hundred guineas. It was totally inappropriate for the climate, but perfect for the pomp and circumstance of the occasion. Flora was dressed in a long, white and gold dress, the latest fashion in Edwardian London, and together they looked the epitome of glamour to the intrigued spectators eager to see the celebrity couple.

They stood on the deck as the steamer passed the outlying islands and weaved its way through an armada of creaking Chinese junks; permanent homes to 50,000 floating residents. Lugard and Flora watched with curiosity as the Chinese welcomed their new Governor with exploding firecrackers. In Victoria harbour, a flotilla of Royal Navy gunships and European trading ships greeted them with cheering crews. The docks, wharfs and low colonnaded buildings, recovering from a devastating typhoon that hit Hong Kong the previous year when about 10,000 people died, were framed by the mist-covered hills of Hong Kong Island.

On the north side of the harbour was Kowloon, still a village, with the newly-built Nathan Road, dubbed *Nathan's Folly* by the sceptics who could see no future north of the island. An iconic Star Ferry chugged slowly across the harbour in front of them before they docked at the Kowloon terminal, where they transferred to a government launch for Hong Kong Island. To the north were the shimmering hills, thick forests and ancient villages of the New Territories, leased by the British Government from a reluctant China, only nine years previously.

They were given a seventeen-gun salute, with the warships joining in the cannonade of fire as they stepped off the launch at Blake's Pier onto the red carpet under an elegantly-carved awning. They were greeted by the Acting-Governor, Francis May, a tall, athletic Irishman with a serious demeanour, who escorted them down the palm-lined carpet to inspect a smartly turned out guard-of-honour. It was made up of an interesting mix of Indian, Chinese and British troops. An enthusiastic military band played the national anthem in the background. A line of senior civil servants and business representatives from the 'hongs' of the colony were introduced, before Lugard and Flora were shown to sedan chairs.

After a welcoming speech, the sedan chairs were hoisted into the air, Lugard carried by eight bearers in scarlet dress and Flora by four. They were ceremoniously paraded through the streets of Central district, with the crowds massed on the pavements and hanging out of windows to catch a glimpse of the new Governor, to see what manner of man he was. Flora noted, '…*it was a strange atmosphere for they were silent, not a word, not a cheer and yet not hostile. The crowd, as a corporate body had a curious way of conveying that it was pleased.*' There were fleets of rickshaws, no cars, but the first trams were running along the seafront.

They were carried to the Peak railway terminus at Cotton Tree Drive, and taken up in the steep funicular railway, climbing past thick sub-tropical jungle either side to arrive at the Peak station. Further bearers conveyed them to Mountain Lodge, the smaller of the two Government houses. It had originally been built as a sanatorium, but had been closed due to the walls trickling with condensation from the swirling mists that frequently engulfed the Peak. When the mists did clear, there were fine views over the harbour. The house was surrounded by pristine lawns and exotic flowering shrubs and trees. Here at last they could relax. Lugard threw off his '*soaking armour*', walked around the garden, and sat on the verandah with a cool drink to contemplate the task he had taken on.

The next day he was taken to Government House in Central, swore the Governor's oath and started work on the mountain of files at his usual frenetic pace. He had the luxury of Francis May as his highly-experienced Colonial Secretary, and a large number of officials in tow to run the mature economy, a stark contrast to the conditions in Nigeria.

Hong Kong had a population of 400,000 people in an area of 400 square miles, and was the second busiest port in Asia. Approximately 14,000 non-Chinese merchants, lawyers, bankers and engineers ran the back-up services and infrastructure, to keep the goods rolling through the port.

Lugard took an instant liking to Francis May (who became Governor when he left in 1912) and thought him a '*somewhat stolid, slow-thinking sort of fellow, quite good - devoid of Vaseline – gives you the idea you must play up to him, than he to you. Plenty of sense. I like him.*'

It is not known what Francis May thought of Lugard. He had been in

Hong Kong for twenty-six years, and had been running the colony for months since the previous Governor, Sir Matthew Nathan had been posted to Natal. He was not going to let this wild man of Africa upset things. May was certainly not slow-thinking when he was the target of the only assassination attempt on a Governor in 1912. The bullet lodged in the chair in which he was sitting, and he escaped unscathed.

Lugard soon realised that with a well-established government in place, he was merely a figurehead. He wrote to Ned, *I realise my role will be to endure fools gladly, and sign my name perpetually.* He was shielded by May from interfering in the well-oiled machine running Hong Kong. His main role was to manage the Legislative and Executive councils and to conduct a busy social schedule with his wife, a task that he hated.

After a short time he felt he had made a grave mistake. He could not see any big projects he wanted to get involved in, and without Ned, depression crept back. Flora wrote to Ned, *'...and you know without my telling you how difficult life grows for the rest of us when that it is the case.'*

Flora had a different perspective on this new life, seeing it as a journalist. Hong Kong was a busy, commercial centre, with many important figures passing through the colony. She saw the social functions as her ears to the colony. She started to learn Cantonese, and read extensively on Chinese history and culture. She quickly realised that the new century had ushered in big changes and dangers for China.

There had been the Boxer rebellions with attacks on foreigners in 1900, which led to the capture of Beijing by commercial powers, and resentment of the Manchu rulers by the Chinese. Concessions were being given to European powers, with Britain leading the way opening up the ports and building railways, causing further resentment among the Chinese populace. China was a bubbling cauldron. If it boiled over, Hong Kong would be the first to be affected, with peace and trade threatened. Flora helped Lugard understand his role, the importance of helping the local Chinese as well as the merchants, and pointed towards projects in which they could both be involved.

Within a few months Lugard felt growing confidence managing the Legislative council. Flora was working flat out, doing the social rounds, interviews with the press, making speeches and spending time supporting local clubs and societies.

With Hilda's help, Flora transformed the two Government houses that had laid forlorn for the previous fifteen years under Nathan, a resolute bachelor. They supervised the redecoration of every room, and the construction of a large connecting staircase to the garden, with illuminated arches.

The refurbished ballroom allowed for banquets for up to 200 people. A new social era dawned. Regular dinners for forty guests were held, with invitations being highly sought after by the influential and decision makers of Hong Kong.

Government House became the centre for a continuous stream of foreign dignitaries, officials, generals, admirals and diplomats visiting Hong Kong. They included Chinese and Japanese princes, Indian Rajahs, the President of the United States William H. Taft, Kier Hardie, and Mrs. Alice Keppel (mistress to Edward VII). A number of Flora's old literary friends passed through Hong Kong, and Sidney Webb, a British socialist, economist, reformer and co-founder of the London School of Economics.

Although uncomfortable in the role, Lugard did the rounds of the sporting clubs, including cricket, football, yachting, tennis, polo, and the popular horse racing at Happy Valley, all of which were mired in the stultifying class divisions of England. Lugard noted, '*Flora does all the right things, talks to the right people, admires the pretty, is nice to the dull ones and kind to all the lame ducks.*'

Although he had been used to the hectic social life in London, he was embarrassed being the centre of attention, saying, '*It gives me a curious feeling of having suddenly been withdrawn from a life of work I understand, to act a part in a stage play which I have not worked up. I feel it is not I who is being saluted when I come into a council or at a racecourse with God Save the King, but some other idiot in whose place I am masquerading.*'

He accepted that Hong Kong was a commercial colony where '*the men are all frankly here to make dollars and the women to amuse themselves in a reasonable and proper way.*'

Soon after they arrived in Hong Kong, they entertained a new Viceroy, Chang Jen Chun, who arrived in a Chinese warship on his way to Canton to take up his post. He had a large powerful face, with a genial disposition and an agreeable smile. He had travelled widely, was used to European food, could understand English but deliberately spoke through an interpreter, and was a man of considerable influence.

It was a pleasant meeting and Lugard and Flora were invited to Canton. They travelled on the Government yacht *HMS Alacrity* which was '*...admirably comfortable, and obsolete as a fighting ship,*' and docked at Shamin in the European settlement of Guangzhou city. They were carried through the granite-paved streets escorted by forty khaki-clad soldiers with sword bayonets, led by a large Chinese officer sitting on a fat, white pony, which mesmerized them as it waddled along.

After formalities there was magnificent lunch, with a large amount of alcohol consumed including champagne, sherry, port, liqueur brandies and whisky, with many toasts, starting with the Empress Dowager of China and King Edward VII. This was followed by a rather confused conversation on the six doctrines of Confucius, due to the inebriated state of the translator.

It was a good introduction for Lugard on the importance of Chinese banquets as part of political functions, and it became clear to him that the prosperity of Hong Kong depended on good relations with Canton. He invited the Viceroy back to Hong Kong again in 1909 for a large banquet, which continued to improve relations between Britain and China. It was the first time a Chinese Viceroy had ever accepted such full hospitality in Hong Kong.

On October 1 1907, Hilda married Captain Mitchell Taylor. The large wedding reception was held in the newly-renovated ballroom, when Lugard opened the proceedings with the State Lancers' dance, having had a few lessons from Hilda. It was a happy family occasion, but shortly after the couple returned from the honeymoon, tragedy struck. Hilda went down with blood poisoning. Her condition gradually worsened, and developed into meningitis. She died suddenly in early December. Flora was distraught, having been present at Hilda's birth and had virtually acted as her mother when her sister Mimi died. It was a miserable Christmas.

To counteract her sadness, Flora threw herself back into her work, but pushed herself too far and became ill from exhaustion. Lugard continued his duties and insisted on nursing Flora as well, surviving on a minimum of sleep. By spring, Flora still hadn't recovered her energy, and reluctantly she returned to England in May to recuperate. Lugard put her in the care of Ned, '*the only absolutely reliable man on earth,*' for six months. Their hopes to be together were once again dashed.

There were four big issues that Lugard wanted to address in his first year of office; to carry through plans for a rail link to China, to improve sanitation in the colony, to deal with the opium problem, and to radically improve education.

He had years of experience on railway planning and construction from his time in Nigeria, so he tackled the Kowloon to Canton railway project with enthusiasm. The Chinese had wanted to develop a national network of railways, a plan which had been presented to the Imperial throne in 1895, but there was resistance to the connection to Hong Kong. China considered it a political and commercial intrusion, possibly a military danger, but the British saw it as essential to develop trade.

In 1905 the Chinese had accepted a British loan to pay for the section of railway from Canton to Hong Kong, and it was from the repayments that the Hong Kong section would be built. It was only twenty-two miles long with five stations, but there were many engineering problems traversing through mountainous territory and complex geology, requiring forty-nine bridges, five tunnels, land reclamation and other land to be acquired.

The project was controlled by the Colonial Office and engineers in London, which to Lugard was too remote. They in turn retaliated that he was interfering. This was probably true, as he immersed himself in the finer detail, but he correctly questioned the design of the bridges, which resulted in new designers being appointed. Lugard also tried to get the rolling stock built locally, a move strongly resisted.

The preliminary cost for the line was £500,000 but this quickly rose to £1,200,000. There were many heated debates in the Legislature on the costs, but Lugard gained respect for his sound arguments for increasing the budget and his intricate knowledge of the details.

He enjoyed visiting the tunnels being driven through the mountains of Kowloon. They used Chinese and Italian tunnellers from projects in China, replacing the original British workers who were unable to stand the heat and humidity, and only lasted a month. The tunnel linings were made from bricks sent from India, as they did not have the right local materials. Steam shovels excavated their way through the hills, and the bridges were constructed using the latest technology - reinforced concrete.

The line was completed in April 1910, and although the most expensive railway per mile in the world, was a technical triumph. Lugard had the pleasure of driving the first engine from the new Kowloon terminal station to the Lo Wu border.

Lugard was unable to attend the official opening ceremony on October 1 1910, as he had to be in London. Tables and chairs were set up at the border, and a colourful group of visitors in Edwardian finery and straw boaters celebrated the opening, eating cucumber sandwiches and drinking champagne as though they were attending Henley Regatta. The first train to Canton ran the following year, and proved an immediate success with three times the traffic predicted. Plans started immediately to extend the lines, which continue to this day.

When Lugard arrived in Hong Kong, there were immense social problems. The majority of the poor Chinese lived in densely populated slums strung out along the rim of Hong Kong Island, overlooked by the prosperous Europeans living on the Peak. There were few water and sewage connections, and plague outbreaks happened at regular intervals.

In 1894, over 3,500 people died of bubonic plague, and special plague medals were given to those in the Army regiments that fought it. The supply of fresh water was a major problem. The Chinese population was always transient, planning was difficult, and so was the control of diseases. New reservoirs were being built, but the council was limited by restricted revenue, and there was concern that if taxes were increased it would drive people away.

Lugard called meetings with the Chinese communities to see where improvements could be made. He suggested ways of saving water. He encouraged the research at the local Tung Wah hospital which combated infectious diseases with Chinese and western treatments, and where they ran a dispensary and mortuary. He instigated a purge on rats, and discouraged the habit of leaving dead bodies in the streets. He set fines for spitting, and was astonished when a petition of 8,000 signatures was submitted against his spitting law, and had to form an anti-spitting committee - which failed.

Opium had been a sensitive issue in China since the Opium Wars of 1858 and 1860, when cultivation started in China on a large scale. It wasn't until 1891 that a vote was passed in Parliament that the Indian production of opium was morally indefensible, and not until 1907 that the British government signed an agreement limiting the export of opium from India, with cessation by 1917. The Empress Dowager also issued an edict in 1907 to cease poppy production over ten years, and to close the opium dens. She did make an exception for the over sixties – which included herself.

In May 1908 a surprise resolution was passed in Parliament initiated by a zealous Mr. Johnson of Nuneaton to close the opium dens of Hong Kong immediately. It ended up on Lugard's desk. There were over one hundred licensed opium dens in the colony, so Lugard asked for time to carry out his own investigation to see how bad the problem was. He visited a large number of divans (dens) in 1908 and was surprised at what he found. He wrote to Flora, *'No-one seemed surprised or in any way resented our entrance, the men smiled good-humouredly and went on chatting...Much more tobacco than opium seemed to be smoked. The divan was a narrow room 20 or 30 feet long with clean lounges on either-side, and a passage down the middle. On each divan two or three men lounged...all were animated and intelligent and there were none that were besotted or stupid...I must say that the net impression conveyed to one's mind was that the so-called vice was really a temperate and satisfactory substitute for alcohol ...You could not find such scenes in English public houses!'*

He carried out further surveys and found that at most, 1.5% of the total Chinese population and 10% of adult males were opium smokers, the majority being casual. This contrasted with the wildly emotional statements of the abolitionists who had most of the Hong Kong males down as drug-deranged addicts. One official in Whitehall described '*how once this vice masters a Chinaman, he sells all he has, his land, his wife and his children…and dies of cold in winter stripped naked in the street.*' On further analysis Lugard found the problem to be with the merchants, the suppliers.

There was a well-organised system in place with £5,000,000 worth of raw opium coming from India per year sold through a 'farmer,' with many people benefiting down the chain. Immediate closure would have serious economic consequences in the colony, including a major tax revenue loss to the British. Lugard therefore proposed a phased closure starting from 1910, and compensation for imperial revenues.

After many months of debate, the majority of Parliament came round to his way of thinking and the phased closures were finally accepted. The result was that it drove the trade underground, created illegal drug barons, and a big increase in morphine and cocaine addiction. Those problems are still with us today.

Lugard felt isolated when Flora went back to England, and struggled for the six months she was away. He found consolation walking the trails being laid out on Hong Kong Island, including a new circular walk around the Peak with magnificent panoramic views across the harbour to Kowloon. This path became Lugard Road, and the walk is still enjoyed by thousands of tourists every year. He spent time in the beautiful grounds of Government House, especially in springtime, when there was a stunning show of azaleas, reminding him of their garden in Abinger. One day, when he was wandering around the grounds he was approached by a visitor and asked for directions. He was so astonished and bemused to be mistaken for a gardener that he directed the way, the visitor continuing on none the wiser for his encounter with the Governor.

He wrote to Flora every day, and made sure to include details of the continuous stream of visitors to the colony, to keep her spirits up. The brother of the Regent of China arrived unexpectedly for lunch one day, along with twenty-two admirals, several generals, and a host of attendants, followed soon after by a Japanese admiral and seventeen captains, complete with geisha girls. He was surprised to be asked by the admiral why the British didn't fight the Germans immediately instead of waiting for them to increase their strength.

Lord Kitchener stayed at Government House during a tour of the Far East, to study the defences of Hong Kong. He was famous for his success in defeating the Mahdi at the Battle of Omdurman in 1898, and chased by the press wherever he went. He was friendly and unaffected, but Lugard found his obsessive passion for collecting porcelain disturbing. Sir John

French visited, another Army general who spent several days discussing the defences of Hong Kong, and the deepening crisis in Europe.

The American fleet called at regular intervals and Lugard was invited to a grand dinner on board the flagship by the admiral. He was disturbed when the admiral highlighted some special oysters that he had procured, of which Lugard had a profound dislike. He thanked him kindly, and spent the meal discreetly disposing of them in his pocket.

In December, Lugard heard the welcome news that Flora was feeling stronger and able to sail back to Hong Kong. He had started work on a new project, and could not wait to get Flora involved.

Lugard wanted to build a University.

CHAPTER 27
Hong Kong legacy

Lugard started taking an intense interest in education, strongly supported and encouraged by Flora. He wrote to her in 1909, '*I have never before in my life, had anything to do with education and as a new subject it interests me immensely. Before I leave this Colony, I hope to make considerable changes - I hope, improvements.*'

He paid frequent visits to many of the seventy schools in Hong Kong, both Government and mission. He saw a strong desire for the 6,000 Chinese children to gain knowledge and learn English. They wanted a better life, and they could see that knowledge was the key to power.

China had been trying to reform, but was in disarray after the closure of the civil service examination halls; Chinese students had turned to Western higher education in Britain, America, Germany, and to a lesser extent in Japan.

Shortly after arriving in Hong Kong, Lugard was approached by Mr. Hormusjee N. Mody, a rich, elderly Indian Parsee businessman, one of many Indians who had contributed substantially to the prosperity of Hong Kong. Mody had already met Flora, and wanted to start an endowment for a University of Hong Kong, and offered £15,000 to start the fund.

In March 1908, Lugard called a meeting of representatives to discuss how further funds could be raised. He estimated that around three hundred students would qualify for University, and maintained studying in Hong Kong meant substantial savings to Chinese parents rather than sending their children to Europe. His vision was a University that taught arts, sciences, engineering and business, and there would be freedom of religion. There would be hostels for the students and he called for preliminary costings.

The Colonial Secretary questioned his estimated building and running costs, and showed little enthusiasm for the project, concerned

Fig 11. Lugard family photograph, England 1864

Fig 12. Sir Edward
Lugard, uncle of FDL,
photo taken around
1890. *'Your advice
has more weight to me
than anyone else in
the world'*

Fig 13. Lugard
around 16 years old
at Rossall school

Fig 14. Edward
Lugard (Ned),
brother and alter ego

Fig 15. 9th East Norfolk Regiment, 2nd Battalion,
'The Holy Boys' Afghanistan 1880

Fig 16. Captain Lugard,
adventurer and writer 1893

Fig 18. Sir George Goldie, founder
of The Royal Niger Company

Fig 17. Sir John Kirk, leading
anti-slaver and mentor

Fig 19. WAFF staff at Lokoja 1898. *'Many would die of fever, hostilities and wild animal attacks'*

Fig 20. The first nurses in Nigeria at Lokoja 1900. Lugard recommended them all for decorations.

Fig 21. Amalgamation Day procession, Lagos 1 Jan 1914

Fig 23. Flora in
Hong Kong 1912

Fig 22. Lugard,
Governor of Hong
Kong, receiving the
Viceroy of Canton
1908

Fig 24. Flora in England
1907. Oil painting by
J.E. Blanche 1907

Fig 26. Hong Kong University
1912

Fig 25. Mr H.N.Mody. Flora made
a last desperate plea to increase his
donation to build the University

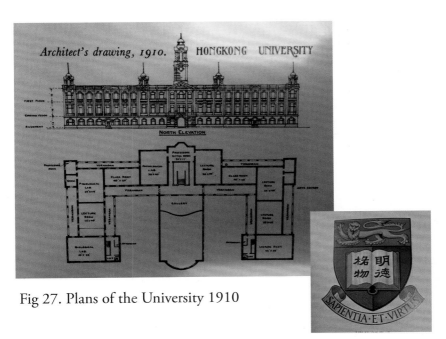

Fig 27. Plans of the University 1910

Fig 28. Coat of Arms of
HKU 'Wisdom and Virtue'

Fig 29. Durbar at Kano 1913. *'Each Emir had a picked band
of horsemen who charged at full gallop halting before us'*

Fig 30. Nigeria Amalgamation Day Lagos 1 Jan 1914

Fig 31. Rudyard Kipling.
Visited the *'Emir of Emirs'*
in 1903

Fig 33. Baron Lugard
of Abinger 1929,
'Me a Peerage! What for?'

Fig 32. Dame Flora 1916, *'I am
loving and appreciating your qualities
more and more every day'*

Fig 34. Emirs' visit to Little Parkhurst 1931. Sultan of Sokotu, Emir
of Kano, Emir of Gwandu, Governors of Nigeria and Uganda

Fig 35. Lugard in his study at Little Parkhurst
'I am always thinking of her, and if I sleep, I dream of her'

Fig 36. Little Parkhurst 1940.
'A centre for lively discussions at the weekends'

at the potential political effects as China became increasingly unstable. Lugard was undeterred, and lobbied for support from the Universities in England, and local hongs such as Jardine Mathieson, and Butterfield and Swire.

He encountered hostility on all sides. Competing schemes in China were mooted, and there were concerns that trade would be switched from the Europeans to the Chinese. Lugard became depressed about the whole scheme, writing to Flora, *'I am by no means liked here. Even the University scheme which you applaud, is unpopular…never, I think in my life have I received such consistently hostile and sneering criticism without even the credit for good intentions…'*

Flora rallied to his cause. She first went to see Lord Crewe at the Colonial Office, and used all her persuasion and charm to win the first grant, and convinced him of the benefits of good relations with China. She followed this with visits to the head offices of all the main Hong Kong companies in London, badgering and cajoling the executives.

Lugard went to see the Chinese British Ambassador, Sir John Jordan in Peking. He supported Lugard's idea and, after an argument with the Colonial Office, got a contribution from the Chinese government, as well as further pledges from the Chinese business community. By December, Lugard had raised enough pledges to go to the Legislative Council and ask for a grant of £5,000. They agreed.

Meanwhile he instructed the consultants to start the detailed building plans, and was disturbed to find the costs had risen to £28,500 pounds. This was well over Mody's pledged donation, due to expire at the end of the month. Mody's health was also failing, so Flora made a last desperate plea for him to increase his donation. She promised to get him a knighthood. That clinched it, and Mody finally agreed on December 31 1909.

Lugard was able to write to Flora, *'I have won my University.'* Separately he wrote, *'All my other public schemes have been my own, emanating out of my own work. This is yours. I took it up at your strong instigation…Mody knows how keen you are about it, and he has profound admiration for you … if it goes through to success, the credit will be yours.'*

Further pledges were promised, with £20,000 coming from the Viceroy of Canton, followed by donations from the merchants of Hong Kong. By February Lugard was feeling much more confident.

The proposed site was agreed, a twenty-minute walk to the west of the Central District in a prominent position overlooking the harbour, and detailed drawings continued. There was a central block for sciences, engineering and business, with a nucleus for Arts, and libraries; and accommodation for Medical and Engineering Faculties, as well as preliminary hostel rooms for seventy students.

On March 16 the foundation stone was laid, watched by an excited audience of two thousand people from the elite of Hong Kong and members of the Colonial service, to the Viceroys of Canton and Nanjing. A frail Mr. Mody was given pride of place. In his speech, he paid tribute to Flora, but was so overcome with emotion that he was almost unable to finish. Lugard, dressed in a fine grey suit and waistcoat, and a top hat finished in silk, rose to give his speech. He took his time to look round and wonder at the contrast to his experiences in Africa. He never enjoyed public speaking, but this time he was enthused with passion and had learnt it by heart. After a tribute to Joseph Chamberlain for being 'the Missionary of Empire' he continued, '*Let us then exercise an imperial imagination in regard to this University and not confine our view to the horizon of the immediate present. We are endeavouring not only to afford the highest educational facilities to the citizens of Hong Kong, but to hold out the hand of friendship and to assist China to educate her sons without exposing them to long exile and the risk of denationalization by sending them to Europe and America. Shall we, by doing so, create skilled rivals to compete against ourselves? I refuse to believe that men of British race have come to be afraid of fair and honest competition. The justification of the British Empire lies in its results. So long as it stands for impartial justice, so long as its aim is to raise and to educate the peoples who are subjects of our King, or who are contiguous to his boundaries, for so long will it prosper ... It will pass away as other Empires have passed away before it, but I believe that history will record of it that it was founded on something higher than territorial conquest or national aggrandizement ...I have been the humble instrument by which the confines of the Empire were enlarged in some directions. These days are past. It is no longer an age of acquisition in which we live, but an age of development, and if this Colony becomes ...the centre of educational progress in South China, you will have achieved a nobler extension of the principles which underlie the British Empire than any which accompany territorial expansion...*'

He emphasised that Mr. Mody had insisted on the best quality materials, and only the highest calibre of staff to be employed. He finished, to the delight of the audience, by announcing the award of a knighthood for Mody.

The foundation stone was lowered from a tripod and with a flourish of mortar from a specially made golden trowel, it was laid to great applause. It is inscribed, '*This foundation stone was laid by Sir Frederick J D Lugard KSMG, CB, DSO on 16 March 1910. This building is erected and presented* to the Colony by H. N. Mody. A Parsi gentleman 50 years resident in Hong Kong.' The stone is still there today.

His Excellency Wei Han, Viceroy of Canton replied with a speech emphasizing China's history and length of civilization, which he read in English. '*Geographically Hong Kong is a portion of China, and what makes for the good of one part must naturally reflect profitably upon the whole of the country. It is a universal axiom that the man that can make two blades of grass grow where only one thrived before, is a worthy citizen, but how much more valuable to the world at large is the country which can ensure the growth of such a tree of learning as is today being planted? China ever has been and always will be, a home of study; the nation has not, of course, developed and pursued the line of march taken in the West...China is a vast empire, which, centuries before the European nations evolved from the barbaric state, possessed her schools and her regulated system of civilization...China is at one with others that feel the impulse at their hearts to acquire what is best of the numerous world-changing advances in scientific, industrial, political and social life...It is for this reason that a University in Hong Kong is welcomed by the Chinese...*'

It was an immensely satisfying day for Lugard, and he could not wait to write to Flora that evening. Ned had written the previous week that Flora had been taken ill again with acute appendicitis. What Lugard did not know was that an emergency operation had been performed, and for a few days she was close to death. He wrote on that memorable day, '*... Well now I have told you all about it. You will like dear old Mody's reference to you – he almost worships you, dear old man – when he read that part in a voice of feeling and an almost reverential tone, there was great applause...I am in great spirits tonight. Physically perhaps, it is the reaction after the double tension of your illness and this ordeal, but it is founded on good cause...The sunshine of the outer world has got into my heart this evening.*'

The design was completed by the chief architect, Alfred Bryer of Leigh and Orange, and construction commenced soon after. The building was completed in February 1912. The search for the Vice-Chancellor started, and when Lugard returned to England, he visited Manchester and Birmingham Universities to study their administrative systems.

It took nearly two years to find the right candidate which eventually came through a recommendation from Lord Crewe. He put forward (later Sir) Charles Elliot, a man of extraordinary intellect, an ex-diplomat who spoke twenty-seven languages, was an expert botanist and Vice-Chancellor of the newly-opened Sheffield University. He had been a High Commissioner in East Africa when Lugard had been in Nigeria, and had resigned after an argument over land rights, so they knew each other. He was an excellent choice and during his chancellorship learnt another two languages before returning to the diplomatic service in 1919.

Lugard returned to England in April 1910, and spent the summer helping Flora recuperate, and acquired more information for his beloved University. In September they returned to Hong Kong together, this time travelling across Siberia by train to Peking.

He was given a surprisingly warm welcome in Peking and had the luxury, for the first time, of a motor car laid on for him. He was invited to a dinner at the Students Club by Chinese students who had been educated in Britain. He was welcomed by Dr. Wu Lien Teh, who was complimentary about Hong Kong University, calling it *'a gateway from Europe to the East'* and welcomed the decision to teach in English. Lugard emphasized the progress and moral aims of the University, which was well received.

With Flora by his side, the next six months in Hong Kong was another happy period for Lugard. Shortly after returning, he learnt that his deputy Francis May had been appointed Governor of Fiji. The two men had worked well together, and he was sorry to see him go. Lugard gave a warm farewell speech in the Legislative Council and to his surprise, the tough and distant Irishman almost broke down and was hardly able to answer.

His successor was W. D Barnes who, after only a short time in office, suffered a colonial death by having a fatal heart attack whilst playing polo. He was succeeded by the brilliant Cecil Clementi, who eventually became Governor in 1925, and was of great assistance to Lugard during the setting up of the University.

On returning to Hong Kong, Lugard looked with increasing concern across the border, hearing reports that law and order was continuing to break down. Riots had started in Canton in October 1909 after Sun Yat Sen, the Chinese revolutionary, had sent a Japanese freighter full of arms to his supporters in Canton. It was seized by a Chinese gunboat and Japan demanded the boat be returned. This led to a boycott and destruction of Japanese shops in the city.

Sun Yat Sen, who later became the founder of the China Republic, was based in Hong Kong with other revolutionary groups taking refuge in the Colony, and determined to overthrow the unpopular Manchu dynasty that had reigned China for 300 years. On November 15 1908, the Empress Dowager Cixi died, having appointed her young nephew Pu Yi successor.

Riots broke out in Hong Kong in support of the popular revolution. Merchants in Hong Kong were extremely concerned, as the economy was already in a slump, and riots made it worse by disrupting trade. They appealed to Lugard to take action. After consulting Francis May, who had been the Superintendent of Police for many years, he sent troops onto the streets, and arrested trouble-makers. This calmed Hong Kong, but underlying ferment simmered in China throughout 1910, leading to a tumultuous 1911.

In April 1911 riots re-erupted in Canton, spreading to the rest of Guangdong. A stream of refugees, including criminals and activists, flooded into Hong Kong. Further plots were hatched and assassinations carried out across the border. Armed robbery and violence increased rapidly with gangs entering houses and junks being robbed. Children were held for ransom and girls were kidnapped for prostitution.

Draconian laws were brought in by Lugard under the Peace Preservation Order, strongly supported by the Chinese legislators, with a minimum sentence of five years in jail for robbery and violence, and fifty lashes for other serious offences. This was too severe for the Colonial Service and they reduced it to a mere twenty-four lashes.

In July and August the revolution exploded in Szechuan, brought about by the battle between Peking and provincial leaders over railway construction by foreign companies, and spread throughout central China. Troops were put on alert in Hong Kong, and they would have been sent to Shanghai if violence had broken out against British citizens.

On November 6 the Viceroy asked for the railway to Canton to be suspended, which was interpreted by the Hong Kong Chinese that the Manchus had fled, and Peking had fallen. Lugard was amazed at the reaction and wrote to the Colonial Office, '*The entire Chinese population appeared to become temporarily demented with joy. The din of crackers (the usual method of rejoicing) was deafening and was accompanied by perpetual cheering and flag-waving – a method of madness most unusual to the Chinese.*'

Three days later, the Viceroy took refuge with the British Consul in Canton, who sent him to Hong Kong by warship, where he arrived in a state of near collapse. It was a delicate situation, but Lugard appealed to the populace for calm and to treat the Viceroy as a guest, which they did. The Manchu government was in disarray and collapsing, and to Lugard's surprise he was approached by the new government in Canton to help draft revised laws, which he took to be a great compliment.

On the streets of Hong Kong there were escalating problems with law and order, with women having jewelry ripped off them in the street, trams being commandeered, police being stoned whilst making arrests, and news-paper offices' windows broken amid cries of '*Hammer the foreign devils.*'

Lugard brought in the Peace Preservation Order again, and had the troops march through the markets of Central and Wanchai every day, and introduced 'the cat' (the cat o'nine tails was a type of multi-tailed whip originated in the Royal Navy for severe floggings) for all offences of violence and intimidation. He kept close contact with the Chinese leaders, listening to their advice, and gradually things settled down. He wrote to Ned in December, '...*I hear many stayed away from the St. Andrews Ball in the fear the place was going to be blown up by dynamite! The Chinese (lower classes) have gone off their heads. Even the prostitutes have announced in posters and in the press that they are paying half their earnings to 'the Cause' and inviting extra custom from patriotic motives! Where, but in China, would you find it an act of high patriotism to fornicate!'*

Lugard ordered arms and munitions to be collected and put into a strongly guarded central store. The Chinese revolutionaries requested to use the harbour to assemble their ships to send to the north, but Lugard refused, which caused further tension. By March 1912, the worst of the violence was over, and Hong Kong settled down.

Lugard had been grateful for the support of the Chinese leaders in Hong Kong. Most had connections with the mainland through family and property and some had lived in fear of assassination. They sympathized with the revolution, and were crucial to maintain the trade between Hong Kong and Canton. For their assistance, Lugard recommended the leader of the Council Dr. Ho Kai be awarded a knighthood, which was proudly accepted.

Lugard was worried about Flora. She had taken a trip to Japan in May, before the monsoon season started, having been entranced by its beauty on their previous journey. The journey didn't start well when her maid Dodson broke her leg, and ended up in hospital in Kobe. After a short stay, they went up to Yamoto to visit the volcanic sulphur springs and walk in the surrounding hills. It reminded Flora of Abinger, and she was feeling energetic and her old self. When they were about to return in early September she started feeling sharp abdominal pains again. She went to see an American doctor in Tokyo who examined her, and immediately recommended an operation. It was carried out speedily, but was botched, and was to have serious repercussions for her.

Lugard wanted to go to her when he realised how serious her condition was, but the situation was still tense in Hong Kong. He wrote to her the day after the operation, '*I have travelled with you how many times through the Valley of the Shadow of Death but I have never penetrated so far into its gloom and terror as I did yesterday.*'

Flora returned to Hong Kong a month later, but they were now faced with another major decision. Sir John Anderson had just been appointed the new head of the Colonial Office, and had written to Lugard whilst Flora was in Japan. '*We are anxious to amalgamate the Nigerian Administration making one Governor and say, three deputies, one for the East, West and North. But our difficulty is to get the right man for the job. We are agreed you are the man, if you would take it even if only for a sufficient time, say three or four years to give it a good start. We should not be difficult about the salary, but the figure in our minds is 6,000 pounds with a duty allowance of 1,500 pounds. Will you kindly let me know what you think?*'

Lugard now realised how difficult it was to live without Flora, and would have to make a heart-rending decision between love and duty. He wrote to Flora, '*First and foremost – indeed nothing matters in comparison to it – it is the question of separation and your happiness... The strain of anxiety, and of single-handed personal responsibility (of Hong Kong) are as Nil compared with Africa, and I have grown fat and well-fed and lazy and self-indulgent... Must I confess to you, who can read all my thoughts, that the task does not appeal to me ?...It is the biggest job in the whole British Empire and one of the most difficult...it is the turning point in the destiny of that vast country.*'

Flora read his anguish with a sad heart. She telegraphed him before she returned, '*Sorrowfully accept.*'

On her return they discussed every aspect, with Flora's health in mind, and together composed a reply. They proposed revised terms with six months in Nigeria, and six months in London. This was not initially accepted by Sir John Anderson, but after further exchanges he agreed to eight months in Nigeria with four months leave.

During that time, Flora received a letter from (Lord) Lewis Harcourt, who was Secretary of State and an old friend. He flattered her by saying that if Lugard did not accept the offer, he would postpone the amalgamation of Nigeria. He also confirmed that he could not accept their first proposal, but added, '*I cannot tell you what great importance I attach to getting your husband to complete his great African work.*'

This convinced Flora that her husband must accept the post and wrote to Ned in December 1911, '*Fred must accept. African Lugard! He is asked now to complete his work, to do the biggest thing that remains to be done in tropical Africa...our personal happiness must not stand in the way...I am not hurrying to communicate my views to Fred. His own will form parallel to mine.*'

As Lugard entered his final three months in Hong Kong, he was surprised at the outpouring of appreciation that came from many quarters. His relationship with the China British Ambassador, Sir John Jordon, had been volatile during his term, mostly due to Lugard using his own initiative with the Viceroy and not informing the Consul in Canton. Despite this, Jordan could see that Lugard meant well, and held him in '*high esteem.*' Lugard in turn said to Flora, '*He is a good, earnest, real man with whom it is a pleasure to deal.*' On Lugard's departure from Hong Kong, the Ambassador sent a generous tribute to him from Peking.

The start of the farewells came five days later on March 11 1912 when he officially opened the University, his crowning achievement in the Colony. To raise more funds, they combined the opening with a large fête and bazaar. Many eminent figures attended the ceremony, both local and international, including the newly-appointed Vice-Chancellor Sir Charles Elliot.

They wound their way up the paved steps, passing through the tall colonnades, the fresh white stone sparkling in the sun, flanked by the fire-red brick walls and crowned by the clock tower. They entered the great hall, surrounded by impressive teak pillars, stained-glass windows and a fine domed roof. The newly-designed coat of arms looked down on them with the motto '*Sapienta et Virtus*' meaning wisdom and virtue through moral and intellectual enrichment. It was taken from the Confucian classic '*The Great Learning.*'

Lugard took centre stage, flanked by the two major sponsors. On one side was Nowrojee Mody, the son of Sir Hormusjee Mody who had died a few months earlier, and on the other, Warren Swire, the representative of Butterfield and Swire. The National Anthem was played. Mody rose and gave a heartfelt speech thanking Lugard for all his support, and presented him with a fine silver model of the main building.

Lugard replied, sincerely thanking all the donors for their generosity and those that had made the University possible. Finally he confirmed the award of a knighthood for the leader of the Council Dr. Ho Kai, which was warmly applauded.

A University song in the form of a Latin ode had been composed by Cecil Clementi, and Denman Fuller, the cathedral organist had composed the music. It was sung by a combined choir and played by the Philharmonic Orchestra and a military band. After the enthusiastic rendition, Lugard led the guests out to a large, raucous crowd waiting impatiently outside, who let out cheers and set off fireworks.

He opened the fête and bazaar, and thousands of people rushed to see the hundreds of stalls, exhibitions, displays, Chinese plays, folk dances, military spectacles, tombolas, restaurants and film shows. The celebrations lasted for days and were a great success, raising tens of thousands of pounds for the University.

During his last year, Lugard had become popular with the Legislative Council, both with the Chinese and European representatives. On his last day in the Council he made a modest speech, which was replied to by Dr.

Ho Kai. He extolled Lugard's achievements, including winning the respect and confidence of the Chinese, and praised him for being accessible to all classes in the community. He added, '*You have during your tenure of office, done everything you could to foster trade and industry. It is due in great measure to your interest in commercial affairs that the position of the Colony is better than when you came.*'

On March 16 Lugard and Flora departed Government House for the last time. They left as they had arrived, taken to City Hall by sedan chair, escorted by the King's Own Yorkshire Infantry and the Sikh Regiment. Flora was still recovering from the operation and had to be carried onto the platform at City Hall in a chair. She was frail, but elegantly dressed in a cream satin costume and a black picture hat with a large upstanding ostrich feather.

The Council was gathered, and their leader Sir Paul Chater gave another warm speech listing the Governor's achievements, and paid special tribute to Flora. Chater presented Lugard with a scroll of the speech, bound in blue morocco, enclosed in a box embellished with the Coat of Arms of Hong Kong in gold. He was visibly moved, especially by the tribute to Flora, and had great difficulty replying, saying in an almost inaudible voice, '*There is one abiding regret with which we both leave Hong Kong. It is that Flora has been unable, through ill health, to play her part here as she would have wished to play it, by my side every day, since I have been in the Colony. But it was not to be so, and you can only faintly know how deep and sincere has been her intent in every single thing connected with Hong Kong. We are as one, as you said, in all things. The only claim I can make, was that that I have done my best and I have not spared hard work.*'

After a lengthy round of applause, they were carried down to Blake's Pier with crowds thronging on every street, cheering and letting off fireworks as they passed. By the time they reached the pier, Flora showed unrestrained emotion, sobbing audibly. She could see the genuine, warm, spontaneous appreciation from the people for all the hard work and sacrifices that her husband had made for Hong Kong.

They boarded the government launch and as they sailed out to the waiting liner, more fireworks burst across the skyline to end a truly memorable day.

Their Chinese servant, Ah Yeu, accompanied them, setting off to the next great challenge - the formation of Nigeria.

CHAPTER 28
Completing the circle

The long voyage from Hong Kong gave Flora time to recuperate, and for them to plan their future. They agreed that a new London base was required, and with the help of Ned, they found a spacious, terraced, colonnaded house at 51, Rutland Gate in Kensington. Today it still nestles in the diplomats' quarter of London, near the Royal Geographical Society, and bears a blue plaque commemorating the time they were there. It was going to be their base for the next six years, so it was redecorated and furnished, supplemented by the Chinese furniture sent from Hong Kong.

They arrived in England on April 19 1912. After a short break at Little Parkhurst, Ned and Lugard headed back to London to start the daunting preparations for the amalgamation of Nigeria from a basement office in the Colonial Office. Lugard knew northern Nigeria well, but he had little knowledge of the more complicated south and was given six months to study it in detail.

The dapper and lascivious Lord Lewis Harcourt (nicknamed Loulou) was the new Colonial Secretary in the radical Lloyd George Government. On June 27, Harcourt made a speech on Nigeria in the House of Commons announcing the amalgamation, and the appointment of Lugard as Governor. '…*Northern Nigeria is in the truest sense the product of his foresight and genius. He reclaimed it from the unknown; he gave it a legal code, differing only in its civilization from the essential lines of native custom; he established a land system which combines altruism with revenue, may well be a model and inspiration to other Protectorates …On my earnest solicitation he returns now to the field of his early labours, to complete and consolidate what has been proved, I think, to be the greatest tropical province of the Crown.*'

On September 18, Lugard set sail from England with Ned. He called on the Governors of Sierra Leone and the Gold Coast and arrived at Lagos on October 3. He received a very different welcome to that given to him in Hong Kong. The steamer had to anchor two miles out to sea because of the shallow sand bar, where Lugard was transferred to the government boat, which was tossed around in the choppy seas whilst the tropical rains lashed down. There were twenty ships in the harbour, with sodden, bedraggled bunting, and subdued cheers as they landed at the Apapa wharf. They were met by an equally drenched line of representatives and officials.

They transferred to official cars and drove round the lagoon, crossing two bridges linking Iddo Island to reach the centre of Lagos, the home of 80,000 people. The procession drove slowly along the long marina lined with local people cheering and waving. Lugard noted, '...*the crowds of natives shouting and seemingly very delighted ...I must say there seemed a dash of genuine intention about all this, and I believe the common people who all knew me by repute...seemed genuinely glad – the women flung up their arms and shouted things in Yoruba at me ...*'He thought it would have pleased Flora, adding, '...*even though, like myself, you might have judged it to be of little meaning, and that they may be hooting me in the streets before long.*'

The procession swept through the gates of Government House to the imposing, but not inspiring, two-storey, square, white building that would be his office and home for the next six years. It had been built thirty years earlier, designed with galleries running around a central well, with rooms radiating from the galleries. Lugard's office was at the front, overlooking the busy harbour so evoking pleasant memories of Hong Kong.

Lugard made his first priority to visit the northern capital Zungeru, to meet the Consul and show his solidarity. He set off, now having the luxury of a government train. It was composed of six carriages designed by his predecessor Sir Walter Egerton, comprising luxuriously fitted rooms, bathrooms and servants quarters. However, it was not a comfortable ride, as the inadequate suspension of the carriages was unable to cater for the undulating, narrow 3ft 6in gauge, making it difficult to read or write. It was a slow, tedious journey, with animals and people often on the line, and it took a day to reach Jebba.

There was still no bridge across the River Niger so the whole train had to be ferried across the river, taking another six hours to reach Zungeru. On disembarking, he looked up and saw the wooden government house he had built on the hill looking rather forlorn and much the worse for tropical wear.

He was met by Charles Temple, the Acting-Governor of Northern Nigeria, the son of Sir Richard Temple, an eminent member of the Indian Civil Service. He was a distinguished geologist and surveyor, had travelled across South America as a boy, and became an expert on Hausa society and language. He was tall and charming, but undisciplined, a bit vague and rather disorganised, which did not fill Lugard with confidence. Temple had not prepared a room for Lugard, assuming he would stay on his train. As a result *'I had a small bed with a tiny camp mosquito net on four sticks and the <u>necessary</u> arrangements were abominable.'* Not a good start.

After a short conversation, Lugard quickly reminded him that he was Governor, and that Temple was the Deputy Governor, and going to have to adapt to his policies. Despite this, Lugard could not help liking him and wrote to Flora, *'He was most nice; not bumptious or disagreeable at all, but simply muddle-headed, and had addressed me a long series of letters speaking as Governor of N.N.'* Temple made an important contribution to the amalgamation of the region over the next five years.

Within a few days Lugard returned to Lagos to study its working systems, which he found bureaucratic and cumbersome. The differences between the north and south were deeper than he realised, and had major hurdles to overcome. Hong Kong had given him the experience of dealing with a Legislative Council, the commercial community and social gatherings at Government House. He met with local African leaders who were Legislative members, barristers, doctors and members of professional bodies and listened carefully to their views. They were mainly Yoruba, some highly educated and all politically astute.

One of his first inspections was of the new infrastructure works being built around Lagos. These included an extension to the harbour, and wharves being built for a new railway connection to Apapa. He needed to assess and price a new tram system, new coal and petroleum wharves, and considered the use of private enterprise.

His old enemy, malaria soon came back to visit him. It was a particularly virulent strain, but he had Ah Yeu to nurse him, and Ned to watch over the administration. By November he had recovered and set out on tour through the south.

He took the train to Ibadan, which had a population of over 170,000 and was (and still is) one of the largest cities in Africa. It was a major commercial centre, and he met with groups of local officials and traders to hear their views. He quickly detected opposition to any imposition of the system he had installed in the north, especially to taxes.

He drove on to Oyo to visit the new Alafin and pay his respects. His demeanour was in marked contrast to his last visit in 1894, when he startled them by appearing out of the bush from Borgu in an alarmingly disheveled state.

His last stop was at Offa, a key political town, before heading back to Lagos, where he attended his first meeting of the Legislative Council. There followed an always popular three day race meeting, where home-bred ponies competed against imported stock brought in by British and Syrian traders.

In December, he undertook a tour around the south coast with Ned, sailing in the government boat to Forcados on the mouth of the Niger, and headquarters of the marine department. The town was still competitive with Lagos despite the new railway, with thousands of barrels of palm-oil stacked on the wharf waiting for shipment to Europe.

As they sailed further east, Lugard looked for a suitable location for another port to link the eastern railway. He was shown various inlets by canoe and his preference was for an area near Okrika. Later he named it Port Harcourt after his old chief, which has since become Nigeria's second port and a major export terminal for oil.

He continued to Calabar, the old capital of Southern Nigeria before Lagos, and close to the border of Kamerun (the German Cameroons). Half the population turned out to greet him, with forty large canoes each holding thirty to forty rowers manoeuvering skillfully around his boat.

His car was unloaded from the boat, and he drove slowly past the crowds with thousands of schoolchildren pressing forward to see him. He was introduced to the chiefs who were regaled in a startling variety of dress. There was no national dress in that region, so everyone had their own preference, from Savile Row suits with tinsel crowns, to strange admiral regalia with gold crowns.

These were important people representing many thousands of tribesmen, whom Lugard treated respectfully, and he made time for long discussions with them. Some were nervous of him because of the stories they heard from the north, but their biggest concern was the introduction of tax.

The famous Mary Slessor lived here, and Lugard was determined to meet her during his visit. She was born to a poor family in Aberdeen and raised in Dundee. When Livingstone died in 1875, she decided she wanted to be a missionary; the following year, after brief training, she went to Calabar at the age of twenty-eight.

It was a wild place, notorious for cannibalism, the killing of twins and the drinking of poison to prove guilt. She went to live with hostile tribes for fifteen years, gained their confidence, learned the language, combated witchcraft and helped to make social changes. She adopted many children, established a college for vocational training, and 'Ma' as she was known, was highly respected by the local tribes. So great was her influence, the Government made her a local magistrate to rule over the native courts.

Mary lived in the area, but was reclusive and often just disappeared into the bush. She had to be fetched when Lugard arrived, and made a special effort of wearing shoes, stockings and a battered hat for the occasion. Lugard was very moved by this tiny, fierce, determined, shabbily-dressed woman, as he stood there in his ridiculous plumed hat and breeches. He was determined to see her rewarded for her amazing work and dedication, which he knew she would resist if offered. When he returned to Lagos he asked Ned to prepare a recommendation for an Honorary Associate of the Order of St. John of Jerusalem.

When Ned read her life story, he was moved to tears and greatly regretted not seeing the award presented himself. It was awarded by the Provisional Commissioner H. Bedwell, and on receiving it Mary said, '*May this be an incentive to work and to be better than ever I have been in the past.*'

Congratulations flooded in from around the world and when she died of malaria two years later, she had the equivalent of a state funeral, with flags being flown at half-mast and Lugard sending a warm tribute, '*with my deepest regrets… appreciation of this well-earned reward for her life of heroic self-sacrifice.*' Her legacy continued, and many statues of her were erected, and schools named after her in Nigeria and Scotland. In 2009, she was still not forgotten, with the Clydesdale Bank featuring her on the back of a ten pound note.

Lugard returned to Lagos in December and attended further meetings with the elite of the city. He met with the Eleko, who was the head of the White Cap chiefs of the former royal dynasty of Lagos. He noted, '*He came attired in a hat trimmed with heavy silk lace and a silver crown in front of it, also a heavy brocade or taborette cloth such as you have for heavy curtains. It was gorgeous but I think, hot.*'

On Christmas Day he took the government train north to Zungeru. On the way he stopped at Abeokuta, the capital of Egba state to meet the Alake. They enjoyed a high degree of self-government, which Lugard admired in one way, but was concerned in another. The Alake greeted him '*…in an arrangement of different coloured plush cloaks, feathers, gold lace and tinsel, and his hands were massive rings of gold like the links of an anchor chain and massive necklets of gold.*' The introduction of tax here was to give Lugard major problems.

On arrival at Zungeru he met with Charles Temple again, this time with a much clearer perspective on the differences between the running of the north and the south. The north was almost able to run itself, whilst the south was sunk under reams of bureaucratic paper and bogged down by endless hours of policy debate.

On January 1 1913, the Emir of Kano held a special Durbar festival inviting all the other Emirs. Lugard agreed to involve the West Africa Frontier Force (WAFF) and the Mounted Infantry. It was a magnificent occasion. Fifteen thousand horsemen gathered in all their finery, plus thousands of splendidly adorned footmen, each grouped around their chief. There were 800 WAFF troops with three hundred mounted infantry in smart turbans, holding lances with coloured pennants.

Long trumpets were sounded, and they paraded proudly in front of Lugard, who was sitting under a canopy with the Emir. Lugard described the spectacle in a letter to Flora. '...*Then each Emir came past with all his horsemen, and some of them had most interesting processions, led horses most wonderfully clad in rich clothes - court jesters mounted and unmounted, heralds and trumpeters and native bands. In one there was a company of women jesters to entertain the Emir on his travels. In some there were camels, in some there were men in chain armour... Then came the Pagans, almost naked, skipping and dancing and yelling and brandishing clubs - some in a most weird array. When the last had gone past they began the salute. Each Emir had a picked band of horsemen ...who charged down at full gallop halting a yard or two off* [in front of us] *in a whirlwind of dust. The Emir dismounted and came and knelt on the ground and made obeisance.*'

The Durbar lasted for three days and during this time Lugard met each of the chiefs individually, using Temple as his interpreter. On the last day there were sporting exhibitions and competitions. In a letter to Flora later that day he wrote,

'*All the Emirs were seated together - a marvellous sight when one recalls the bitter jealousies which formerly possessed them ...Even the Chinese have little or nothing to teach these Emirs in the way of courtesy and good manners... But the Pagan dancers were simply wonderful. There were tumblers and contortionists from Ilorin, and wrestlers and also pugilists... The blows were so heavy that I wondered if serious damage had not been done, but the surprising thing was the absolute good humour with which it was taken, and the genial way in which when a man was knocked down and vanquished, he accepted defeat ...During all these three days belonging to rival Emirs who had grievances against each other, and each trying to aggrandize their own lord — not a single quarrel or even altercation did I see or hear of! Everyone kept saying to each other that it was a really marvellous sight which they would not for the world have missed. And so it was!*'

In the quiet of his room he wrote again, '*I have hardly heard your voice at all this last day or two, what with the dust and the shouting and braying of trumpets, and the noise. I have been treated here as if I were a King, and I am wanting to get back into my own proper sphere, and on to my office stool... This is somewhat demoralizing and fatiguing...I should like it better if you were here and I could lay at your feet.'*

Before he left Kano, Lugard made an inspection of the city that he had not seen since it was captured in 1903. He was shown the new, clean prison and treasury, the reorganized market, and the first schools being built, all being administered by the Emir's government. In addition, it had attracted two hundred Europeans traders. He also noticed that the red walls of the city were crumbling in places and in need of repair, and was told quietly that this work had always been done by slaves.

Continuing his tour of inspection by car, Lugard went to Zaria to look at a cotton mill and a light railway to serve tin mines on a nearby plateau. From there he drove back to Zungeru to catch up on the dispatch boxes from Lagos.

To complete his tour, he sailed down the Niger, stopping at Onitsha, heard about potential coalfields at Udi, and drove on to the ancient kingdom of Benin.

He was welcomed by the chiefs, who were stripped to the waist as a sign of respect. Lugard was well aware of the recent sensitive history; in 1896 there had been a massacre of British officers and 250 African soldiers after a bungled military expedition to take the city. Only two British officers survived. This led to a brutal reprisal by a British force of 1,200 marines led by Admiral Sir Harry Rawson in 1897. The city was burned, and thousands of priceless religious relics and pieces of art, including the famous Benin bronze heads, were looted. Lugard was keen to establish a good relationship.

He held long discussions with the chiefs. In a letter to Flora he wrote, *'They had, like the Buganda, established a regular form of government and, like them, their kings had degenerated into monsters of cruelty. It must be a very ancient kingdom, dating no doubt back to the thirteenth or fouteenth century, and the home of the highest art discovered in Africa outside Egypt ...Of course we talked much of the massacre...and of the subsequent army under Rawson which broke the power of Benin. It took a strong force, of, I believe, upwards of 2,000 blue jackets with artillery etc ...and there was heavy fighting. That was in 1897, just when I came from South Africa to raise the WAFF...The chiefs only raised one question - the water-rate, for Benin has a laid-on water supply.'*

From Benin he returned to Lagos by car, to prepare to leave for England. He had covered a lot of ground in five months. Confiding in Flora he said, *'...It seems impossible that it is less than five months since I landed here.*

I think I can claim I have done a year's work in that time... Yes it has been an eventful year, and counting our lives as one and our interests as one and indivisible - all our years as each goes by, are eventful and even this is hardly more eventful than its predecessors for many years back...'

Lugard had established a good rapport with his southern secretary Alexander Boyle, who he regarded as *full of common sense and as loyal as a man can be,'* but he was still struggling with his northern secretary Charles Temple, who he thought *'...works partly for himself and partly (I think) for ideals and objectives of his own creating, and not for the policy of the chief.'* They had quite different views over native administration.

On February 2 1913 Lugard set sail for England with Ned. By April 6 they were back in the basement of the Colonial Office working on the amalgamation details, with one typist. When he sat down, Lugard had a clear plan in his head of how he wanted the implementation achieved. Less than one month later, he sent the Secretary of State thirty-seven foolscap pages with the plan for the amalgamation of Nigeria.

At the beginning of October, Lugard and Ned returned to Nigeria after a frantic five months, to prepare for the changeover. January 1 1914 was chosen for the historic amalgamation ceremony to be held in Lagos.

On the day, he wrote to Flora in an almost detached way. *'The ceremony went off, as the Commandant said 'like clockwork', and I received congratulations on every side regarding it, as well as my new appointment as Governor-General. We started sharp at 9 at the Court House, and I made my speech first, then the instruments of Government were read, then a 21-gun salute, then I was sworn in - 17 more guns - then Boyd and Temple, and I read the King's and Harcourt's telegrams. Then I addressed the populace from the balcony, and drove home. I came all alone, the streets being lined with soldiers, blue jackets and police. I returned with Boyle and Temple and Ned - then I swore in James and the C.J. [Chief of Justice] at Government House then the Legislative Council, and we finished I think about half past twelve. It was suffocating hot in the Court House and I was wet right through.'*

Lugard's first aim was to create a new capital. Lagos was in the wrong place for the new Nigeria; it had endless problems with the silting harbour, poor communication links and woeful sanitary conditions. Lugard wanted it to be Kaduna. It was centrally situated, at a higher altitude, offering a healthier climate, it was in a fertile region, and was already the headquarters of the WAFF. He asked Flora to help prepare a town plan, and sent his officers to consult with her when they were on leave. His plans did not materialise.

In 1914, war loomed in Europe, and Africa was not going to be spared.

CHAPTER 29
The forgotten war

On April 25 1914, Lugard returned to England with Ned, who brought with him a number of tropical birds including an elegant Crested-Crane, a Secretary Bird and a huge jet-black Ground Hornbill which according to Ned '*talked continuously and sounded like a creaking wheel.*' He presented the first to Lord Harcourt and the others to London Zoo.

Lord Harcourt was a Liberal, and Secretary of State for the Colonies from 1910 to 1915. He was from an old aristocratic family, his father William a highly-respected politician and his wife, a fabulously rich American heiress. He was sophisticated, a Trustee of the British Museum and the Wallace Collection, and a well-known roué with both sexes. He was also a lesser known paedophile. He was shielded by his friends, but after an attempted seduction of a twelve year old Eton schoolboy in 1922 which was about to be made public, he committed suicide at his luxury home in London.

Harcourt disagreed with Lugard on many of his policies, and in a later conversation with Margery Perham, Lugard complained that '*he constantly reversed my action as Governor...the Service under him was intolerable.*' Flora spent much time with Harcourt in London trying to influence him and discussed Lugard's dispatches in detail. Her entreaties helped, but Harcourt just thought Lugard too sensitive to criticism. In 1915 Harcourt was succeeded by Bonar Law, but the criticism of Lugard continued with further opposition to his policies.

A topic that Flora and Harcourt fundamentally disagreed on was Ireland. The Third Home Rule Bill for Ireland had been presented to the House of Commons in April 1912. It proposed that Ireland should have its own autonomous Parliament in Dublin, but the Protestants in Ulster had no wish to be governed from the south. The Ulster Unionist Party under the leadership of Sir Edward Carson fiercely opposed it, and a paramilitary group, the Ulster Unionist Force (UUF) had been formed. The Nationalists, the Irish Parliamentary Party, under John Redmond were preparing an army and there was talk of civil war. Ireland was at boiling point.

Flora's large Anglo-Protestant family still lived in Clonmel and around Dublin, with many political and military connections. She was seriously concerned about their safety, and was not convinced that the Home Rule Bill would protect Ulster.

Immediately Lugard returned in April 1914, he was drawn into the debate by Flora, and supported her passionate and persuasive Unionist arguments. In July, Flora asked him to go to Belfast for a few days to see the situation for himself. He could stay with Lord Castlereagh and give support to Sir Edward Carson, who was to make a speech. Lugard thought this would be a pleasant break from the office basement, but totally underestimated the consequences of his visit.

Lugard and Carson travelled by ferry, and on entering Belfast, every shipyard and boat was crowded with men cheering for Carson. Lugard wrote to Ned, '*Carson is worshipped here. It is extraordinary.*' As they drove in an open-top car which had been decorated with orange lilies and Union Jacks, Carson stood and waved, relishing the adulation of the crowds of supporters thronging in the streets.

On July 10, a few days after the anniversary of the Battle of the Boyne of 1690, Lugard accepted an invitation from Lord Castlereagh to address a group of special service troops. *The Irish Times* reported the following day, '*…Sir Frederick Lugard who also addressed the men, said he came to Belfast that morning with the object of seeing for himself what he had heard so much about…He was not an Ulsterman nor an Irishman, but he had served his country almost entirely overseas. He wanted to tell them that the example they were showing in Ulster, of the grit and determination in the people of the United Kingdom, would never be forgotten…He could assure them that the attitude they had taken up had rung through the Empire from one end to the other. He wished them God speed, and hoped the time would never come when they would be called upon to fulfil the terms of their Covenant. Should that time come he knew that there would be men who would do all they should. He warmly congratulated them, in the name of the Overseas Dominion which, perhaps, he may claim to represent, he thanked them heartily for the encouragement they had given.*'

Almost immediately Lugard uttered these words, he knew he was in trouble. He wrote to Ned the following day, '*The fact is I got carried away at an inspection of the special troops last night…and it is in all the papers this morning. My host Sir Robert Kennedy, an ex-diplomat, assures me that I need have no fear, but that the Nationalist Members will ask a question in the House as to what right I have to engage in these polemics and it is probable that Harcourt will agree with him! Unfortunately I thanked them in the name of the Overseas Dominions. This show is enough to carry any man off his legs...'*

When Lugard returned to London on July 15, there was a terse message waiting from Lord Harcourt stapled to *The Irish Times* report. '*The enclosed report of a supposed speech by you in the neighbourhood of Belfast has only just reached me. I shall be obliged if you will, at the earliest moment, send me any explanation you wish to offer, and at the same time return the cutting.*' Lugard attempted a weak explanation with an official reply within the hour, and followed it with a personally written letter, and further apologies.

He had a sleepless night, not knowing whether his career had come to an abrupt end. The answer came back that afternoon. '*Sir Frederick Lugard. After anxious consideration - and consultation with the Prime Minister (Asquith) - I have decided to accept the apology in your letter of last night for your very grave breach of the best traditions of the Colonial Service. If your speech becomes a matter of public comment and criticism I shall have to state that I have received and accepted this apology. I am sorry to be obliged to add this incident must in the future gravely affect my estimate of the value of your judgement and discretion. L. Harcourt.*' Lugard took no exception to the reprimand and said, '*I think he was fully justified.*'

His relationship with the Colonial Office was about to get that much harder, but the outbreak of the First World War soon overshadowed this incident. The Home Rule Bill was suspended until the war was over.

On August 3 1914, Germany invaded Belgium on their way to France. Britain declared war on Germany the following day. The German troops brutally razed many towns and murdered thousands, punishing Belgium for not allowing access to France.

Tens of thousands fled their homes and waves of refugees were on the move. Flora was incensed at their plight, and immediately sent out urgent requests to her contacts to see what they could do to help. Within five days she had set up an organisation to find accommodation. An insurance company gave their empty offices in Aldwych, and a team of clerical staff was assembled. They launched an appeal, and on the first day received over one thousand replies offering money, accommodation and food.

The first Belgian refugees arrived on ferries at Folkestone in Kent on August 24, (see Fig 3). Within a few weeks over 250,000 refugees were in England, distressed and destitute. Flora worked with the War Refugees Committee set up by the Government until the end of the war, tirelessly helping wherever she could. After the war most of the refugees returned to Belgium, hardly leaving a trace - except a lot of goodwill towards the generous British people.

Lugard returned to Nigeria in September. He sat in his Liverpool hotel, waiting to board the boat to Lagos, with the thought of German gunboats lurking off the West African coast. He reflected on the memorable summer spent with Flora, and the joy she gave him. He wrote, '*My own darling wife … You are forever in my thoughts. Yes, we had a very happy summer, the motor drives to Abinger, the games of Patience, the times you kept looking in my study and interrupting my work, you sitting on my knee, chatting and getting (and giving) many kisses…I am loving you all the time. Your loving husband, Fred.*'

As the boat neared Lagos, he entered his own war, in Africa, thousands of miles from the western front, of which few knew or cared about. The Germans were in the adjacent Kamerun (now Cameroon) on the east side of Nigeria, with a common border of over 1,000 miles. On the west side of Nigeria was Togoland which had been swiftly taken by a combined French/British expedition. It was expected that Kamerun would follow soon after, as it was reported there were only 170 Germans and 2,000 Africans under arms. The strategy was clear, to take the capital Douala, the only deep-water port between Sierra Leone and South Africa.

Lugard was Governor, which included being Commander-In-Chief, but the Colonial Office was quick to remind him that in this wartime situation, the troops would be under its command. This did not stop him from reviewing the preparations and making his views known. As the invasion plans were being discussed, Lugard soon came to the conclusion that the commander sent by the Colonial Office was totally unsuitable for the job in Nigeria.

He was in a quandary, because it was a serious matter to have a senior officer removed. He wrote to Flora, '*The situation was very grave. Perhaps you can hardly realise how serious it is to interfere with the Commander of a force a few days before it takes to the field.*' He telegraphed the Colonial Office, who passed the communication to the War Office. They agreed with him. It was Lugard's unpleasant duty to break the news to the unfortunate commander. Afterwards he wrote to Flora, '*In my private heart, I believe I have saved many lives, perhaps a disaster.*'

Whilst waiting for the replacement, Brigadier-General (later Sir) Charles McPherson Dobell, Lugard was temporarily in charge, with Colonel Frederick Cunliffe at his side, in whom he had the greatest confidence. The strategy had been agreed, that there would be a four-pronged attack on Kamerun; the first from the north-east at Maiduguri to attack a mountain post at Mora, the second from Yola to take the town of Garua and a third to take Itom from the south. The capital Douala, was the last and would be taken by the Navy led by Admiral Sir Cyril Fuller.

The land attacks were in difficult terrain and did not go as planned. They were beaten off at Mora and Yola, and soundly defeated at Itom, suffering heavy casualties. It was essential the attack on Douala went well.

Brigadier-General Dobell sailed along the west coast and picked up contingents from other colonies, along with French and Senegalese troops, 4,300 in total. The WAFF contributed another 1,260, with sixty-five British officers and NCOs and seventy-nine British volunteers. The little expeditionary force set sail from Lagos on September 20. They swept aside the German mines and scuttled ships in the harbour, and much to everybody's astonishment, took Douala after only a short bombardment. They concluded that the Germans were convinced the allies would be swiftly defeated in Europe, so had limited any damage to the port.

Lugard was immensely relieved, but now faced the problem of dealing with the hundreds of German prisoners, both men and women, being sent to Lagos. With lingering memories of South Africa, Lugard ensured they were treated well, but they still complained, and by the end of October they had all been shipped to Britain for internment.

At the end of November, Lugard sailed to Douala to inspect the port and the forty mile radius around it which was now occupied. He wrote to Flora, '... *Then as I approached the wharf, guns rang out from the cruisers and from a tremendous salute. Everything was done with the most perfect precision and seamanship, we were alongside the pier and the gangway, down in a jiffy, and the whole length was a double guard of honour, French along one side, British on the other. I think you would have felt a little thrill if you had been with me...*'

In Douala he stayed at Government House, which had sustained only minor damage, and toured the stores, hospital, magazines and wireless station which were untouched. Lugard wanted to see how the Germans laid out the new native towns they had been building. He found '...*they are excellently planned, with the waterworks having a wonderful new principle. We have a lot to learn from these Germans.*'

He went to the front line outside Douala, and saw the results of a small battle that had been fought a few days earlier in dense forest and swamp. The next day he continued into the Cameroon Mountains through miles of well-kept cocoa and rubber plantations, crisscrossed with light railways. At the top was the Governor's *Schloss*, which was well-designed and nestled elegantly in terraces of gardens full of cascading flowers. Everything here was also intact, including the silver, linen, and pictures, ready for the occupants' early return, or so the Germans thought.

Lugard returned to Lagos in December, sent his inspection report to London and waited to hear what they wanted to do with the captured territory. He was hoping they would at least retain Douala, being such a strategic port. A second round of fighting had started in the heavy seasonal rains, and the casualty rate was mounting, most of the deaths being from malaria and other tropical diseases. This worried Lugard, as there were now serious staff shortages in Nigeria. He was working eleven hours a day, with minimal staff, to keep the Nigerian forces supplied and administer the country.

The northern Nigerian chiefs stayed loyal to Britain throughout the war, even when Turkey came in on the side of Germany. The southern states were more complex, infiltrated by German agents, who spread rumours that the allies were losing in Europe, and that the British were going to leave. To counteract this, Lugard undertook a major tour of Nigeria covering 1,000 miles.

He started in February 1915, covered around 550 miles by sea and boat, 450 by car and forty miles by train. He encouraged his Residents to push on with the small amount of infrastructure works being put in place, met the chiefs, and boosted moral.

That year neither side made much progress. Garua continued resisting, and even counterattacked into Nigeria, with strikes on Yola at one stage. A heavy twelve-pounder gun had been ordered from England and once it arrived, Garua fell under a siege.

Lugard returned to England for four months in August, to see Flora and the progress with her refugee project. She had worked relentlessly, and because she spoke fluent French, had made many Belgian friends and became extremely popular with the refugees. This had created tensions with the War Refugees Committee, so she continued her work under the Local Government Board, giving her more independence. Refugees had been living with families for nearly a year and the crisis had moved into a new phase. Goodwill was tested and put a strain on households, making the refugees feel uncomfortable. They longed for places of their own.

Flora looked for more houses that could be used, with the first lent by Lord Harrington in Kensington Park Gardens, which housed thirty-five refugees. Many more empty houses were found, opened up as hostels and looked after by Belgian managers. This gave temporary employment to the Belgians, and they started to earn some money of their own, and recovered their self-respect.

Lugard marvelled at what she had achieved in such a short time, but was still concerned about her health. She was working too hard, still suffering from the after effects of the operation in Japan. He was immensely proud when he heard that, for services to the refugees, she was to be created a Dame of the British Empire (DBE) in the Honours List in 1916.

He continued his work in his bunker in the Colonial Office with Ned. Whilst there, he received an invitation from his old comrade and friend from Nigeria, General Willcocks, to visit the western front in France. He spent a week near the front line, and despaired at the waste of lives and resources.

By the time Lugard returned to Lagos at the end of December 1915, the fighting in Kamerun was coming to an end. In February 1916 the last mountain stronghold at Mora was taken from the Germans, who escaped capture by fleeing to Rio Muni, a small Spanish territory to the south, still within Kamerun.

In March the Colonial Office confirmed that Kamerun was being handed over to the French, apart from a small strip adjacent to the Nigerian border, which the British called Cameroons. This agreement was eventually sealed at the Versailles Treaty in 1919. In 1961 the country regained its independence to become the Federal Republic of Cameroon. The troops returned to Lagos, and were given a warm welcome. From the 9,000 British, French and Belgian troops that had started out, there were 917 British and 906 French casualties. There were approximately 5,000 German soldiers killed, mostly African - many dying from disease, not bullets.

On the troops' return, Lugard received an urgent telegram from the Colonial Office to send 2,000 men to East Africa. This was a much larger campaign involving 400,000 allied troops and support staff, covering a vast area over many borders. They had been bogged down since 1914, and by 1916 the battle was not going well for the allies. General Smuts, (who had fought against the British in the Boer War) was brought in as the commander, along with a large contingent of troops from South Africa.

Lugard was unhappy with the request, as half his soldiers were sick or lame and still recuperating. The Colonial Office agreed to postpone the move, but in November, 3,000 Nigerian troops sailed for East Africa under General Cunliffe. Lugard addressed them at the dockside before they embarked, and wrote to Flora '*I addressed the sea of black faces with their little woollen green fatigue hats, wishing them good luck etc. ...I ended up by asking them if they were ready to go and conquer just to give them a chance for the yell of applause which they love. The interpreter rendered 'Governor wants to know if you are ready to kill all the bastards' and the yell of applause was great, and then they gave the usual three cheers for me with splendid enthusiasm! They are a fine lot - as good as any we have sent, and fully trained.'*

Lugard was there to meet the troops when they returned the following year. They had been engaged in some of the fiercest fighting and had taken heavy casualties. Men were dying of pneumonia even as they were being taken off the boats. The rain lashed down, but the bunting was up, food, drink and cigarettes were dispensed, and the weather did not dampen the joy of the soldiers, who cheered as they saw the red coats of their comrades, and heard the bugles sounding. The walking wounded limped behind with bandaged feet and legs, and the weary British officers and NCOs came slowly down the gangplank in the remains of their tattered uniforms.

Lugard's view of the East Africa campaign was not complimentary. He believed the losses were excessive, and that the administration had been muddled and expensive - the war cost the equivalent of 12 billion pounds today. Lugard was proud of his Nigerian force, saying, *'There is no doubt that it was the Nigerians who won the campaign. They alone could stick the starvation and the malaria, and showed indomitable pluck in action.'*

The war overshadowed the civil reforms that Lugard tried to make during his tenure. Hong Kong had opened his eyes to the importance of education. When he arrived in Nigeria in 1912 he wrote to Flora, *'I regard the education question the most important both at Home and in our Colonies and I read anything of importance regarding it.'* He constantly referred to it in his papers over the years in Nigeria, and well into his retirement.

In 1914, education was entwined with Christianity. The majority of children were taught in missions. A small number of Government schools provided education to the rest. Lugard estimated that in southern Nigeria only one child in 180 was in any kind of school. In the north it was entirely different, with six million Muslims and 25,000 Koranic bush schools. Lugard set down his ideals in a paper in 1914. *'The primary function of education should in my judgement be to fit the ordinary individual to fill a useful part in his environment with happiness to himself, and to ensure that the exceptional individual shall use his abilities for the advancement of the community and not to its detriment or to the subversion of constituted authority. ...It should be the aim of our new system to train up a generation... who shall be able to recognize and achieve ideals of their own, without a slavish imitation of the European and be proud of a nationality with its own clear aims and future.'*

There was general criticism from leading Africans of the time, describing pupils coming through the system as ill-educated, unreliable and lacking self-control. Others such as Sapara Williams, the senior African member

233

of the Colony Legislative Council said, '*Sometimes parents feel that it is far better children do not go to school at all than come out as they do filled with ignorance, pride and stupidity.*'

Lugard needed educated pupils for his new, expanding government. He needed clerks that could read, write, count and use a typewriter, and felt it was a waste of local resources using Europeans. Nigerian children needed secondary education and at that time, only a pitiful number were receiving it.

He set out a series of measures strengthening government controls, improving and building more schools, introducing school inspectors, and working with the missions. He set up a Board of Education, with a Lieutenant Governor in the chair and school committees in each province on which local Africans sat.

It was a slow and painful process working with the Colonial Office, but by 1917 he proudly wrote to Flora saying that his measures in the south had received a consensus of approval from the education department, the Protestant missions and the Roman Catholic bishop.

One aspect on which he was not supported, was his idea of trying to introduce moral instruction not based on religious teachings. In 1915 he wrote, '*I conceive that if a short daily* (period) *be devoted to placing before children, in an attractive way, the social and other incentives to gentlemanly conduct…with similar lessons by the aid of illustration and anecdotal biography, it would form a valuable adjunct to the inculcation of the same ideals of right living as enforced by religious precept and sanction.*' The missionaries strongly opposed this, and it was the only item on education that the Colonial Office questioned. In 1916, after much delay by the Colonial Office, his new education law was passed - without moral instruction being on the syllabus.

Northern Nigeria had to be treated entirely separately, but Lugard tried to set up a similar administration. He had the capable assistance of his old friend (later Sir) Hanns Vischer (1876-1945).

He was the son of a successful Swiss businessman, went to Cambridge, and was a deeply religious follower of Saint Francis of Assisi. In 1901 he had travelled to Northern Nigeria to work with the Church Missionary Society, but shortly afterwards applied to join the administration. Lugard was a bit apprehensive employing a foreigner, so he set him some conditions. He was to become naturalized, fluent in English and Hausa, know the Maliki law, and to gain a diploma in surveying with the RGS. To Lugard's astonishment, he passed all these tests in two years, and was immediately employed. It started a brilliant career in Africa and a lifelong friendship with Lugard.

Vischer was the real initiator of government education in northern Nigeria, and after an epic crossing of the Sahara by foot in 1906, (publishing *Across the Sahara from Tripoli to Bornu* in 1910) he became the Director of Education in 1908. By the time Lugard returned to Nigeria in 1912, Vischer had started a multi-faceted experiment just outside Kano, working closely with the Emirs. It included building an elementary school, a school for sons of chiefs, scribes and clerks, workshops for local crafts and a surveying school. He started with 320 pupils with ages ranging from six to sixty from a variety of emirates. He was popular with the people. Not only was his Hausa good (when he spoke in the dark he was mistaken for a local, and gained from the people the nickname *Dan Hausa* or son of a Hausa), but he could also play the African drums.

The experiment was a success, and Vischer continued to expand it with his principle of *'the preservation of the native'*. It was a delicate balance - there was still resentment of the British occupation among many Muslims. It was common to move out of the shadow of a non-believer, or spit on the ground after he had passed. Vischer showed his understanding and respect for Islam and its culture, and continued to foster and develop good relations with the Emirs.

Lugard and Vischer agreed to limit the expansion of the missions, but expanded the use of English, without diminishing Arabic, so producing long-term benefit to all.

By 1918, approximately 40,000 children were attending school, but still only 4,600 in Government schools. There were six hundred European missionaries with five thousand African assistant teachers, with most schools unaided and under little government control.

Lugard had instigated changes that would help Nigeria develop in the twentieth century, and although he faced many critics, by the time of independence in 1960, Nigeria had one of the best education systems in Africa, that produced notable statesmen, writers and eventually, Nobel Prize winners.

Lugard saw a fair tax system as an essential part of his Indirect Rule philosophy. The revenue raised would be ploughed back into the country to create better infrastructure, schools and hospitals, improving the health, education and business, creating a framework to prosper. This was not how the African business elite viewed it. Lugard met a lot of organised opposition in Lagos, where there was resentment and suspicion of any tax system. This was to lead to many arguments, riots, and eventually to his downfall.

In 1915 he sent his northern Resident, Richard Palmer to carry out a taxation study in the south. He produced a detailed report, which Lugard sent to the Colonial Office, recommending that taxes be introduced into select urban areas, and starting with the relatively prosperous towns of Benin, Oyo and Abeokuta. The Colonial Office was wary of implementing such a scheme after the tax riots that had occurred in the Gold Coast (Ghana), and opposed the proposals. Lugard pushed on anyway, and introduced taxes into Oyo in 1916.

In October, riots broke out in Isyeyin, sixty miles west of Oyo, and there were a series of murders, of some new District Heads and a judge of the new native court. They were put down swiftly by the quick action of the area Resident with the support of the Alafin before it spread further. Eight men were charged with the murders. Lugard decided that to discourage further violence, they were to be executed in the town in front of the people. It had the opposite effect and created more resentment. The next serious outbreak at Abeokuta in 1918 was a disaster for Lugard.

Abeokuta, was a major town in Egbe state that had a special history in the early development of Southern Nigeria. In 1893 the Governor of Lagos, Sir Gilbert Carter (1848-1927) signed a Treaty of Independence with the Egbe chiefs which recognized Egbe as an independent state. In return they accepted a British Commissioner, maintained freedom of trade, abolished human sacrifices (but not slavery), and maintained good order and cooperation with the Lagos government.

Lugard was concerned about the status of the state; its independence did not fit into his plans, and he wanted Egbe integrated into the south. He also had doubts about the security of the railway which passed through the state.

In August 1914 there was minor conflict that escalated into a blood bath. A young, inexperienced officer panicked and ordered his troops to shoot. A fusillade of shots rang out killing a chief and six of his followers. It became known as the Ijemo massacre. Anger and resentment increased when Lugard declared the 1893 treaty void.

In May 1918 Lugard introduced taxation to Abeokuta, which he thought would be welcomed as an improvement on the existing corrupt scheme. He was wrong. The old resentments came bubbling back up, and riots broke out later that month. A rebel group formed, dissatisfied with the advisor and the chiefs. They resented the British occupation and wanted revenge for 1914. They destroyed railway stations, property and rolling stock, ripped up railway lines and killed one of the chiefs that refused to join them. Lugard received reports that many Europeans and soldiers had been killed, later found to be exaggerated. One European had died and had been decapitated.

The Nigerian troops had just returned from combat in East Africa, so he sent 1,000 troops to put down and punish the rebels. He increased the number to 2,500 when the rebels moved outside the city and spread over a larger area. Between June 11 and July 10, fighting continued in torrential monsoon rains and 564 Africans were killed before peace was restored.

The war in Europe was coming to an end, and the Colonial Office had far more important matters to deal with. However, the London weekly publication, *West Africa* headlined the riot and demanded a full inquiry. It strongly criticised Lugard as an autocratic governor taking power into his own hands. The Colonial Office was tired of Lugard continually challenging them, wanting to implement Indirect Rule on his own terms, and saw this as a chance to remove him.

A commission was set up, chaired by Dr. James Maxwell - one of Lugard's own Residents, and included a Wesleyan missionary, a police magistrate and an African barrister, Eric Moore. They produced a thorough and detached report collecting a vast amount of evidence. The conclusions were damning.

It found the main fault lay with the administration, that Egbe's grievances were valid, and that disorder was the only way illiterate people could show their disapproval. They especially condemned the officer in charge, Resident Syer, as completely out of touch with the local people. It concluded that the tax system Lugard wanted to implement was unsuitable for the complex structure of the tribes in that area.

By the time the Egbe report came out, Lugard had returned to England. The fighting and jousting with the Colonial Office had taken its toll on him. He was sixty, exhausted, and tired of Lagos politics. His idea to unite the two systems of the north and the south had failed. He admired the straight and dignified Moslem leaders of the north, but still found the sophisticated, well-educated and often corrupt Yoruba leaders difficult to work with. (He added '… *Nor do I find it any easier to get on with the European agents of the Liverpool merchants.*') The vocal press supported the Yoruba chiefs and criticised him at every turn. Moreover, he was becoming increasingly concerned for Flora, who had been trying various treatments to cure her ailments resulting from the Japan operation, and was having little success.

The final straw came when the influenza pandemic of 1918 spread to Lagos in October. Lugard was not affected, but many of his staff went down with the deadly virus, including his loyal secretary, Mr. Browne, who died. His military officers were also affected creating instability and leading to desertions in the ranks. He wrote to Flora on September 2 1918, '*But to all men the moment comes when they have to lay down the trowel…..I have done over the usual time for which a Governor holds office….I believe in my own secret heart that I am regarded with so much dislike (and perhaps jealousy) by the CO officials they would be delighted to see the last of me. I hope by the grace of God to temper that pleasure by making them devoutly sorry that they released me from the galling control of the COs red tape – but that is another story.'*

He wrote a protesting letter to the new Secretary of State for the Colonies, Viscount Walter Long, concluding that he felt his task in Nigeria was complete. The minister took this as his resignation, and offered him thanks for his work and a Grand Cross of the British Empire. Lugard turned down the honour, saying he had not meant to resign, and offered himself for further service. He was swiftly rejected.

After further terse exchanges, a disconsolate Lugard finally left Nigeria on a sad, sour note in November 1918, as Europe celebrated the signing of the Armistice.

CHAPTER 30
Sunny days and sunsets

Lugard's disappointments in Nigeria were soon outweighed by the joy of being back in Abinger with Flora. The next ten years were full of new, shared projects and this period would be the happiest of their lives.

Flora sold their house at Rutland Gate in Knightsbridge in April 1920 whilst Lugard was on a short, fact-finding visit to Ethiopia. '*I woke up for the last time in the green room …I wish you were here on the pillow beside me, so that we might say goodbye together to the house where we have been so happy…Now we have to concentrate on our little corner of paradise.*' They settled down in Little Parkhurst to write, renew relationships with old friends and family, and enjoy the house and garden they had built together.

There was always a car parked in the drive, visitors coming and going, lively debates going on in the study, and the sound of laughter echoing from children in the garden. Their visitors came from many walks of life. There were politicians, foreign diplomats and colonial governors, writers, media, missionaries, scientists and academics. That year they included Austin Chamberlain, (son of Joseph Chamberlain), Winston Churchill, Lord Scarborough and friends from *The Times*. They had a special visit from Princess Clementine of Belgium, the wife of Napoleon Victor Bonaparte (1879-1926), to thank Flora for her work in Belgium. The Emir of Katsina, Mohammed Delio swept through an astonished Abinger with his entourage in 1921 and 1923. They took tea in the garden, and as the sun set, laid out their prayer mats on the lush lawn to pray to Mecca.

Lugard completed the report on the amalgamation of Nigeria for the Colonial Office, and set about writing a book on his ideas for colonial government. He called it '*The Dual Mandate in British Tropical Africa*'. The words flowed easily, as all the ideas had been in his head for years, derived directly from his experiences. Flora was now by his side. He consulted her on every chapter, principle and point of style, and dedicated the book to her when he completed it in 1921.

He wanted the book to be a practical volume that could be consulted by other colonial administrators, and it was divided into two parts. The first part was called '*Europe and Tropical Africa*' and gave a brief introduction to the history, people and types of government. Part Two he called '*Special Problems*' which was the majority of the book and went into the details of administration. The subjects were split into chapters and covered methods of ruling the local people, taxation, land tenure, minerals, slavery, labour problems, education, transport, economic development and law and justice.

He showed that administration had to be broken down into its components, each to be adjusted to the particular requirements of the country, and sub-divided into ethnic or tribal requirements. He stressed the importance of Indirect Rule, of keeping the existing tribal structures, thus softening the contact, and ensuring the regime was mutual and positive, to the benefit of both sides. He concluded, '*When I recall the state of Uganda at the time I made the treaty of 1890 which brought it under British control, or the state of Nigeria ten years later, and contrast them with today, I feel that the British effort - apart from benefits of trade - has not been in vain.*'

In 1921 he could already see the beginnings of the desire for independence in various countries in Africa. He wrote, '*If there is unrest and desire for independence among Africans, then their very discontent is a measure of their progress,*' adding '*that the benefit can be made reciprocal and that it is the aim and desire of civilized administration to fulfil this dual mandate.*'

When the book was published in 1922 it was generally well-received by the reviewers and newspapers, including Lugard's old adversary, Sir Harry Johnston. He wrote warmly in *The Times*, '*I am almost everywhere in agreement with the author.*' The critics agreed it was original and its merit was, '*that it had not only been written, it had been lived.*'

Not all agreed of course. The Labour Party came out strongly against. Their chief spokesman was Leonard Woolf, who condemned all European occupation of Africa, and advocated the placing of all colonies under international control. Despite the book costing a hefty two guineas, it sold well and by 1929 had run to four editions.

Flora was still writing reviews for *The Times Literary Supplement*, and articles for *The Manchester Guardian*. By 1921 the majority of the Belgian refugees had returned home, and she was able to draw a close on that chapter with a lot of satisfaction.

Her new project was the development of a large scale market garden at Little Parkhurst. Flora started it in 1913, renting a small acreage on the adjacent land from the estate of Sir John Evelyn to grow vegetables for the war effort. She wanted to experiment with the land to see if she could increase the output on the relatively poor sands and greensands of this part of Surrey. She tried different types of fertilizers, and looked at French methods of production.

By 1919 she was cultivating thirty-seven acres. She had a water supply installed, sheds and cottages built, and a link road constructed. A whole variety of vegetables and flowers were being sent daily to Covent Garden for sale. At peak production, a quarter of a million lettuces were produced in one year, with large quantities of apples, plums and soft fruit. A poultry farm was added, and rabbits and a herd of pedigree Berkshire pigs were bred for which she had particular affection, winning many prizes.

Lugard could see this brought Flora immense pleasure, and was unable to resist her requests, even when most of the venture was losing money. Ned helped with the running of the business and noted, '...*no wonder the lettuces look splendid - they were manured with five pound notes!*' Lugard needed new ways of increasing his income, and he took the traditional route of taking on some directorships.

The first was with Barclays Bank on its East African Sub-Committee, and later the central board. Until well into his seventies he attended weekly meetings, and on his return from London, walked the three and half miles from the bus stop. He pressed Barclays to bring in policies that would help the people directly, and encouraged the staff to work closely with local companies. He advocated scholarships and pushed the company to give educational grants. He enjoyed the weekly lunches, where he listened to leading business figures invited to speak and discuss the latest topics.

His second appointment was with the Empire Cotton Growing Corporation, of which he became Vice President and Chairman of the West African Sub-Committee. He became involved with the Kassala Cotton Company which was developing irrigation schemes in Sudan.

He was also a director of the Huileries du Congo Belge, an off-shoot of Lever Brothers, involved in the development of palm plantations in the Congo. There had been many complaints about the exploitation of workers in the Congo by the Belgians, and Lugard watched carefully to ensure everything was done correctly.

In 1922, Ireland again hit the headlines, and Flora followed the unfolding events closely, keeping in regular contact with her family. Sinn Fein were pushing for Irish independence, and carrying out bombings, kidnappings and assassinations to try to achieve it. Flora deplored the violence, but felt it was the inevitable result of the mishandling of Ireland by successive governments. In 1923 she heard from sister Lulu, that her husband Jack Bagwell had been kidnapped. It was a fraught time, but thankfully he was released unharmed a short time later.

Flora felt the press was being muzzled and that the British people were being kept in the dark. She wrote, '*The conspiracy of silence upon Irish affairs in the British Press should come to an end. Instead of trying to hide the sore, the situation in Ireland should be fully exposed and discussed in order that public opinion in America, as well as in our own dominions should be informed.*' Her plea fell on deaf ears, and the violence continued.

Lugard maintained his involvement with the anti-slavery movement right through to his death, when he was probably the world authority in the field. In 1920 he made a short trip to Abyssinia (Ethiopia) for a British company, the Abyssinia Corporation. He aim was to promote trade concessions, but Lugard also used the trip to expand his knowledge on serfdom, slavery and the slave trade in this ancient kingdom. Slave trading was still practiced then, and to this day has not been eradicated. He never stopped writing articles for the Anti-Slavery Society and was a leading figure on the Slavery Committee until 1933.

Whilst Lugard was in Ethiopia in 1920, Flora wrote a long and warm letter to him from Little Parkhurst, reflecting on their eighteen years together. '*We have been longer together this time than ever before in our marriage – and we have never been so close together. Let this be the last separation…we have earned the right to be happy together…Robinson has just come in with the letters and among them I find to my delight one from you – a love letter – the sweetest and dearest that any woman could wish for…You speak of your age writing love letters – I think of mine receiving them! It is a happy time for both of us…I am now loving and appreciating your qualities more and more every day…the last year is always the happiest of our lives…to rest on each other fills life with joy.*'

Education remained high on Lugard's priorities. Having been inspired by Flora, and seen the enormous benefits in Hong Kong and Nigeria, he maintained his interest with great enthusiasm. He never lost contact with Hong Kong University, keeping in close touch with the new Chancellors, and serving on the London consulting committee. In 1927, he was celebrated in the 15th anniversary of the opening of the University at a ceremony in Hong Kong.

After retirement, Lugard developed a close friendship with Dr. Joseph Oldham (1874-1969), a Scottish missionary born in India who became a highly- respected ecclesiastical statesman, writer, and teacher. He linked up again with his old friend from Nigeria, Hanns Vischer, and they all joined the Advisory Committee upon Education in Tropical Africa set up by the Colonial Office in 1923. It had a wide remit, and Lugard threw himself into the work to ensure it was focused and productive.

The inaugural meeting was held in June 1923, and by 1925 a White Paper was produced, 'Educational Policy in British Tropical Africa', which laid down principles that were the basis for education policy for many years. Lugard was enormously proud of his work, and Dr. Oldham said, '*We should never have had it at all unless you had started us on the track and your original framework has remained unchanged.*'

The paper was sent out to all African governors, and became one of the principle landmarks of imperial policy in the twentieth century. In 1929 it was considered so successful it was renamed the Advisory Committee on Education in the Colonies. Lugard continued to serve on the committee until 1937.

From 1923 to 1936 Lugard served on the Permanent Mandates Commission, set up in 1921 to deal with the fourteen territories which had changed hands in the First World War. Britain was responsible for six territories, and Lugard was one of the representatives. He went to Geneva every year for three months to sit through lengthy and often tedious meetings, many in French, listening to experts and officials debating new international laws.

Lugard sat through each meeting absorbing the detail. He was described as patient, courteous and inquisitive, occasionally forming a bloc with the Belgian and Dutch representatives to counter the French. He fought the South Africans over their treatment of Africans and was listened to, but hit a political wall when he was advised not to criticize the French when they attacked Syria in 1926.

Flora came with him to Geneva for the first conference in 1923, and had a six week holiday whilst he sat through the meetings. She toured Geneva, took a boat on the lake and managed '*to drag Fred away from the clutches of the Mandate*' for an idyllic drive under the shadow of Mont Blanc to Chamoux. It was their last overseas trip together.

In September 1926, Flora suffered a serious heart attack and was confined to her bed for seven months, nursed by Fred. In the bitterly cold February of 1927, when Leith Hill was covered in snow, Fred went down with bronchial pneumonia. He was critically ill for a month, but struggled back to his feet before Flora recovered.

The following June, on a fine summer's day, they celebrated their silver wedding on the lawn of Little Parkhurst. Surrounded by their families, a wedding cake was produced, warm speeches were made and they toasted each other's health. Flora wrote, '*My beloved Reg* (Brackenbury) *with his wife and his brother, represented my side of the family and Fred's brothers and sisters were here to represent his. We had a really happy day. Everyone vied with everyone else to make a charming festival, and they succeeded.*'

On January 1 1928 Flora handed him a letter, beaming, knowing what was inside, and watched his reaction as he opened it. Lugard had been elevated to the peerage and took the title, Baron of Abinger. She watched his reaction of astonishment when he opened it. '*I can't understand this. What does it mean? Me a peerage! What for?*' He decided he must refuse it, and added, '*I am terrified at the idea of the House of Lords and I shall never dare open my lips!*'

Two hours later he came back after a long bath and breakfast, and said to Flora, '*Do you know, I believe the Lordship is coming out in me. I am finding that I am liking it very much… This is going to make a great difference to Africa; the African Service has been neglected.…This has raised the African Service to the level of the other services.*' Flora was delighted and kissed him with passion, exclaiming, '*My Lugard of Africa!*'

They designed the coat of arms together, and to humour Flora, he ordered a box of linen handkerchiefs from Ireland with the baronet arms embroidered in the corner. She was delighted. '*This is the kind of present I like, one which has taken a lifetime to win.*'

Over the next twelve months, Flora's strength diminished from the effects of the heart attack, and she went into a slow decline. Her sight deteriorated and she could no longer read or detect colours. Being near Fred brought immense comfort, and she faced up to the inevitable end with calm and a feeling of peace. She wrote to a Belgian friend, '*…my husband's public life brought into mine, a continuous stream of interest which carries on for me all the interests of my own public life, without the labour and fatigue…I am so happy that nothing seems to matter. A peace which passeth understanding seems to have come to me.*'

There were two outstanding concerns she wanted to resolve. She was keen to see the start of Fred's biography, and with the help of Ned, had already collated a lot of his letters and correspondence. She wanted Professor Reginald Coupland to write it, as he had just completed a trilogy on East Africa and knew Africa well. After a long correspondence and visits to Abinger, he reluctantly declined, saying he had just completed his recent trilogy, and felt the biography was so important it had to be approached with freshness and vigour. Flora was disappointed, but she would have approved the eventual biographer, Dame Margery Perham, who possessed both those attributes, and more, and in 1956 produced one of her finest publications.

It was also important to Flora to know that Fred would cope when she had gone. Only one person could help him though this, and that was Ned, who had shared so much with him throughout his life. She wrote to Fred, *'He knows my affection for him, and the absolute dependence with which I leave you to his devoted care.'* Flora also suggested that her nephew Reg Brackenbury and his family come to live with him when she was gone, to ensure Little Parkhurst still felt like a home. Lugard agreed.

Over the last few years Flora and Fred had discussed faith and morals, trying to make sense of their beliefs. She had studied physics, astronomy, biology, and The Bible, reflected on Meredith's doctrine of acceptance and turned to various philosophers. She did not believe in God, having lost her faith before she met Meredith, but preferred 'Eternal Spirit' or 'Absolute or Ultimate Reality'. The war challenged her agnosticism and she wrote to Fred a month before she died, *'...I have no theories, only a great and growing trust in the goodness of God. The war has, I think, greatly strengthened the feeling that Death is not what it generally seems to be, but something sweeter, simpler and in the order of expanding life.'* She added, *'As we feel towards the edge, everything has a golden vision...It seems impossible that I shall know nothing of you when I have passed. Absolute truth must exist somewhere.'*

In December Flora enjoyed her last birthday with Ned, his son Cyril and wife Kitty and their four daughters, who were about to depart for a new life growing coffee in Kenya. On January 22, she was preparing for Fred's seventy-first birthday when she went down with a chill, which rapidly developed into pneumonia. Three days later, on January 25 1929, at the age of seventy-six, she passed away peacefully.

She left behind a final note to her dear Fred, *'A word of farewell and love and gratitude for all those last happy years that we have enjoyed together. I want you never to remember anything but the joy and peace of it.'*

CHAPTER 31
Laying the bricks

Lugard was stricken with grief when Flora died. He collapsed, and one week later the newspapers were reporting that the family feared for his life. He could not attend the funeral at Woking crematorium and was represented by Ned and close family. A small number of dignitaries also attended, including the Belgian Ambassador, an Army brigadier, a few lords, and Mr. and Mrs. W. M. Meredith.

Tributes to Flora poured in from all over the world for her work as a pioneering journalist, a brilliant and knowledgeable writer, an ardent proponent of Positive Imperialism and a perfect partner for her beloved husband.

A few months later Lugard wrote to Ned, *'You who know me better than any other living soul, must know that the blow that fell on me is one which can never be healed. I do not do things by halves and my love for her was part of my very being…I am always thinking of her and if I sleep I dream of her, as I did last night, and the vividness of a dream is more painful than thought…to the outside world I am no doubt just what I was a year ago. Life is still interesting even though all the sunshine and pleasure has gone out of it. Leave it at that.'* Over the next two months Lugard slowly pulled back from the abyss, and returned to his meetings and travelling to the Mandate Commission.

On March 13 1929 he made his maiden speech in the House of Lords. He was nervous, still disliking public speaking, and wished he had Flora's support. He need not have worried. He was introduced by Lord Olivier, an ex-Governor of Jamaica who gave a glowing account of his career. Lugard's maiden speech was long, discussing a disputed report *Closer Union of the Dependencies in Eastern and Central Africa*. He was particularly concerned about too much power being given to the white settlers in Kenya while limiting the African participation.

The speech was authoritative and knowledgeable and everyone listened. When Lugard sat down, the Archbishop of Canterbury complimented him and considered the speech of permanent importance. Lord Buckmaster also congratulated him, but as he supported the white settlers, he could not agree with Lugard's sentiments. His old friend Doctor Joseph Oldham, with whom he had been researching and working on the speech, watched him in the gallery and wrote the next day, '*Lugard was splendid. The outstanding feature of the debate was the extraordinary expression of confidence in him from every quarter of the House. It is literally true to say that, in the opinion of the House, he was the debate. The impression he made gives him a position of commanding influence which will be of great value in the future.*'

As a result of Lugard's speech, the report was delayed and Sir Samuel Wilson was sent to Kenya to investigate further. Labour came into office at the General Election and Lugard found new allies, including the newly-appointed Colonial Secretary, Lord Passfield (Sidney Webb 1859-1947), who he had met in Hong Kong, and invited him to dinner.

He was a socialist, economist (he founded the London School of Economics) and one of the early members of the Fabian Society, and married to Beatrice Webb. The two men got on immediately, and talked until past midnight. Passfield was inspired by the meeting, and took a lot of notes. In June 1930 Passfield issued two White Papers which accepted Lugard's proposals. They insisted on African rights and emphasized the importance of prioritising native interests, outraging Kenyan settlers.

A further Joint Selection Committee was set up, which Lugard served on for the whole ten months it was in session. It called fifty-one witnesses, including three Governors and for the first time, three African witnesses from three territories. The Africans made a deep impression on the Committee, especially Mr. Kulubya from Uganda. They presented themselves with dignity and intelligence, and changed many opinions that day. Africans could no longer be ignored but were to be fully involved in the decision making.

Little Parkhurst became a centre for lively discussions at the weekends. All the members of the Select Committee visited during this time, as well as various Governors, (later Sir) Julian Huxley (1887-1975), the brilliant scientist, eugenicist and founding member of the World Wildlife Fund, and Professor Bronislaw Malinowski, (1884-1942), one of the most important anthropologists of the twentieth century. The house buzzed with conversation and ideas, exactly what Flora would have wanted.

Lugard maintained his interests in other parts of Africa. On his visit to Ethiopia in 1920, he was appalled how much slave-trading was still prevalent. He had met Emperor Haile Selassie on his visit, and after frank discussions the Emperor asked him to be an advisor on the abolition of slavery. He helped appoint Colonel Sandford as an advisor, and kept in touch for many years.

The International African Institute had begun research into the effects of European influence on African languages and culture in 1924. Lugard had always had an interest in the subject and became Chairman of the committee, working with his old friends Hanns Vischer and Joseph Oldham, and attended meetings regularly to 1944.

In August 1933 there was a horrific massacre of three thousand Christian Assyrians in Simele, Iraq. A stream of destitute refugees fled the country looking for a safe haven. Neighbouring Syria took them in, where they lived safely until the devastating civil war eighty years later. Lugard raised money for the refugees and helped with their resettlement in Syria.

On a warm June day in 1934, a cavalcade of limousines wound its way through Surrey to Abinger Common. They drove through the village, up the hill and into the drive of Little Parkhurst. It was a rare and privileged visit of the Sultan of Sokoto, the Emir of Kano, and the Emir of Gwandu, accompanied by Sir Donald Cameron, the Governor of Nigeria, and Sir William Govers, the Governor of Uganda.

The Sultan and the Emirs looked splendid in their finery and lined up for photographs in front of the house. They took tea on the lawn from a large silver urn, and were given a guided tour around the house. They showed particular interest in the artifacts collected from Africa and the Far East. Lugard apprehensively showed the Emir of Kano the elegant screen that had been carved from the Kano gate taken in 1903. The Emir looked closely at the screen for a few minutes, and to Lugard's relief smiled. He was not offended. The meeting was emotional for Lugard - he was able to warmly welcome his old foes into his house, and talk of peace and prosperity for the future.

Lugard was shocked and angered when the fascist Italian government under Mussolini sent troops into Ethiopia in 1935. He wrote to *The Times* on July 30 1935 calling for Britain to give a strong lead for international action against the Italians. As the war worsened, he became Chairman of a committee to organize a Red Cross ambulance service in Ethiopia. The Italians bombed the Red Cross camp, and continued their occupation, forcing the Emperor to flee the country.

In 1939 Lugard gave his last speech in the House of Lords. He dreaded attending because of his increasing deafness, but had been following developments in Southern Rhodesia (now Zimbabwe) with concern. Godfrey

Huggins (later Lord Malvern) became the fourth Prime Minister in 1933, and Lugard had been encouraged when Huggins had read aloud from *The Dual Mandate* in the Rhodesian legislature. He invited him to Little Parkhurst and soon realised the country was unlikely to flourish with over half set aside for Europeans. By 1939 a colour bar had been introduced into Southern Rhodesia, and in his speech Lugard strongly opposed any extension into the northern Protectorates. He could foresee the problems that would develop over the following decades.

By 1937, it was clear that from the Fascist rhetoric coming out of Germany, Britain was heading for war again. On September 30 1938, Neville Chamberlain, desperate to avoid war, came back from Munich waving a piece of paper declaring peace, whilst Germany annexed Sudetenland. When Germany invaded Poland and war was declared on September 3 1939, Chamberlain was an ill and disillusioned man, and in May 1940 he resigned.

Winston Churchill took over, but brought Chamberlain back into the Cabinet, appreciating his contribution. Lugard had never forgotten Neville Chamberlain's father, Joseph Chamberlain, whom he considered a great man, and felt immense sympathy for his son. By making the decision to delay the start of war, it gave Britain valuable time to prepare. He wrote to Neville Chamberlain from Abinger on October 13 1940, giving his support, saying,

'*Dear Mr. Chamberlain,*
    …Your absence from the Cabinet is a grievous loss to the country, and the nation is at last beginning to anticipate the undoubted verdict of history on the splendid effort you made to avert war.
    Circumstances, which no human foresight could have anticipated, have made it clear now that it was inevitable, and better that it should come now, than be longer postponed, and it is increasingly realised how much the country owes to your untiring efforts since it began…'

Lugard received a swift reply on October 19.

'*Dear Lord Lugard,*
    It was a delightful surprise to me to receive your letter of 13th instant and I am indeed grateful for you writing in such generous terms.
    I do particularly value your good opinion, and your letter was therefore most welcome to me.
    I don't suppose you ever realised what a tremendous hero you were to me in those far off days when you came to Highbury.

Yours very sincerely,
Neville Chamberlain'.

A few weeks later Chamberlain died of cancer aged seventy-one.

When Hong Kong was invaded by the Japanese in December 1941 it was a short and bloody fight. After only eighteen days, the colony Governor, Sir Mark Young, surrendered to overwhelming forces, and the colony entered a dark, savage period. The occupation lasted three terrible years. The Japanese carried out over 10,000 executions. The Europeans were interred in concentration camps, and tens of thousands of Chinese were deported to labour camps or died from starvation. The population of Hong Kong dropped from 1.6 million to 600,000. Lugard followed the news with great sadness, and sent letters to Hong Kong offering help where he could, including to the family of his old servant Ah Yeu.

The University was ransacked and most records destroyed. Classes were abandoned, and Lugard did not live long enough to see them commence again after the Japanese surrendered on August 30 1945. He would have been proud of the resilience of the Hong Kong people, who rebuilt Hong Kong at a frenetic pace, and continually expanded the University, now ranked in the top fifty of the world.

In January 1943 Lugard received a letter from the Controller of Overseas Services of the BBC asking him to contribute to a series on Empire biographies. He was astonished and helped to put a script together. It was broadcast but it is not known if a copy of the broadcast exists.

In Britain, 1945 started particularly cold, with deep snow drifts in Scotland, and freezing temperatures across the country. Lugard wrapped himself in a blanket and put on mittens whilst he was writing, to save electricity. He was tired of this war, now in its sixth year, with his journeys to London being continually interrupted by bombing and blackouts.

Travelling was no longer a pleasure, and his latest journey had been a particularly sad one. His old and dear friend, Sir Hanns Vischer, had died on February 19, only two weeks after his youngest sister Charlotte. He felt deep shock at this loss. Hanns had helped him so much since the early days of Nigeria with his knowledge, ideas and smooth social skills. He had been there for Lugard at awkward moments at the International African Institute when encountering people he had little time for, and helped him with his increasing deafness. The funeral was held at Newport Pagnell. The train journey had been tiring. Lady Vischer noted a few days later in a letter to Margery Perham, *'He was in a kind of daze. He sat disconsolately upon the stairs, a true picture of grief. Twice I had to plead with him to come and sit with us in the library.'*

At the next meeting of the International African Institute in London on March 28 he resigned, and handed over to Lord Hailey. It was a long meeting, with critical discussions on plans for when World War Two was over. When he came out into Lower Regent Street the blackout had started, and he had a long wait for a taxi to Waterloo station. At Dorking, there was another wait at the cold, bleak station, and he was glad to get home to the warmth of Little Parkhurst.

Letters continued to flow from his pen for the next few weeks, and he was touched by the letters of thanks he received for his work at the Institute, especially one from Joseph Oldham, who wrote, '*...my feelings were so deep that I felt any expression of them would be inadequate. What you have done for the African Institute cannot be measured and the association with you in its work for a period of years is among the happiest memories of my life.'* Lugard replied he was deeply moved by his letter.

The following day, on April 1, he sat down to write his last letter to Margery Perham. Over the years that Margery had been working with him, gathering information for the biography, they had formed a strong and affectionate bond. Lugard wrote in his neat, firm hand, thanking her for all the work she had done, enquiring after the health of her family, and looking forward to her next visit. He leaned back in the chair, reflecting on ageing and how it affected his writing. He mused, '*...I am increasingly conscious of the ineffectiveness which age brings with it, and one must learn the meaning of 'acceptance' as my dear wife used to say. You say I have too rigid standards and have adopted Lord Strafford's motto. What was it? My dear mother taught me as a child that the verse in the Bible – 'Whatever thy hand findest to do, do it with all thy might,' should be the right motto, and I have tried to adopt it. I must not write more now.*

Very affectionately yours,
Fred'

On April 2 the old man had little energy and felt increasingly weak. He called for Ned, and was helped up the oak staircase to his bed by his staff. Across the landing was Flora's bedroom, untouched since she died. She had surrounded herself with her most treasured possessions. There were many books, including personal copies from George Meredith and Ruskin, various periodicals and cuttings, collections of letters, blank writing paper and a pen ready for use. A small tea set was in the corner, given to her by Mrs. Tolley, a remarkable old lady she met in Woolwich when she was setting up the food cooperative with Ruskin. On her bedside was the pocket watch that Ruskin gave to her all those years ago, which she carried with her all her life. Lugard had written to a friend a few weeks earlier, '*You would have found no change in the house and in our way of life as she left it. Her spirit and the harmony she created has lived after her.*'

Within a few hours he had lost consciousness, and on April 11 1945, with the picture of Flora by his bedside, and surrounded by Ned and his close family, Lugard died peacefully, after eighty-six tumultuous years.

Five days later, four black limousines slipped quietly out of Little Parkhurst on a beautiful spring day, following the hearse down the Surrey country lanes to Woking crematorium. The cars carried Ned and his family, Agnes his remaining sister, various nieces and nephews, and three of his loyal house staff, including Violet Townshend. The coffin was covered with a Union Jack and on top were his Orders, medals and decorations, along with his sword, plumed hat and a wreath of flowers. After a mile, the cortège halted for a few minutes at the main entrance to a wartime military camp where, at their own request, the soldiers lined the road and a guard of honour presented arms and sounded The Last Post. The commanding officer, Major A.J. Baldwin laid a wreath of laurels and a number of villagers gathered to pay their last respects.

The chapel at Woking was full of family and friends to pay tribute. The Colonial Office, the International African Institute, the Royal African Society and the Secretary of State all sent representatives. One missing face was an extremely disappointed Margery Perham, who had been taken ill. In a moving service led by the Rector of Abinger, the Reverend Lionel Meade, (who had survived the doodlebug attack on St. James Church a few months before) and the local chaplain the Rev. C. E. Sylvester, 'The Earnest African' was laid to rest. The fever of life was over, and his work was done.

On April 26 a memorial service was held at Westminster Abbey, led by the Dean. People from all walks of life came from Peers to African students to celebrate his life in the closing stages of World War Two.

The Times obituary was written by Sir Reginald Coupland, who had also made an overseas tribute on April 17 1945. Tributes flooded in from all over the world. They reflected all the countries he had visited and where he had made a difference, including Kenya, Uganda, Sudan, Hong Kong, and there were many from the chiefs of Nigeria including the Sultan of Sokoto. Haile Selassie never forgot his kindness and actions, and after Lugard's death, sent a cable to Ned with his sympathy. '*On the death of your brother, a great Englishman and a valued friend of ours.*' In addition, the myriad of societies that he was involved with sent their tributes, including the International African Society, the Royal Geographical Society and the Save the Children Fund, founded in 1919 when he was Patron.

It is not known where his ashes were scattered, but when repairs to the church in Abinger Common were completed in 1950, a simple copper plaque was fixed to a wall inside, inscribed with the details of Flora and himself and finished with his motto,

All I did was to try and lay my bricks straight

In the same churchyard are buried his sisters Charlotte and Agnes, and very close by, his brother, Ned.

EPILOGUE

Eleven years after Lugard died, the first volume of his biography, *Lugard: The Years of Adventure 1858-1898* was published by Margery Perham in 1956. It was well-received by the critics. His brother Ned considered it *'A wonderful book – an amazing story.'* Ned died in 1957, so he did not see the second volume, *Lugard: The Years of Authority 1898-1945*. Almost certainly he would not have been so enthusiastic.

This was published in 1960, and was more critical of Lugard's conduct and his decisions in Nigeria. The handling of the massacres at Satiru in 1906 and Abeokuta in 1918, the preference for the system of the North over the South and his attitude to politicians in the south all came under scrutiny. Lugard's inability to delegate work caused immense frustration to some of his subordinates, but at the same time his strong, quiet style attracted great loyalty to their 'chief.'

After World War II there was a rising swell of anti-colonial views around the world and strong criticism of the leaders. So much exploitation and brutal subjugation had been carried out in the name of colonialisation, especially in different parts of Africa, which overshadowed the many successes that had been achieved in establishing law, education and health systems, and new infrastructure.

Lugard's views on Indirect Rule now looked outdated and were discarded. In the 1960s there was a rush to unload the African colonies, and a desire from the emerging nations to cast off the yoke of their colonial masters to enjoy a free and democratic future. The new generation of politicians struck out in different directions.

This did not happen in Hong Kong which continued as a British Colony until it was handed back to China in 1997. The legacies Lugard left there were built on, creating one of the most prosperous countries in the world in the twenty-first century. Hong Kong University expanded dramatically to become one of the best in the world. The health system is envied by many, with tropical diseases that Lugard had seen, now conquered. The excellent transport and communication systems have made Hong Kong a top financial centre, attracting professionals from around the world to work and live in, creating a lively, cosmopolitan city of seven million people.

Lugard's qualities as a man are still to be admired. He was a Victorian and had some of the best characteristics of that era. He remained a modest man all his life, but driven after his first visit to Africa by an intense desire to stamp out slave-trading in Africa, he wanted to make changes. He was brutally honest, almost incapable of deceit, and his own worst critic. His work ethic and stamina were legendary, setting very high standards that many found difficult to work with. He had little time for those Kipling described as '*jelly-bellied flag-flapping*'.

Many of his early expeditions were failures, but the confidence he inspired in those that worked with him enhanced his reputation. In return he gave total support and loyalty to those he respected, including Joseph Chamberlain, and Sir John Kirk.

Lugard always looked to the future. He was not interested in living in the past. Even in old age, there was a continuous stream of politicians, writers, academics and family coming to Little Parkhurst to discuss and hear his views well into the night. In 1945 he was calling for a World Charter after the end of World War II, urging for human rights and fundamental freedoms for all independent peoples.

Despite the iron image, his friends also talked of Lugard's sensitivity. When he fell in love, he gave himself completely. This almost broke him mentally with Catherine, but also brought him the greatest happiness with Flora. He was kind and generous to his family, not a man for small talk, but someone whose presence gave reassurance and strength. There are some elderly relations in the family still alive, who remember him with fondness for his kindness and help right to the end of his life. He was one of the outstanding men of his era, saluted at the time by the many nations and people from all walks of life, but now largely forgotten by the present generation.

Flora was a pioneering journalist of her time, overcoming enormous prejudice to become the first colonial editor of *The Times* through her own remarkable abilities. She was not afraid to ask awkward questions and was passionate in all she set out to achieve. She was a role model for women of her time, and is being looked at again by a new generation of women looking for inspiration.

They were an outstanding couple of their generation, fighting adversity, trying to make the world a better place.

ACKNOWLEDGEMENTS

Many people have assisted me in my research for this story, and I would first like to thank the archive staff at the Bodleian Library, Oxford for their patience in directing and furnishing me with numerous boxes from the Lugard, Flora Shaw and Perham Papers. Also to Iris Chan and Dr. David Ponfret at the archives department of Hong Kong University, the staff at the Royal Geographical Society archives, and to those at the National Portrait Gallery finding prints not seen for many years.

Also to Dr. Brad Faught, the biographer of Dame Margery Perham, for starting my search for the mysterious Catherine, to Professor Jan Montefiore for her views on the Kipling and Ruskin letters, and to Giles Jackson who worked with me in Nigeria and helped me discover Abinger and Little Parkhurst. Here we met the present owners Steve and Maria Walton who very kindly gave myself and various members of the family a tour of the mansion and garden, where the layout has changed little from 1945.

Many thanks also to descendants of the Lugard and Shaw families who allowed me access into their private archives and memories. Especially to Gillian Kelly, Anthea and Robin Haig, Lucinda Meade and her treasure chest, Kathleen and Jenny Thomas, and Elizabeth Johnson, all in England, Jos Scharrer and George Shaw in South Africa, and my mother's cousin Elizabeth Richmond, who started it all from a box under her bed in Brisbane, Australia. Special thanks to Russell Kilmister my editor who also travelled to Australia, put up with and deflected my assault on the English language, and listened to my stories in the Red Lion in Chalgrove so patiently.

Finally, great thanks to my editor and publisher James Essinger and to Charlotte Mouncey for her excellent cover and hard work and diligence on the typesetting.

TIMELINE

Frederick Lugard

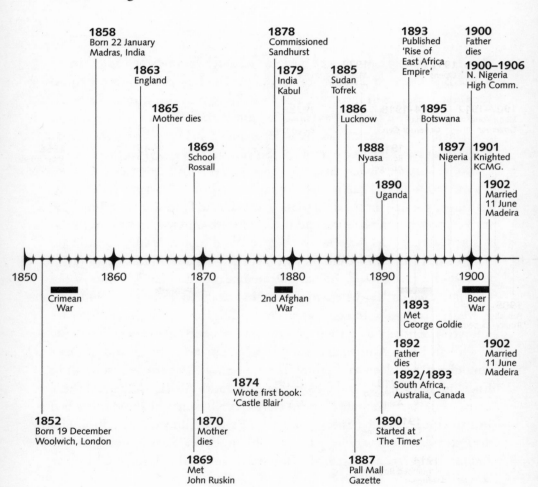

1858
Born 22 January
Madras, India

1863
England

1865
Mother dies

1869
School
Rossall

1878
Commissioned
Sandhurst

1879
India
Kabul

1885
Sudan
Tofrek

1886
Lucknow

1888
Nyasa

1890
Uganda

1893
Published
'Rise of
East Africa
Empire'

1895
Botswana

1897
Nigeria

1900
Father
dies

1900–1906
N. Nigeria
High Comm.

1901
Knighted
KCMG.

1902
Married
11 June
Madeira

1850   1860   1870   1880   1890   1900

Crimean
War

2nd Afghan
War

Boer
War

1893
Met
George Goldie

1892
Father
dies

1892/1893
South Africa,
Australia, Canada

1874
Wrote first book:
'Castle Blair'

1890
Started at
'The Times'

1902
Married
11 June
Madeira

1852
Born 19 December
Woolwich, London

1870
Mother
dies

1869
Met
John Ruskin

1887
Pall Mall
Gazette

Flora Shaw

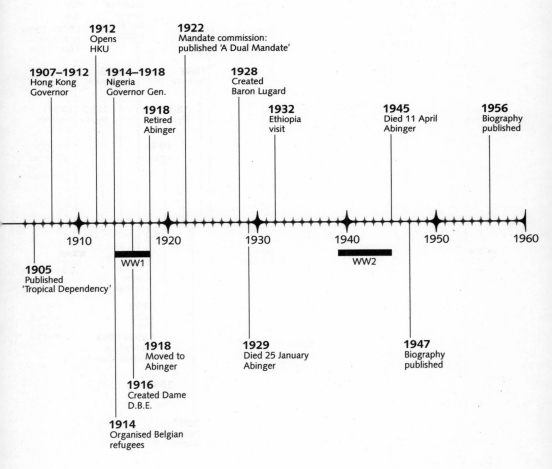

1912
Opens
HKU

1922
Mandate commission:
published 'A Dual Mandate'

1907–1912
Hong Kong
Governor

1914–1918
Nigeria
Governor Gen.

1928
Created
Baron Lugard

1918
Retired
Abinger

1932
Ethiopia
visit

1945
Died 11 April
Abinger

1956
Biography
published

1910   1920   1930   1940   1950   1960

WW1

WW2

1905
Published
'Tropical Dependency'

1918
Moved to
Abinger

1929
Died 25 January
Abinger

1947
Biography
published

1916
Created Dame
D.B.E.

1914
Organised Belgian
refugees

BIBLIOGRAPHY

Books referred to in the text
ALLEN, C., 1979, *Tales From The Dark Continent*
BARRIE, J.M., 1911, *Peter Pan and Wendy*
BELL, E.M., 1947, *Flora Shaw*
CARLYLE, T., 1841, *On Heroes, Hero-Worship and the Heroic in History*
CURICH, P., 2012, *University of Hong Kong 1911-1945*
FAUGHT, C.B., 2012, *Into Africa: the Imperial Life of Margery Perham*
FERGUSON, N., 2003, *Empire*
FLINT, J., 1973, *Sir George Goldie and the Making of Nigeria*
GALLOWAY, W., 1887, *The Battle of Tofrek: Fought Near Suakin March 22 1885*
HAGGARD, R., 1885, *King Solomon's Mines*
KIPLING, R., 1888, *Plain Tales from the Hills*
KIPLING, R., 1901, *Kim*
KNIGHT, D., 1989, *Dorking in Wartime*
LUGARD, F. J. D., 1893, *The Rise of Our East African Empire Vols 1 and 2*
LUGARD, F. J. D., 1922, *The Dual Mandate in British Tropical Africa*
PERHAM, M., 1956, *LUGARD The Years of Adventure 1858-1898*
PERHAM, M., 1960, *LUGARD The Years of Authority 1898-1945*
PERHAM, M., 1959, *The Diaries of Lord Lugard Vols 1-3*
PERHAM, M., 1963, *The Diaries of Lord Lugard Vol 4*
SCHARRER, J., 2014, *The Journalist*
SHAW, F.L., 1877, *Castle Blair, A Story of Youthful Days*
SHAW, F.L., 1903, *A Tropical Dependency – An Outline of the Ancient History of the Western Sudan with an Account of the Modern Settlement of Northern Nigeria*
STANLEY, H.M., 1890, *In Darkest Africa*
STEVENSON, R.L., 1882, *Treasure Island*

THOMPSON, A.A., and MIDDLETON, D., 1959, *Lugard in Africa*
PAKENHAM, T., 1991, *The Scramble For Africa*
VISCHER, H., 1910, *Across the Sahara from Tripoli to Bornu*
WELLESLEY, D., 1934, *Sir George Goldie*
WELLS, H.G., 1901, *First Men in the Moon*
WELSH, F., 1993, *A History of Hong Kong*

Papers, Articles and Letters referred to in the text
ADVISORY COMMITTEE ON EDUCATION IN TROPICAL AFRICA
1925, *Educational Policy in British Tropical Africa*
BODLEIAN LIBRARY, Oxford University, *Papers of Frederick J. D. Lugard 1871 - 1969*
BODLEIAN LIBRARY, Oxford University, *Papers of Flora L. Shaw, Lady Lugard 1847-1945*
BODLEIAN LIBRARY, Oxford University, *Papers of Dame Margery F. Perham 1844-1980*
CHAMBERLAIN, N., 1940, Private Collection, *Letter from Chamberlain to Lugard Oct 1940*
CHURCHILL, W., Private Collection, *Letters from Churchill to Lugard 1906-1938*
HOUSE OF LORDS PROCEEDINGS, March 13, 1929, *Lugard's Maiden Speech - Closer Union of the Dependencies in Eastern and Central Africa*
HELLY, D.O., 2003, Memorial Lecture for Helen Calloway, *Travels with Helen 1927-2003*
HONG KONG UNIVERSITY ARCHIVES, *Hong Kong University Memories 2013*
KIPLING, R., 1903, Private Collection. *Letter from Kipling to Lugard 1903*
LUGARD, E.J.L., 1946, *A Book of Remembrance Lugard 1858-1945*
PALL MALL GAZETTE 1887, *A Lady's Interview with a Captive Chief*
PARLIAMENTARY COMMISSION REPORT 1897, *Select Committee of Inquiry into the Jameson Raid*
ROYAL GEOGRAPHICAL SOCIETY, London, *Proceedings 24 Dec 1890 - Report of Captain F. D. Lugard on his Expedition to Uganda*
ROYAL GEOGRAPHICAL SOCIETY, London, *Proceedings 15 Nov 1892 - Report of Journey from the East Coast to Uganda and the Great Equatorial Lakes of Africa*
ROYAL GEOGRAPHICAL SOCIETY, London, *Proceedings Jan 1904 – The Campaigns in Kano and Sokoto*
RUSKIN, J. 1871, Private Collection. *Letters from John Ruskin to Flora Shaw 1870-1883*

SHAW, F.L., 1893, *Letters from South Africa*
THE IRISH TIMES, Dublin, July 10, 1914, *Report of Lord Lugard in Belfast*
THE TIMES, London, January 25, 1929, *Obituary of Lady Lugard*
THE TIMES, London, April 12, 1945, *Obituary of Lord Lugard*
VANITY FAIR Magazine Dec 1895, *Men of the Day No 639 Captain F. J. D. Lugard*

Other References in the Text
BBC ARCHIVES 1960, Reith Lecture, *The Colonial Reckoning*, by Margery Perham
GILBERT AND SULLIVAN 1882, Light Opera, *Iolanthe*
MEREDITH, G., 1881, Poem, *The Lark Ascending*
PUNCH MAGAZINE, 1894 and 1897, *Cartoons of Flora Shaw*
WAGNER, R., 1865, Opera, *Tristan and Isolde*

INDEX

C

Campbell-Bannerman, Sir Henry 157, 192, 195

Cameron, Emma 29, 33

Carson, Edward 226

Carter, Sir Gilbert 236

Carlyle, Thomas 25

Castlereagh, Lord 227

Cather, Colonel 54

Chamberlain, Austin 239

Chamberlain, Joseph 102, 104, 108, 109, 128, 137, 145, 147, 148, 153, 154, 156, 157, 178, 183, 210, 239

Chamberlain, Neville 249

Chang, Viceroy Jen Chun 202, 209, 213

Chater, Sir Paul 217

Churchill (later Sir) Winston 192-197, 239, 249

Cixi, Dowager Empress of China 199, 203, 205, 212

Clapperton, Hugh 162, 180

Clementine, Princess of Belgium 239

Clementi, Sir Cecil 212, 216

Cole, Brigadier-General Arthur 160

Coupland, Professor Reginald 244, 252

Crewe, Lord 209, 211

Cronje, Piet 109

Cross, Dr. 63, 66, 68,

Cunliffe, General 229, 232

Curzon, Viceroy of India, Lord 175

D

Dealtry, Bishop of Madras 29

Decoeur, Capt. 115, 116, 127,

D'Estournelles, Baron 100

De Winton, Fenwick 75, 97

De Winton, Sir Francis 73

Dicksee, Frank 103

Digna, Osman 45, 48

Dikko, Emir Muhammadu 185

Dillon, John 157

Dobell, Sir Charles McPherson 229, 230

Dodson, Miss 214

Dualla, Indris 75, 80, 81, 85, 97, 99

E

Eaglesome, Sir John 165

Egerton, Sir Walter 219

Eleko, Chief 222

Elgin, Lord 192, 195, 197

Elliot, Sir Charles 211, 216

Euan-Smith, Col. Charles 58, 71

F

Farrar, Lord 41

Fitzgerald, Colonel 146, 151, 154

Flint, Joseph 160

Fodio, Bello 162

Fodio, Shehu Usuman 162

Fort George (Uganda) 87, 88, 92

Fort St. George (Madras) 29, 31

Fort Goldie (Nigeria) 152

Fort Kivari (Uganda) 92

Fort Waverley (Uganda) 91

French, Sir John 207

Friker, Edmond 169

Fuller, Admiral Sir Cyril 230

Fuller, Denman 216

G

Galloway, William 46

Gambier, Frances Catherine 79, 51-53, 84, 85, 129, 146, 150, 167, 171, 173, 188, 255

Gladstone, William 38, 44, 45, 48, 101,104, 115

Goldie, Sir George Dashwood 108, 109, 110, 113-116, 121, 127-132,